End of the Line

End of the Line

Autoworkers and the American Dream

**EDITED BY *Richard Feldman*
AND *Michael Betzold***

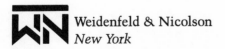 Weidenfeld & Nicolson
New York

Published by Weidenfeld & Nicolson, New York
A Division of Wheatland Corporation
841 Broadway
New York, New York 10003-4793

Published in Canada by General Publishing Company, Ltd.

Photographs by Robert Buchta.

Excerpt from "Dream Deferred" by Langston Hughes Copyright © 1951 by Langston Hughes. Reprinted from *Selected Poems of Langston Hughes*, by permission of Alfred A. Knopf, Inc.

Lyrics from "Union Sundown" by Bob Dylan are Copyright © 1983 by Special Rider Music. All rights reserved. International copyright secured. Reprinted by permission.

Lyrics from "Respect" by Otis Redding © 1965 Irving Music, Inc. (BMI) All Rights Reserved/Int. Copyright Secured.

Library of Congress Cataloging-in-Publication Data

Feldman, Richard.
    End of the line / edited by Richard Feldman and Michael Betzold. — 1st ed.
        p.   cm.
    Bibliography: p.
    ISBN 1-555-84170-8
        1. Automobile industry workers—United States—Interviews.
    2. Ford Motor Company—Personnel management.   I. Betzold, Michael.
    II. Title.
    HD8039.A82U643   1988
    338.7'6292'0973—dc19   88-4108

Manufactured in the United States of America

Designed by Irving Perkins Associates

First Edition

10 9 8 7 6 5 4 3 2 1

To Eugene G. Betzold, who knew life was more than work

To Myron H. Feldman, an honest, gentle man

To our sons, Micah Fialka-Feldman and Patrick James Betzold, who are the future

To Keith Peterson, a co-worker who cared

Contents

Acknowledgments

WE COULD NOT HAVE WRITTEN this book alone. Most important have been the steadfast support, patience, love, ideas, and encouragement of Janice Fialka and Kathleen Conway, who are our wives and our friends.

Many people at the Michigan Truck Plant, especially Richard Olack, "Sugar" Ray Wilson, Tim Schulte, Calvin Rachal, Larry Mayberry, Ron Adam, and James H. Brodie, provided ideas and encouragement in discussions.

Special thanks go to Michael Castleman, who showed us the ropes of agents and publishers. Raphael Ezekiel helped get us going. Roger Goodman, Neal I. Gantcher, Sidney Elliott Cohn, and Steve Brier took us farther down the road. Katinka Matson of John Brockman Associates went out on a limb for us and made it happen. John Herman of Weidenfeld & Nicolson had confidence in our vision, and William Strachan's editing helped tremendously.

The sponsorship necessary for the project was provided by the Michigan Council for the Arts, Aaron "Ike" Krasner and the Progressive Artists and Educators Committee, the Jaffe Foundation, and the Detroit Council of the Arts.

Doris Johnson of Datastran did outstanding work in transcribing interviews, and Cici McLay and Kathleen Conway pitched in. A number of friends read drafts of the manuscript and offered suggestions: Susan Eggly, Debbie Hejl, Gene Fairchild, Jeff Grabelsky, Laurence Peters, Albert Fialka, Shea Howell, Janice Fialka, Kathleen Conway, and Wendy Watson. Fred Miller read various drafts of our introduction and conclusion and helped us clarify our concepts.

Also helping us sharpen our ideas were James Boggs, Grace Lee Boggs, and Freddy Paine, who deserve thanks for their activism, commitment, and continued search for new ideas.

Robert Cohen, Michael Weinstein, and Rosa Naparstek read the initial book proposal and gave us valuable help.

Dan Luria spent hours with us sharing his knowledge of the automobile industry. Nathan Head, Marcy Burstiner, and David Cole provided us the latest research and statistics. Peter Stine helped with interviewing and writing in the early going. Mardge Cohen and Ellen P. Frank gave us valuable resource materials and feedback.

UAW Local 900 President Walter "Jeff" Washington and staff members Bobby Teague and Judy Atkinson provided whatever we needed. Michigan Truck Plant industrial relations manager H. W. Hess, Jr., and Ford public affairs official Rex Greenslade arranged for us to shoot photos in the plant.

Robert Buchta not only lugged cameras around Detroit and took powerful photos but gave us a fresh perspective on our work. Donald Neiman drew us a great map on short notice.

End of the Line first got public exposure in *Metropolitan Detroit* magazine, thanks to Kirk Cheyfitz, Hillel Levin, and staff.

Finally, Rich thanks Harvey and Arlene Feldman, and Albert and Dolores Fialka and family for their love and encouragement, and his mother, Pearl J. Feldman, for providing the confidence to dream and the values to care. And Mike expresses appreciation to friends and relatives for their support, especially to Patrick, for understanding why Daddy stayed upstairs in the office on so many days when he could have been outside playing catch.

Foreword

by Richard Feldman

WHEN I WAS GROWING UP in Brooklyn in the 1950s and 1960s, I had no interest in cars; working in an automobile plant was the farthest thing from my mind. But as I became involved in the civil rights, antiwar, and women's movements at the University of Michigan, I grew committed to organizing American workers for social change. I decided that if I was going to help radically change my country, I should live and work with the people who sang "Solidarity Forever" and who had built our country into the wealthiest nation in the world. When I left Ann Arbor, Michigan, in 1970, I moved to the Detroit suburb of River Rouge so I could live near the historic Ford Rouge Plant—the site of crucial battles that had helped forge the United Auto Workers. Eventually, in December 1971, I got a job at Ford's Michigan Truck Plant in suburban Wayne.

I am not a typical autoworker. I came to the plant because of political principles, not for the money. In doing so, I was part of a larger group of students who were moving from the campus to the cities in the 1960s, following a long tradition of college-educated activists who since the 1930s had gone into the auto plants to organize. In the truck plant I helped start a rank-and-file newsletter, participated in walkouts, encouraged people to stand up for their contractual rights, and discussed my ideas with anyone who would listen.

I am one of only three Jewish workers in my plant, a real switch from my childhood, when I had only two non-Jewish friends among a large group of peers.

While some of my co-workers have arms as thick as my thighs, and others can reach under a dashboard or into an engine with the dexterity of a surgeon, I have trouble changing a light switch in my house. I remember my father having three cigar boxes full of screws, nuts, and bolts; two screwdrivers; one pair of pliers; and one hammer. After seventeen years working in an auto plant, I don't have any more tools than he had.

Despite all this, I have found that I am not so different from my co-workers. We share many of the same concerns: our parents' health; our neighbors' welfare; our children's future. Over the years I have introduced some of them to different ways of thinking, and they have given me a broader and deeper understanding of America's soul and mind. Our discussions have been respectful, passionate, and sometimes heated.

The plant has given me a continuing education. I have been challenged constantly to develop and advance my ideas. In all my activities I have listened to and learned from people of very different backgrounds from mine: whites and blacks from the South; immigrants from Europe and Latin America and the Middle East. I have come to realize more clearly how important our little daily discussions in the plant are to an understanding of the present and the future. I am fortunate to be so close to the pulse of America.

In 1985 I had an awakening. I came home one day, tired and sore after working ten hours on the line, lifted my 18-month-old son, and realized it was time to find a new job. I thought about how my father had worked hard six days a week and had died when he was 57. I made a commitment to quit the plant within a few years.

But before I left, I wanted to make sure that I would have something more to remember than the backaches and the sore arms of seventeen years on the line. I wanted to remember the stories, the faces, and the personalities of the people who had been my friends and co-workers for so long. I didn't want to forget a black man from the South telling me how he couldn't get a drink of water at a department store in the days of Jim Crow, or the pain on a Vietnam veteran's face as he told me about the war while we sanded trucks, or the Motown imitation of fellow painters doing a line dance between the moving trucks. Together we had shared monotonous hours on the line, dinners at each other's homes, births, weddings, and funerals.

I had often heard co-workers say, "I wish somebody would write a book about this plant." In February 1986 I took up the challenge. I started to interview co-workers with the idea of writing a book about their lives and how they viewed the changes that were taking place in the auto industry and in the world. Over the next year, on the weekends when we weren't working, I interviewed about three dozen of them. Some I had known since I first started in the plant; others were just passing acquaintances. My goal was to get a cross section of workers and their views.

Some people didn't want to be interviewed because they didn't trust me or thought they had nothing to say. Some spilled out vivid stories of their lives, their families, and their dreams. Others were less articulate, but their views are no less important. Each shared what was important to him or her.

This book is not a modern history or a sociological study. The people who share themselves in these pages do not represent a clinical sample of American workers. These are oral histories, and as such they are filled with contradictions, prejudices, discrepancies, and widely divergent views of the same events. Some people bared their souls and revealed very intimate thoughts and feelings, while others spoke in guarded or even self-serving terms. While some may say we have exposed too much dirty laundry, I believe we have let people tell it like it is.

All the people who speak in this book have worked at the Michigan Truck Plant. The plant opened in 1963 and in its early years made bus chassis and light trucks. It now produces the Bronco and the Ford pickup. During 1988 it will turn out its three millionth vehicle.

Many of the workers in this book have also worked at the Wayne Assembly Plant, which is next door to the truck plant and is often referred to as simply "the car plant." Wayne Assembly opened in 1952 and for some time produced full-size Ford Galaxies and LTDs. During the late 1960s and 1970s the plant assembled Mavericks, Grenadas, and Monarchs. Today it makes the Escort, the Lynx, and the EXP.

Both plants are represented by Local 900 of the United Auto Workers of America. While this book contains much criticism of and cynicism about the UAW, it could not have been written without the union. Regardless of whether workers speak for or against the union or the company, the union protects their right to speak. I couldn't have done these interviews in a Nissan plant, where there is no union and employment is contingent on being a loyal member of the team.

Only a few dozen women work in the truck plant, and all of them are low-seniority employees. Ford did not hire women at the truck plant until it was pressured to do so by the federal government in the 1970s, so hundreds of women were among the lowest-seniority workers who permanently lost their jobs in the layoffs of 1980.

In March 1980 there were 2,800 people working two shifts at the truck plant. That month one entire shift was laid off, and it remains out, while the other shift works forced overtime. The plant now employs 1,100 people who work ten hours a day, five and often six days a week, making forty-eight trucks an hour.

During the 1984 contract negotiations I organized a picket line at Ford World Headquarters to protest forced overtime during a period of layoffs. No one else from the plant showed up. Today Ford Motor Company employees are working millions of hours of overtime per month. In 1987 the company had 43 percent fewer people working than in the 1970s, but it had nearly the same level of production while making record profits. This situation raises important questions about our values and directions.

Based upon my political principles and commitments, my primary involvement is now in the community rather than in the plant. My major question remains: What principles and values will help guide us in the years ahead? I hope this book will contribute to my search for answers.

Detroit, Michigan
December 1987

Foreword

by Michael Betzold

I HAVE LIVED most of my life in Detroit, but the only factory I ever worked in was a bakery where I loaded bread into ovens. After two nights I quit because I couldn't stand the heat. I had never been in an auto plant until my friend Rich Feldman took me on an insider's tour of the Michigan Truck Plant a few months after I had begun working on this book.

When I walked in the front door, I was struck by how bright, spacious, and clean the place seemed. My image of an auto factory was of a dark, cramped, grimy sweatshop. I was also surprised to see the series of signs hanging next to the assembly line that detailed rational steps in problem solving. I had figured factory workers communicated by grunting and throwing tools.

As I spent the next two hours squeezing past moving trucks, dodging welding sparks, ducking under automated machinery, and meeting the people in the book, I realized my preconceptions had not been so far off the mark after all. The din was so loud that you had to shout—a difficult tone of voice for problem solving. And the bright lights, clean floors, and spacious aisleways didn't make a whole lot of difference on the line itself, where people bent and twisted in narrow spaces, worshiping the relentlessly advancing trucks with their own contorted genuflections.

There were so many twists and turns in the line and so many feeder-line appendages that it seemed a miracle that each truck came out the front door in one piece with its own particular colors and options. The work seemed to be divided arbitrarily. Most assemblers did a little of this and a little of that—a screw here, a clamp there. Some jobs looked a lot harder than others. I watched one poor middle-aged man hustling to keep up—picking up parts, setting down tools, climbing on and off the truck. He was frowning and sweating, repeating dozens of movements that seemed too complicated to become rote. I watched and thought: He does this every day, every day, every day. These parts and tools and motions—this running to catch up and never getting ahead— are half his life.

When I left the plant, I felt weary. Something about the grinding machinery, the noise, and the endless automatic movement of the trucks had made me tired through and through. I went back to my computer with a new respect for the people with whose words I was wrestling.

Their words and their ideas had astounded me from the time I first started reading transcripts of the interviews Rich had done. These were caring, thinking, complex human beings, not the mindless, macho factory rats I had imagined autoworkers to be. I was heartened in my hope for humanity by how deeply and widely their minds and emotions ranged, how quickly they could cut through the crap to get to the heart of an issue. But I was sobered by their despair about the future. My fears about what kind of world my son will live in have deepened as a result of this book.

The process of editing these interviews has been governed by two main principles: respect for the people in the plant and what they are saying, and the desire to present their views as clearly as possible. We have tried not to let language get in their way. That means that many of the rough spots and redundancies in their stories have been smoothed out, but not completely leveled; that their hems and haws and grammatical and dialectical detours have been avoided, but the nuances of their words and storytelling style preserved; that their profanity and uncharitable characterizations of others have been toned down, but kept when necessary to preserve the power of their views.

In reducing nearly one million words of interviews to about 100,000, we have tried to eliminate irrelevancies and repetition while keeping the diversity, the integrity, and the scope of opinion. The process of cutting was sometimes painful.

Equally sensitive was the matter of grouping people into chapters and labeling those chapters. Our goals were to discover what was common among the diversity of people, to highlight the essence of their views, and, in doing so, to give readers some guideposts, while still being respectful of our subjects. This is only one limited way to view these people; the chapter headings are not fixed labels that define who they are or capture their whole beings.

Finally, we are conscious of the irony in our decision to give only name, birth date, birthplace, seniority date, and job description as the introduction to each interview. This is how the workers appear on the company's payroll lists. We have chosen to let them reveal themselves rather than attempt to summarize them in our words.

Writing this book has been a team effort. Rich did all the interviews; I put them into story form. All the major editing decisions, as well as the writing of the introduction and conclusion, were done jointly. The give-and-take has been tremendous—open and forthright, yet always respectful—and we have become better friends in the process. Together, as insider and outsider, we have tried to give voice to a message from the inside of the factory that those on the outside need to hear.

Detroit, Michigan
December 1987

PLANT and HEADQUARTERS SITES

8 Mile Rd.

Livonia

Flint & Pontiac

Warren

Highland Park

Hamtramck

DETROIT

Rouge River

Southfield X-Way

Woodward Ave.

Dearborn

Michigan Ave.

Windsor

Jefferson Ave.

Miller Rd.

Inkster

Wayne

Taylor

Southfield

Flat Rock

Gibraltar Rd.

1   Ford Michigan Truck Plant
and Wayne Assembly Plant

2   Mazda Flat Rock Plant

3   GM Hamtramck (Poletown) Plant

4   Chrysler Jefferson
Avenue Assembly Plant

5   Ford Rouge Plant

6   Ford World Headquarters

7   UAW Solidarity House

8   Ford Highland Park Plant
(birthplace of assembly line)

9   Ford Saline Plant

10 Milan Federal Corrections Institution

N

Introduction

The Dream and the Dollar

What happens to a dream deferred?
    Does it dry up
    like a raisin in the sun?
    Or fester like a sore—
    And then run?
    Does it stink like rotten meat?
    Or crust and sugar over—
    like a syrupy sweet?

Maybe it just sags
like a heavy load.

Or does it explode?

—Langston Hughes, "Harlem"

On April 29, 1987, Ford Motor Company reported another quarter of record profits and new plans to explore a joint venture with Japan's Nissan Corporation.[1]

The next day, at the Michigan Truck Plant, ten miles from Ford's World Headquarters, a fifteen-year assembly worker was found hanging from a roof beam. It was the third suicide in two years by a worker from the truck plant.

These are amazing times. Corporate earnings soar and yuppies stride through the land mines of Wall Street, while victims of economic Darwinism starve on the streets. In automobile plants, where the twentieth-century American dream was built, there is deep fear about the future. The confidence of record profits and the despair of the hanging noose dangle side by side.

After a decade of layoffs and plant closings and the promise of more to come, autoworkers who still have jobs are survivors, desperately holding on. This book is about their work and their lives. It is a view from inside an automobile plant, but it is about all of us—where we have been, where we are now, and where we are going.

Ever since Henry Ford's assembly line started rolling, the automobile has powered America's journey to the good life of material abundance. The auto industry has been so vital to the strength and spirit of America that its interests were long considered to be identical to the nation's. "What's good for General Motors," went the saying, "is good for the country."

Now there is a roadblock on the highway to a better life. The links between profits, production, jobs, and prosperity have been shattered as our nation becomes deindustrialized. The United States is no longer the unchallenged leader of global manufacturing, and the automobile has lost its place as the linchpin of the American economy. Autoworkers, builders of America's dream machine, are being squeezed out of the driver's seat.

Historically one of every six jobs in the United States has revolved around the automobile industry.[2] When the assembly line was humming, unskilled and semiskilled workers could easily find jobs that paid good wages. Now, growing numbers of high school graduates flip hamburgers for minimum wage because thousands of auto factories, parts plants, tool shops, steel mills, and rubber and glass factories have shut down, like electronics and textile plants before them. Millions of Americans have lost their livelihoods and their status, and millions of others who still have jobs have been caught between wage concessions and the high cost of living and have seen the buying power of their paychecks dwindle. More Americans are being thrown out of the middle class than are gaining admittance.

For the first time in the long cycle of postwar economic ups and downs, the recovery of the mid-1980s has made expendable a large part of society while enriching a small number of entrepreneurs and speculators. "We have created hundreds of paper millionaires and quite a few billionaires," investment banker Felix Rohatyn has observed. "But alongside the wealth and glamor of Manhattan and Beverly Hills, we have seen the growth of a semipermanent and permanent underclass."[3]

From its founding this nation had a vision: that the have-nots could become the haves and the disenfranchised could become citizens. The dream has been that through hard work rather than birthright, by acquiring property and wealth, all could advance beyond their station in life and that all could attain freedom from subservience to monarchs through the rights of full political participation.

Critics of the dream have called it flawed and hypocritical, pointing to the contradictions between the rhetoric of democracy and the reality of the enslavement of Africans and the massacre of Native Americans, between the promise of material abundance and the reality of devastated cities and foreclosed farms. The dream's defenders have praised it for creating prosperity unprecedented in human history, freeing millions of people from poverty and granting rights and freedoms to citizens on a scale never before achieved. Both the critics and defenders are right because America is both the practical and the ideal, the myth and the reality, the dream and the despair.

There have always been Americans who have been outside the dream. Now even insiders are being displaced. If this is indeed the end of the line for autoworkers, who is next to be left behind? If ahead is an economy in which only the privileged can participate, a society run by robots and computers, the question becomes: Can America work without its workers?

In 1913 Henry Ford installed the first automatic conveyor belt in his new automobile plant in Highland Park, Michigan. His invention changed our nation, our work, our families, and our values. The assembly line turned the horseless carriage from a curiosity to a commodity; it cut the time necessary to build a chassis from fourteen hours to ninety-three minutes.[4]

Mass production of automobiles was a driving force in the United States' rise to global domination. American labor, technology, and ingenuity built an economy unsurpassed in human history, centered on the automobile. During World War II, while every other industrial power was being devastated, the United States hummed with productive might. Detroit was called the "arsenal of democracy" as its auto plants turned out the tools of war. With its industrial base intact, the United States in the postwar era achieved a monopoly on heavy manufacturing and a culture of prosperity that was the envy of the world.

One key to that prosperity was the market of consumers that the automobile industry had created and sustained through a national dealer distribution and credit network. When Ford introduced the $5-a-day wage in 1914, some called him a socialist. But he recognized that good wages were needed not only to attract reliable workers to run the costly new machinery but also to create car buyers. The new economy needed a working class that could afford more than bread and milk.

The Roaring Twenties, when the middle class started spending beyond its means, was a precursor to the debt-powered, consumer-based culture that emerged fully after the Great Depression and World War II. Looking for material security and for dignity, working-class Americans used the GI Bill to buy houses and go to school and used the credit card to go shopping. The automobile was the big-ticket item in an industrial economy that focused its might on the production of consumer goods while military spending continued at wartime levels.

With the rise of the largest middle class in history and the annual production of millions of automobiles, the landscape of America changed. Endless ribbons of pavement tied together the nation and made railroads and mass transit systems obsolete. Increased mobility for car owners meant immobility for those without cars. Freeways opened up the suburbs, decimating urban neighborhoods and gobbling up farmland. The flight of consumers and capital deprived cities of their tax bases while creating prosperous suburbs.

As cars changed the face of the nation, the struggle for dignity in the plants transformed the workplace. Until the 1930s the auto companies ran factories like fiefdoms. Each morning men lined up at the gate, and if there was no work, they were sent home. If they worked, they did not know when quitting time would be until the whistle blew. They were so tired after their long shifts that they fell asleep on streetcars, and the drivers had to wake them at their stops. Some foremen were so intimidating that workers had to go to their homes on weekends to do yardwork and had to bring along their daughters to provide sexual service.

The company ruled by terror. Ford and other automakers hired prizefighters and goons to enforce the feudal system. Workers could not smoke or talk during lunch or take bathroom breaks without being watched. Michigan Truck Plant worker Don Mushinski recalls the stories told by his father, a UAW organizer at the Ford Rouge Plant: "If you had to go to the bathroom, you had to raise your hand. They didn't have doors on the bathroom, and sometimes the supervisor would follow you and watch you. And if you didn't have anything in that toilet, you would get fired on the spot."

Such indignities made workers ready to support union organizers, and other technical developments also favored the UAW's cause. Scientific management and time studies broke down skilled work into repetitive, monotonous fragments, increasing alienation and frustration. Mechanized production meant heavy capital investment in machinery that could not be moved easily to other plants. Workers performing different tasks on the assembly line all shared the ability to disrupt the line. The production system was extremely vulnerable, and the concentration of autoworkers who had migrated from the South to northern cities like Detroit provided strength in numbers.[5] Their collective power formed the basis for a union that, unlike the old craft organizations, organized an entire industry across the lines of skill and race.

To gain dignity and representation for workers, UAW pioneers fought for basic workplace rights that are now taken for granted by most Americans: the right to bargain for wages and benefits and for improvements in health and safety; job security; seniority; pensions. Union solidarity was the way each worker gained protection from the whims of management.

The triumph of the UAW led to the widespread organization of North American industrial workers. In unionized regions even nonunion shops were forced to give workers more rights and better wages. The union victory compelled sweeping social reforms, from the New Deal to the Great Society, that tried to keep America faithful to its promises of social justice and economic equality.

Over the years the UAW was challenged continually to live up to its rhetoric by the growing demands of blacks, immigrants, and women for full participation in workplace rights and decision making. Through political struggle in society, in the plant, and in the union, black workers who had been denied advancement won greater access to skilled-trades jobs, supervisory positions, and union posts. And female workers fought off sexual harassment and abuse from the company, the union, and fellow workers in an effort to gain the respect and rights due them.

As the UAW grew more established, it evolved from a scrappy champion of the worker, a child of the depression, to a respectable partner in progress. Walter Reuther became a household word as the bargainer who took on the Big Three automakers and won the best wages-and-benefits packages in history. In step with the culture of upward mobility, the UAW concentrated increasingly on wages and benefits and downplayed working conditions and health and safety issues.

The expanding economy of the 1950s and 1960s meant increased production in the plants and unlimited overtime. The assembly line was rolling full speed ahead, and it was hard to imagine it would ever slow down. One particular former Michigan Truck Plant employee describes how it was in the boom times: "America was making money. Everybody was buying cars. You didn't have an import problem. No matter what the American companies built, people would buy it."

In reaction to the overtime and the speedup, many young workers started to demand time, freedom, and a little respect. They could buy what they wanted on three days' pay, so absenteeism soared and the work ethic crumbled. Workers sang the blue-collar blues and used drugs and booze to escape the monotony. Individual acts of sabotage and neglect replaced collective action. And a new wave of wildcat strikes disrupted the established system of bargaining through the union.

All this was part of a challenge to the values of the postwar age of affluence. Critics said the nation had sold its soul for the dollar: that a society based on consumption had elevated materialism above the human values of love, cooperation, and justice; that people had lost touch with family, self, and community in the drive to earn a buck. Environmentalists blamed the automobile and industrial production for turning the face of America into a scarred landscape of freeways and shopping malls polluted by exhaust fumes, acid rain, and chemical wastes. Ralph Nader blasted the auto companies' products as unsafe at any speed. And a few isolated voices decried the deaths of more than two million Americans on the highways in this century, the silently accepted cost of unlimited mobility.

Meanwhile, economic forces that were to end America's automobile manufacturing monopoly were already in motion. Other industrialized nations grew more competitive as U.S. corporations sold them manufactured goods and technologies for huge profits. Germany's Volkswagen Beetle was the first invader to pierce the armor of the Big Three automakers' control over the U.S. car market.

With the OPEC boycott of 1973–74 America realized that its love affair with the automobile had made it dependent on foreign oil. It was the end of the illusion of limitless growth and prosperity and of American self-sufficiency. A wave of efficient, economical Japanese imports shocked American automakers from a long complacency based on high profits from big cars. The American romance with size, style, speed, and comfort cooled, and gas hogs suddenly became dinosaurs. American industry scrambled to adjust to the new consumer demands amid double-digit inflation and record postwar unemployment resulting from foreign competition and increases in the cost of oil.

In 1950 the United States made 80 percent of the world's cars; today it makes 30 percent.[6] Other countries have the know-how, the discipline, and the cheap labor costs to compete. Changes in communication, transportation, technology, and manufacturing have made possible an international system of research, design, and production. Quality automobiles can be assembled and parts made more cheaply outside the United States. By 1980 starter motors could be made in Korea and delivered to Detroit for 35 percent less than they cost to make in Detroit.[7]

As automakers ship more and more work out of the country or to nonunion sweatshops, a two-tier system is being established in the United States. Union members in General Motors, Ford, and Chrysler plants get full benefits and job protection but are losing work to suppliers and to the U.S. plants of foreign automakers, whose employees are not covered under the Big Three contract.

Because corporate profit is no longer linked to domestic production, the United States has become a debtor nation even as the earnings of multinational corporations rise.[8] We used to be able to sell more goods abroad than foreign manufacturers sold here; now the balance of trade has tilted out of our favor. The internationalization of automobile production epitomizes this change.

In addition, the domestic market has stopped growing. The prices of cars have risen while real wages have declined, so cars are no longer as affordable. Consumers are demanding cars that last longer and buying new models less often. And foreign manufacturers are gobbling up domestic sales. By 1991 the Big Three will control about half the domestic auto market, down from 71 percent of the market in 1987.[9] Foreign automakers will continue to find it economically and politically wise to build plants in the United States because of currency fluctuations, trade debates, and "Buy American" campaigns. The result will be a huge production overcapacity in the United States, projected to reach seven million units by 1991.[10]

The auto industry and the American economy have had ups and downs for decades. In the past, periods of belt tightening have been followed by recoveries in which laid-off workers have been called back to their jobs and the standard of living has advanced.

But 5.1 million Americans lost their jobs between 1979 and 1984, and most have not regained their places.[11] Some now work for lower pay in union or nonunion factories. Many are security guards, janitors, or cooks. Others are sleeping on the streets. In the "recovery" of the 1980s the work force in the automobile and related industries has shrunk drastically and real wages have declined. There is increasing competition among Americans for a dwindling number of good-paying jobs. The jobs that are being destroyed pay an average of $444 a week, while the jobs being generated pay $272 a week.[12]

This is not just another cyclical adjustment, but the end of a way of life. In a contracting economy most jobs no longer pay a "family wage" to one wage earner, forcing parents to work over-time or to hold two jobs. Children are being increasingly neglected in the bargain. Single parents or working couples do not have enough time or energy for their children, and they have trouble finding reliable child care.

Deindustrialization means the demise of a large, prosperous middle class and the loss of the economic prosperity and protection that Americans have grown dependent upon in the last two generations. You don't get hospitalization, stock options, and pensions working at a fast-food joint. The abundance we have taken for granted since World War II is at an end, and so is an economy based on a large number of well-paid industrial workers who buy designer clothes, power tools, boats, campers, CB radios, microwaves, VCRs, and personal computers.

Throughout this century American workers have sacrificed freedom, dignity, family, health, and time to gain economic security and a higher standard of living for their families. For some, the deal has seemed worth it. Truck plant worker Gary Shellenbarger admits, "I'm trading my life for a dollar," but gets satisfaction in the material goods he has bought for his family. Many workers, however, regret the bargain. Long hours have robbed them of time with their families and the leisure to enjoy the fruits of their labor. Hillory Weber blames Ford for ruining his marriage and his health and says working in an automobile plant has been "hell."

The indignity of assembly-line work has extracted a great physical and emotional toll. "It's a very unnatural system and a waste of human talent. It is very demeaning," says truck plant worker Al Commons. "You're tied to a machine, and you're just another cog." Harold Coleman says, "To have the human body work like a machine—hour in, hour out, to produce a product—is inhuman."

Many autoworkers say they would rather do something else—if there were something else that paid so well. The hope that their wages will buy a better life and a more secure future keeps them on the line despite the monotony and sweat.

Life in today's factory is much different from the days when Henry Ford's goon squads ruled and from the era of union solidarity. A culture of company-union cooperation has muted the antagonisms of the past. Plants are using more robots and integrated technology to cut labor costs and increase flexibility to customer demands. Copying the success of the Japanese, U.S. companies are changing management methods to get maximum production out of a declining work force. At the General Motors-Toyota joint venture plant in Fremont, California, jobs are structured so that assemblers work 95 to 97 percent of each minute, compared with the 80 to 85 percent standard that has existed throughout the domestic industry.[13] Most workers accept such speedups, as well as increased work loads and the loss of co-workers' jobs, in exchange for perks, participation, profit sharing, and job security. Layoffs have made workers fearful of losing their jobs and more cooperative with the company. These sorts of changes are not confined to the automobile industry. Every American worker faces the same issues.

The men and women in this book are survivors who work fifty to sixty hours a week, trying to get what they can before the doors close for good. Their power to refuse work has diminished because jobs are scarce, machinery is more mobile, and companies are willing to close down plants and move. The survivors work next to robots that have eliminated the worst jobs and their best friends. They walk on rubber mats instead of grimy cement floors, eat in air-conditioned canteens, and exercise in factory gyms outfitted with the most modern equipment. On the line, hydraulic lifts raise batteries for installation so that workers don't have to break their backs bending over. The line moves faster, and more work has been added to each job; but operators have been told they can stop the line if they get a bad part. Foremen no longer run their turf with an iron hand, but there is peer pressure from fellow workers who have a stake in the company and who see laggards as cutting into their profit-sharing pay. Favoritism has replaced rigid adherence to contractual rules. Some workers volunteer to come in early to make up losses in production. They pick up screws from the floor rather than leave the job for maintenance people. They can get free counseling for stress and substance abuse and take free classes in computers, vocational skills, and small-business management or earn college degrees tuition-free.

The pay and benefits autoworkers get have lifted many families out of poverty and provided their children the chance to become teachers, engineers, and lawyers. But this is the last generation of industrial workers to enjoy these opportunities for economic advancement. And confidence in the health of the economy has been shattered by massive budget and trade deficits and plummeting stock prices. Even as we continue to cling to boom time values, the choices we made based on growing prosperity and a rising middle class are no longer available. The making and eating of hamburgers at McDonald's doesn't compare with making, buying, and driving cars and trucks. We find ourselves, at the end of the Automobile Century, still trying to ride a dream that has stalled out.

The autoworkers interviewed in this book, and their counterparts across the country, have seen their friends and relatives become outcasts and know that they could be next. Things workers once took for granted—contractual rights, health benefits, pensions, full-time jobs, a high standard of living, personal safety, and a secure future for the next generation—are now in jeopardy, and not only in the automobile industry.

When an auto assembly plant is shut down and 5,000 line workers lose their jobs, many others are affected: engineers, restaurant owners, truck drivers, maintenance workers, teachers, municipal employees, advertisers, secretaries, concessionaires, accountants. When the core industry of an economy sinks, many are threatened with drowning. The water is rising for everyone. Jobs are disappearing and wages are being reduced as even hospitals and schools join business and industry in cutbacks dictated by cost efficiency—the new buzzword in an era of shrinking expectations. Once only the concern of low-seniority, low-paid workers, layoffs now threaten salaried engineers and administrators. The threat of disenfranchisement is moving up the economic ladder.

In their many opinions about how to respond to this crisis, autoworkers reflect the diversity of a divided, confused, and questioning nation. Like all Americans, each person in this book has a central set of concerns that colors a variety of complex and sometimes contradictory views. Team Players believe in company-employee cooperation; the Disenchanted don't believe anything the company or the union says. Renegades see the continued need for action to change society; the Battle-weary have given up for now on fighting. Breadwinners concentrate on making money; the Pressured, on surviving the hassles of work life. Union Advocates want to revive and rework the principles of unionism to fit a new era; Sages say selfishness and materialism have irreparably damaged those principles.

Listen now to the voices of painters and welders, mothers and fathers, southerners and northerners, native-born and immigrants, sons of coal miners and daughters of farmers, Democrats and Republicans, the religious and nonchurchgoers—builders of America. Their cries and their whispers must be heard and understood if we want to create a new dream.

NOTES

[1] According to a Ford employee bulletin, Ford earned $1.5 billion in the first quarter of 1987, beating the previous record of $1.1 billion in the second quarter of 1986. The *New York Times* of May 3, 1987, reported Ford and Nissan had agreed to study a joint venture to produce a minivan in North America.

[2] William Serrin, *The Company and the Union* (New York: 1974), p. 5. By 1979 government data showed 9.1 percent of the U.S. work force in auto-related jobs, according to an MIT report, Alan Altshuler et al., *The Future of the Automobile* (Cambridge, Mass.: 1985), p. 6.

[3] Felix G. Rohatyn, "Ethics in America's Money Culture," Op-ed page, *New York Times*, June 3, 1987.

[4] Steve Babson, *Working Detroit* (Detroit: 1986), p. 30.

[5] Jeremy Brecher, "Crisis Economy: Born-Again Labor Movement," *Monthly Review* (March 1984), pp. 1–3.

[6] John B. Rae, *The American Automobile Industry* (Boston: 1984), p. 165.

[7] Altshuler, op. cit., p. 177.

[8] Robert E. Lipsey and Irving B. Kravis, "Business Holds Its Own as America Slips," *New York Times*, January 18, 1987.

[9] Harold K. Sperlich, "The Second Chrysler Comeback," *UMTRI Research Review* (September–October–November–December 1986), p. 5.

[10] Ibid.

[11] David Bensman and Roberta Lynch, *Rusted Dreams: Hard Times in a Steel Community* (New York: 1987), p. 204.

[12] Luther Jackson, "UAW Says Job Security Affects the Whole World," *Detroit Free Press*, August 10, 1987.

[13] Personal conversation with Jim McBride, UAW representative.

Chapter One

Team Players

This is not a time for old solutions, or a time to renew old habits of confrontation. This is a time to move forward as a Ford team, to find new and innovative ways to work together for the common good and a shared future.

> —*Donald Petersen,*
> *chairman of the board,*
> *Ford Motor Company,*
> *May 14, 1987*

Jeff Cooper

Born December 30, 1957, in Detroit
Hired May 12, 1976
Editor of World Class Classic, *the official newsletter of the Michigan Truck Plant*

FOR YEARS there was a stereotype of autoworkers as big-bellied, beer-drinking, loudmouthed troublemakers. That image was possibly accurate back when the unions were forming and the company was the enemy. But as times have changed, the people in the plants have changed. As the auto industry gets smaller and smaller, our jobs become more and more important. And workers react to that in different ways. In the plant now there are the far-right people, who are very much into change; they are willing to accept the industry the way it is today. Then there are the liberals, who don't want to change; they think it should still be dog-eat-dog, the company is the enemy, and the union's always right.

Most people are going along with the changes. They realize that for us to survive, we have to be competitive and that by working as a team, we can save jobs. If we build good products, people will buy them and we can keep our jobs.

The bottom line is we have to build so many trucks a day in order for the plant to make a profit. A lot of people in the plant say that quantity is really more important than quality, and to a

Jeff Cooper

degree that's true, because if each plant can't make a profit, then the whole company goes down, and everybody loses.

American autoworkers must decide that we are the industry, that workers and management together have to make it or break it. I work for Ford Motor Company, but I work to make money. I go there because I need so many dollars to survive. Ford is the vehicle to pay my bills. The auto companies and related industries employ millions of people. So, to some degree, what's good for GM is good for the country.

There are so many of us compared with management. We're the ingredients in the soup. We're a very necessary evil to the company. We're the means by which they make profits. And profits are good for all of us. The better Ford Motor Company does, the more people have jobs, the better our salaries are, and the easier it is for our union to negotiate benefits.

The company's starting to realize that we're a lot more important to the industry than they thought. It's because of us, not management, that there are profits. It's the attitude of the people. The guy who puts the bolt on, 99 percent of the time now he wants to build quality. Pride is coming back, and that pride benefits all of us.

The company has finally recognized that the person who has done a job for ten years knows more about it than some engineer. And they're letting him do things his way. That makes him feel like his job is important, not just a menial way to make money. He feels like he's contributing. Quality goes up, attitude goes up, cooperation goes up, and things are better for everybody.

Some people are against the Employee Involvement program. They see it as a downplaying of their UAW rights, as a company propaganda program. They say you're giving up your union identity to conform to company standards. I don't understand that way of thinking because we are the company. We are the people who determine whether profits are made.

I think we'll always have the UAW. There has to be a voice for the workingmen. The union is the watch guard, keeping lookout for all of us. But in the future the union will just protect human rights in the plant.

Eventually everybody in the industry will be a salaried person. There won't be an hourly and a management work force. There will be salary grades. That way they can get commitments and get the quality they want.

*   *   *

I first got involved in the Employee Involvement program after I was laid off from Wayne Assembly in March 1983 and got called back a few weeks later to the truck plant. In my new department there was a strong EI group. People met for an hour on Wednesday afternoons after work up in the conference room, and we got paid for it. We talked about all kinds of problems—anything from oil coming out of hoists to bolts not going in, case nuts coming off, bad clips, bad metal. We discussed how the company could improve quality and improve our jobs.

In the past nobody was taking care of these problems. It was dog-eat-dog. You came in, you hated your foreman, your foreman hated you, you did your job, and you hoped they didn't mess with you. They used to write you up for stupid things. The foreman would tell you to go somewhere and you would go get a drink of water on the way and he would write you up for not following a direct order.

Those days are gone, and EI helped get rid of them. You don't see people these days deliberately trying to make life miserable for their foremen. EI makes conditions better for everybody.

EI is good right now, but it's not as good as it should be because there are a lot of foremen who, like a lot of hourly people, are stuck in the old way of thinking. For EI to work, the foremen have to become totally committed to quality work and human relations like a lot of the hourly people already are.

The Japanese have been using EI for years. If used properly, EI can be a very good thing. But there's abuse. I don't feel somebody should use EI to eliminate a job, but I've seen it happen.

When I'm running EI meetings, I make sure we stay away from contractual issues. EI is not supposed to touch anything that's in the contract between union and management as to how jobs are performed and people are treated. EI is supposed to deal with quality issues: bad parts, bad stock, and other things that get swept under the rug in the rush to keep up production.

We're seeing a lot of improvements in the plants today because of EI and because of profit sharing. Profit sharing is much better than the old system of getting a 3 percent annual raise in our wages. It gives everybody an incentive to build better quality, so the company can sell more vehicles and make more profits. It also gives the company an incentive to spend money to improve their facilities, because if they didn't, they would have to pay that money to us in profit sharing.

One example is the computer class in the plant. The company

provides the room and the utilities, and the UAW helps pay the expenses. It costs the company money, but it benefits everybody. That's something that is coming out of the new wave of thinking. Then there's the weight room. They've taken out five hundred lockers and put in exercise equipment, and two hourly employees get paid to run the room. Those things help make the camaraderie stronger. And that's the way of business in the eighties.

Ford and the UAW have a tuition assistance program that is great. Five cents for every hour we work goes into what is called the nickel fund, and then the company matches it. The money pays for an education program which gives autoworkers a way to increase their capacity as human beings. There are no out-of-pocket expenses to get a degree. Other than books and transportation, everything is paid for. It's a shame that only 5 percent of the people use it.

As a result of these kind of changes, quality in the plant has definitely improved. Statistics show that warranty repairs have declined, and there is more customer satisfaction. We're building better quality today with half the work force of ten or fifteen years ago.

Back then quantity was the rule. The public would buy as many vehicles as we built. We had the market sewn up; there was no competition. But after the oil embargo of 1974 the Japanese took over as the small-car makers because they were building something that America wanted.

Today we still might be the biggest; but Americans have a real choice, and they buy what they like. I could go out tomorrow and buy a Toyota pickup truck or a Ford Ranger. They're both very fine trucks. But the Ford Ranger, even though it's built with some foreign parts, is still built in America by American people who have families to support, and the majority of parts are made by American suppliers. So if we buy American, there are a number of American people who are going to benefit.

Of course, it's funny how the company says, "Buy American," and they import foreign cars and put their label on them. We have an affiliation with Mazda, and we get Japanese condensers for the air conditioners on some of our trucks. But we have no control over how Ford chooses to do business. I have as much control over that as I do what kind of hamburger I get from McDonald's.

Americans owe it to one another to buy American. If you go outside the Midwest, which is the heart of the auto industry, it's amazing how many foreign cars you see. People in other areas don't see a direct link to jobs, so it's easier for them to buy a Toyota or a Datsun. Around here most cars you see on the road are American-made. If a guy owns a party store in Wayne, he had better be driving an Escort or a Ford truck. If people see he's buying their products, they'll patronize his store. But if he's driving a Toyota or a Datsun, people are going to say, "Screw this guy. He doesn't care about my job, so why should I care about his?"

If we don't buy, within reason, as many American-made products as we can, we're going to lose our way of life. Whenever I go shopping for shirts, I always try to buy something that says, "Made in the USA." I know then that I'm doing what I can do. It's hard to buy American if you can buy something else for half the price. But your dollar speaks strongest, and if enough Americans buy only American-made products, then prices will come down.

If it was up to me, I'd stop Japanese cars from coming into the country. Trade's killing us. But President Reagan is very much a believer in free enterprise. He feels that Americans are the leaders and it's up to the leaders to turn things around. Until the people decide enough is enough, our trade deficit will get bigger and bigger every year.

It's not just the company that benefits when people buy American. It's every guy on the assembly line who is supporting his family. He's got kids he wants to send to school. He wants to get his children a good life. If we don't buy American, we'll lose jobs, and jobs are not easy to come by. I'd hate to have to work for McDonald's for $3.50 an hour. Having to take that cut in pay would destroy me.

I don't have an unauthorized absence on my record in the last ten years. I get my work ethic from my father, who I have always admired. My dad's in charge of shipping at Fisher Body in Livonia. He's been there thirty-five years. He's only missed two days of work in the last fifteen years. One time he had all his teeth pulled and didn't miss a day's work.

I've been working since I was 12. I didn't grow up thinking: I'm going to build trucks for a living. I never had any intentions of being an autoworker. I had planned on going to college and becoming a writer or a lawyer.

When I was in high school, my mother's best friend was the telephone operator for Wayne Assembly and the Michigan Truck

Plant. In May of my senior year I asked her about getting a job in one of the plants. I was basically teasing. After all, my whole family worked for General Motors, and if I was going to get a factory job, it should be for GM. I was just looking for a job. If I could get one, great. I knew what kind of money you could make in a factory, because my brothers both worked at Fleetwood Cadillac and my father worked at Fisher Body.

This woman got me an interview at Wayne Assembly. The guy who interviewed me turned out to be a good friend of the woman who recommended me. He gave me the job. It just fell in my lap.

The next day I went in after school and worked ten hours. I thought I had gone to hell. I couldn't believe what people were doing for money. At the time they were building sixty-four Grenadas an hour. They had me working on the Trim Line, hooking up wires and metal under the dashboard. I ripped my pants on the third car that went by. I didn't have any coveralls, so I sat on my bare butt for nine hours. I couldn't believe how hard it was. But I thought of myself as a tough guy, and I was determined to stick it out.

When my algebra teacher found out I was working at Ford's, he told me, "That's the worst thing you could have done."

I said, "Why's that? I'm making as much money as most of the adults in this country."

He said, "Yeah, but you know what you're going to do? First, you'll buy yourself a new car. You'll marry that girl from Wayne High, you'll have yourself a couple of kids, and you'll be stuck in that factory for the rest of your life. You're too smart for that. You need to go to school."

I told him, "No, I won't. I'm going to work here a year, maybe two, and then I'm going to go to school."

He said, "You won't."

He was right. I bought a Chevette, married that girl from Wayne High, had a couple kids, and I'm still at the factory.

I don't want to end up spending thirty or forty years in the factory. Some people are comfortable with that, but I'm not. I want more. I'll have thirty years in when I'm 48. My goal is to be set up so that I can retire then and start my own business. I want to write books or, if I have enough money, buy a newspaper. I would love to put out a daily publication with my editorials in it. I also have aspirations of getting into politics.

* * *

I worked at Wayne Assembly for seven years. I was on afternoons and I hated it. I had a family, and I was working ten hours, going in at 6 P.M. and getting off at 5 A.M. It stunk.

My friends thought I was nuts. I was working so much I had no time to live it up. But after the recession hit, my friends were still working for minimum wage while I was making big bucks. Today a lot of my friends are still struggling. One of my friends went to college, and he's making $20,000 a year working for his dad in a restaurant.

When I got laid off from the car plant, I was in shock. But five weeks later I was hired back at the truck plant. There was only one shift, the day shift. I worked in Chassis, building the front ends for the trucks. I worked harder than I had at Wayne Assembly, but I liked days a lot better.

We're still working overtime. That keeps you from getting much else accomplished in your life. But it's incredible how much your life-style improves for two extra hours of work a day. The average income for hourly workers in 1985 at the truck plant was $38,600, working ten hours a day. That's a lot of money. If you're the least bit frugal or smart with your finances, you can save, you can buy property.

We're definitely upper-middle-class, even though we're blue-collar workers. Teachers don't make nearly as much money as we make. We live better than most people in the world. We have nice houses, we can buy new cars, and we can afford to feed our families. I always have driven the car of my choice. If I want to go out to eat, I always have $20 in my pocket to do it.

But working in an auto plant is not a free ride. We work hard, and most of us earn our money. It's not easy to come in here fifty hours, week after week. The hardest part is getting up at 5 A.M., no matter when you went to sleep. You go in, and you know you have ten hours ahead of you. Once you get the first hour in, it's just a matter of time. You did it yesterday, and you're going to do it tomorrow. Once you get in the groove, it's not that bad.

When I got called back to work at the truck plant in 1983, I had just been through a Dale Carnegie course, and my confidence was high. One day I just went up to the EI leaders and said, "Why don't we have a newspaper? I could be the editor." They said they'd keep me in mind.

In December 1984 the truck plant won an award for passing three consecutive Ford internal audits with less than 250 points for defects. We were the first full-size truck plant to get the 250 award. On Friday, the last day before the Christmas shutdown, the plant was going to get a "250" banner and have a ceremony. That Wednesday I was putting front ends together, and this new plant manager came up to me and said, "If you can have me a paper by Friday, it's your job." So I put together a little four-page paper with some stories about the 250 award and another story about a guy in the plant who had just bowled a 300 game. I pulled it off in just two days. I got a lot of accolades for that. They thought it was great that an hourly man could do something like that.

Now I spend one week a month, for pay, putting out the newsletter. I don't have to answer to anybody. I have total control. I'm not censored. But I'm smart enough to realize that there are certain things I don't touch. Sometimes people will approach me to do a story about a gripe they have, and I'll use my judgment whether or not I can touch it, because I don't want to lose my job. I can be very political, and I have a lot of opinions about things I don't like. But I know that doesn't belong in a newspaper that's trying to appeal to both management and hourly people.

As an hourly employee who's the editor of the company-funded newsletter, I have to walk a narrow line. I can't leave my roots and "be company," but I have to be company to a certain degree. I catch a lot of flak from people on the line who don't understand how I try to sit on that fence. I always try to balance things out in each issue of the newsletter. But I catch a lot of the strong pro-union, anticompany resentment that's still around.

The idea of the paper is to show that we in the plant can do anything if we work as a team. I try to keep morale high and instill pride in workmanship. I try to make people feel better about themselves. There's something about getting your name or your picture in print that makes people feel good.

I try to make everybody feel equally important. That's why I don't even mention the words *salaried* and *hourly.* We have to get away from that, from calling hourly people heads, as in "We need four heads in this area." They are human beings. "I need four workers" is a lot better way to describe a teammate, somebody who is important to the system, which we all are.

I'm a firm believer that America is based on the principles of the Bible. "In God we trust" is our basis. When I was growing up,

Jimmy Swaggart was a hero of mine. He's a real hellfire-and-brimstone evangelist who tells it like it is. He's not afraid to point fingers at the liberals in Congress.

What made America strong was our foundation, the family. We were the envy of the world until women started becoming more independent and leaving their families. And the children have been the ones who have suffered. Divorce and abortion have become acceptable. I think that's a disgrace to our society.

When I realized my marriage wasn't working out and divorce was inevitable, I told my attorney, "No matter what the cost, I want my kids." And I pulled it off. I have custody of my two sons. That's unusual because it's taken for granted in our society that if there's a divorce, the woman gets the kids. And that's a shame because nowhere in any rule book does it say women make better parents than men. Most women probably do, but not some modern women.

Girls once were raised knowing they were going to get married, have babies, and run the house. Nowadays women want a career. They want a man to be sensitive and understanding, the Alan Alda type, someone who will let them do their own thing.

But I wasn't raised that way. My dad was the boss in our household. He made the money, and he was king of the castle. My mother was the doting housewife. She was a very good mother who lived for her children. It's hard to find women like that today. They think they have to be more. And that's why the divorce rate and child abuse and abortion are increasing.

I don't believe in the Equal Rights Amendment because there are differences between the sexes. I do believe women are entitled to the same pay as men if they do the same work. I believe women should have the opportunity to work, but their main priority should be the family. That's what the Bible says. That's how God set things up.

In order to be strong again, we have to take care of each other and rebuild a strong family structure. The only thing we can control is our own backyard. If you keep a strong foundation, the whole country stays strong.

I still feel America's strong. Russia's a force to be reckoned with, but in a nuclear age it's a no-win situation. The superpowers realize that if there's a war, nobody wins. Being a human being, I have to feel that way. Otherwise, we have no hope. And I like to think we have hope.

*   *   *

I read [Lee] Iacocca's book recently, and I was very impressed, even though I don't agree with his philosophy of government. I think he leans toward socialism.

I believe in capitalism because it gives everybody an equal opportunity to succeed. Everybody has the opportunity to start a business without government intervention. That's free enterprise. I disagree with the government controlling anything. The government's functions are to provide defense and provide a school system, but beyond that it shouldn't intervene.

I'm basically a conservative. I think Ronald Reagan has done a decent job, even though people are hurting from it. He has put our country back on the right course. He's a firm believer in family and defense and morals, which is what our country was founded on.

Our rights are important. That's why I'm against random drug testing. I don't do drugs, but I don't feel I should have to prove that to anybody. It's my body. Cops can't come and search your house without a search warrant, but now they want to search your body, which is the only thing you have that is yours. By law we are innocent until proven guilty. That's one of the basic principles of our society.

The same thing with pornography. I think that stuff is terrible and it should be restricted. But if people want to view that type of material, they have the right to do that.

We are a very unique society because of the freedoms we afford one another. You can do what you want, and I can do what I want. As long as we don't step on each other, we can get along. People take these freedoms for granted, but if you wanted to walk the street at 3 A.M. in Russia, you couldn't do it.

If you look at our society, our society works. Sure, there are problems. We have crime, and we have poverty; but that's just man's inhumanity to man. Man doesn't always do things the way they should be done. But I honestly feel that democracy is the best way to live.

We have to regain the pride we once had. Autoworkers were very proud once. But people got lax because they were working and making money.

There was great national pride during World War II. Everything was rationed, and everybody was donating scraps and buying bonds, working for a common goal. That's when the civil rights movement really got started. We were fighting a fascist regime in

Germany, and America was practicing discrimination at home. Blacks were still second-class citizens here. And after the war people said, "Hey, wait a minute. If we fought Hitler, how come we have different bathrooms, different buses, different restaurants for different races in America?" It was an issue of national pride.

Our society is better off today because of the civil rights movement. Everybody has an equal opportunity now. And black-white relations are a lot better today in the plant than they used to be. The plant is like a city within a city. It's different than out in the streets because you have to work with people of every race every day. People come in and do their job every day with a certain amount of self-respect, be they white, black, green, or purple. Of course, you'll always have racists and bigots. That's human nature. It's just like you have the diehard union people who can't accept change.

In my lifetime I've seen blacks become equal. It doesn't bother me at all to have a black person as my neighbor. Twenty years ago it would have bothered my father tremendously. And he's not really a bigot; that's just the way society was then.

We probably have more diversity at auto plants than in any other business. It's a real melting pot. That's because people have come from all over the country to get jobs here. I'm a good example of that. My dad's from Mississippi, and my mom's from West Virginia. They came to Detroit in the early fifties to find a job. If the auto industry hadn't been making money, I might not have been born because my dad might not have been able to afford to support a family.

The industry changed our society. And now that the industry is changing, society is changing, too. The auto plants aren't hiring anymore. I think 1978 was the last year in Local 900 that Ford hired anybody.

Robotics is taking jobs. Attrition and forced reduction are facts of life in the eighties and nineties. That's something that we as a union have no control over. It's not our business. We just work here. I don't own this place. I just make my money here, I support my family here, and I hope I can work for a while. If the time comes when I lose my job, well, I lose my job.

The young people aren't getting factory jobs anymore. Instead, they are working at McDonald's or going to school. If I was 18 years old today and didn't have the money for college, I would probably go into the service and get trained in something I wanted to do.

My children's future is important to me. As long as my boys are in my house, they know school is their number-one priority. I'm putting two or three thousand dollars a year into savings bonds for their college education. I hope they'll want to go to college. I want them to do what I didn't. I don't want them to end up in a factory.

Lorenzo Sharpe

Born March 2, 1934, in Cuba
Hired August 5, 1965
Check and adjust person

I DON'T LET PEOPLE at the plant harass me. If they have prejudice, they can keep it in their heart. I look for respect, and I give
respect. I don't care about nationality, color, or anything. I don't
care if you don't like me, as long as you don't tell me to my face.
The company pays me to work, not to get harassed. I'm going to
do my job, and that's it.

A lot of people in this country don't like it if somebody from
another country has more than them. But anything you have
here, you worked for it. Nobody gave it to you. And I think
everybody could have the same if they wanted to.

When I was a kid growing up in Cuba, my dad was in charge of a
farm. I went to trade school in the city to learn how to be a
mechanic. The mechanics used to argue a lot about what was the
best car. I was crazy about Ford. I would say that one day Ford will
get ahead of General Motors. That was my dream, and now it has
finally happened. I'll always love Ford vehicles. I would rather
buy a Toyota than a General Motors car.

After I finished trade school in Cuba, I worked at the Guan-
tánamo naval base. I decided to come to the United States

Lorenzo Sharpe

because they were laying off civilians at the base and I was afraid I would get laid off. First I went to Chicago, where my brother works, but I didn't like it there. I moved to the Detroit area and tried to get a job at General Motors' Fisher Body Plant, but they weren't hiring. Finally a friend of mine told my brother he could get me a job at Ford, and he got me an application.

I started at the Michigan Truck Plant in August 1965, when the plant was just opening up. I was put on the second shift. I had never worked on a line before. It was rough. But I just went to work, and the days started to go by, and then it was no problem. I was a welder in the Body Shop for seven years before I got into Quality Control.

My wife works for General Motors, at the Westland Trim Plant. I have a lot of consideration for women who work in the plant. They are working to make a decent living just like us. I respect them just like I respect the men.

If you don't have an education, the only way to make a decent living today is to work in the plant. I made close to $45,000 last year, plus all those fringe benefits. Where can you make that kind of money?

We deserve the money we make. I work hard. I do the best job I can. I'll even miss lunch sometimes if there's a problem. I do that because the Quality Control manager and the assistant manager give me respect and recognition for what I do. They care a lot about me, and I respect them, too. When I have a problem, I talk to them, and they solve it for me.

It's not like it was fifteen years ago. Then, if you went to the plant manager's office for a problem, they would try to get rid of you. Now you can walk into any office and they'll tend to you.

Another example of the new respect in the plant is the program where some hourly employees are given new Bronco trucks to drive home overnight and check for defects. Before, only the supervisors could do that. The hourly employees can discover a lot of problems taking the trucks home because a lot of them have more knowledge than the supervisors. They are the ones fighting with the problems every day.

I have what's called a check and adjust job. It's a new classification. We find out what the problems are on the line and solve them before they get out of hand.

They say Americans make bad trucks, but we just put them together. It's not the truck that's falling apart; it's the parts. The Bronco is the best truck on the market, and if we had quality parts in there, not even the Japanese could compete with us. But we don't make the parts. The master cylinder comes from Japan. A lot of parts come from Mexico or Canada. A lot of the electronic parts they ship in here don't function and won't last the warranty.

I don't get mad about Mexico and Canada because they buy our trucks there. But I don't like the Japanese sending us bad parts because they make the price on American trucks so high that the average person there can't buy them.

The company created my job to improve quality. In the past, mistakes were going down the line and nobody would catch them. The defects would go out the door and get to the customers. Back then management didn't want to stop the line to fix something because that would hold up production. But Ford finally realized that lack of quality was causing a lot of problems.

For example, for a long time they were having problems with the door locks. The locks had more warranty repairs than any other part of the truck. I used to install the locks, and the foremen would always tell me I was messing up; but I knew it wasn't me. After I got this job, I found out the problem with the locks was the bad parts they'd been getting for years. I got together with the parts people, and we corrected the problem. Now, if a problem comes up with the locks, I show the vendors who sell us the parts and the operators who install them exactly what's wrong, and I make sure it gets fixed.

I'm still an hourly employee, but now I get more respect from the engineers. I used to try to talk to them, but they didn't pay much attention. Now I know all of them, and they're listening to me because they know their jobs depend on the job we do. If we don't do a good job and quality goes down and they stop selling trucks, we're all out of a job. It takes everyone working together and doing their part to get quality out.

Quality suffered in the past because vendors were sending us bad parts. Now I keep an eye on them. And instead of having to wait a month for a new batch of parts to replace bad ones they send us, now they have what's called "just-in-time" service. If vendors send us a lot of junk, we call them and they send somebody out immediately to solve the problem.

If vendors ship us something that falls apart, we'll sit down with them and show them how to make them right. There are operators in the Body Shop who have as much knowledge as any engineer, or maybe more, because they work every day with the parts. The operator can tell you if there's a defective part faster than an engineer can. And he can tell an engineer what design is going to work and what won't work.

Another part of my job is driving to the dealers to see what the problems are with the warranties so we can stop them in the plant. It's an effort to put the customer first.

Customers are tired of dealers who don't uphold the warranty. If I buy a truck that has a major problem from the factory and the dealer doesn't fix it right in the first place and gives me the runaround until the warranty expires, then I'm stuck with it. The Japanese don't do that. They make sure it's fixed right because they want you to come back. When you keep up a warranty, people buy from you again.

The people on the line who don't cooperate with the company's Employee Involvement [EI] program don't seem to understand that you have to produce quality today to compete. Nobody is going to pay $20,000 for a piece of junk that they have to take back and forth to the dealer.

When I first heard about the EI program, I didn't think I'd like it either. At the time I was on medical leave and they were laying off people, and there were rumors of more layoffs, so people were suspicious about the program. But when I took classes to get trained for the check and adjust job, I learned a lot about plant economics and realized the necessity for EI.

Most people think EI is a program to eliminate jobs, but it's not. If EI is done right, it helps people on the job.

I used to see some guys lying down on the job while one guy was trying to keep the line going. But I got them to understand that when they don't keep up with the job, the company loses money and we lose money, too.

If we get quality out, we don't have to be scared about losing our jobs. If we build good vehicles, they're going to sell, and we're going to have a job. But the company doesn't want to have a plant open making trucks that are not selling. The company has to make a profit. Quality is the bottom line.

I've told the people who run the EI program that they should have a meeting and let everyone know the economics of operating the plant: what the cost of downtime is; the way they make profits; where we get wages; where we get benefits. Then people would see why EI is needed, and everyone would get involved. As it is, supervisors tell the operators that they have to keep the line going, but the workers don't know why. They think it's just that the company is greedy. In fact, our wages are based on running a certain number of trucks a day. The company has to pay wages, gas, lights, and water regardless. So if the company loses ten jobs in a day, they don't get enough trucks out to cover the cost of running the plant.

When the company makes money, we make money, because of profit sharing. That's a bonus we didn't have before. Instead of wage increases, we get a lump sum. It's better that way because with an hourly wage increase all they do is raise your taxes and you never see the raise in your take-home pay.

There's still a lot of wrongdoing in the plant with good working people. In the past, if you had a problem on the job and you kept telling your supervisor about it and he didn't respond and you took it to the company's Labor Relations department, the supervisor would lie and the Labor Relations people would take his side. You would get frustrated and wouldn't give a damn about your job. Now Labor Relations people are trying not to take sides. But some of the production supervisors won't change.

It's a big problem when the supervisor won't listen to the guy who is seeing the problem on the job every day. If you don't solve the problem, the guy gets to the point where he doesn't care. You should help him, especially if he's a good operator.

The union is there to provide protection if the supervisors get out of hand. If the supervisor is lying to hurt a guy, the union and the company should make sure that guy doesn't get penalized. Sometimes a supervisor may not like you for some reason, and he gets you suspended without pay just to get even. If you don't work for two or three weeks, you are going to have a hard time. They should put a stop to that.

The union without us is nothing. If we stick together and help the union, it will be strong. The union is important, but only if people are united. We are the union.

I don't have any regrets about being an autoworker. The biggest satisfaction is what I have achieved for my family. I have my home, my cars. My house is paid off. I enjoy life. I've traveled. And my health right now is pretty good.

I never had a problem with working overtime. I'm never bored when I'm working because I keep busy. If you work at a slow pace, you get bored, and it'll be the same when you retire. That's why some people who retire just die or get sick, because they just give up. It's like a new car. If you drive it for five or six years at 30 or 40 miles an hour and then one day get out there and try to drive it at 80 or 90, it'll break down. I'm preparing for my retirement now. I'm going to invest my profit-sharing money in some stock or in the Ford money market funds, so we'll have something extra.

I think the most an autoworker should work is twenty-five years. That way the younger generation will be able to get jobs sooner. If they were offered early retirement, a lot of people at the plant would retire now and make sure they get a pension because they are scared that the plant might lay them off or close down and then they would end up with nothing. Nobody knows what's going to happen to our plant. But I think with twenty-two years in, if this plant closed down, I'd have a chance to go to another plant.

If they raised retirement benefits and let me retire now, I wouldn't work a day more. For what? The earlier I leave, the more I can enjoy life. I don't want to retire and die within two or three years like a lot of people do.

Mander "Lee" Thornsberry

Born December 3, 1944, in Topmost, Kentucky
Hired March 16, 1965
Union coordinator for the Employee Involvement program at the Michigan Truck Plant

WHEN I WAS WORKING on the line back in the sixties, if there was something I wanted from the supervisor and didn't get, I would let trucks go by without doing my job. I was no angel. Like everyone else, I would get away with whatever I could. They couldn't do anything to me, and that was the best way to retaliate against the supervisor: get his ass chewed for shipping incomplete jobs down the line. It happened a lot.

Back then it didn't matter what you said to your supervisor. You could tell him, "Look, this sealer is just not doing the job. Can't we get another type of sealer?" He didn't care, as long as he wasn't getting any flak.

When you got hired, they would tell you, "If you got a problem with your job, say something, let people help you out; we'll stop the line." But when you got on the line, you would catch hell if you did that.

Quality at the plant was pathetic in the past. Guys back then were instructed by supervisors: "Get it out of here. We don't care what kind of shape it is in, as long as we get our quota." I worked

36

Mander "Lee" Thornsberry

in Quality Control then, and I saw it. I once saw a truck leave here with an automatic transmission *and* a clutch in it. People didn't care back then. We worked a lot, and the trucks were selling even though they were bad trucks. Management's main theme was: "Get it off the line. Give me forty-two an hour, and I'm happy; I don't care how they are." As production workers we felt the same way. If they didn't care, why should we?

We would have lost it all if we had continued building the type of trucks we did then. If people hadn't gotten concerned about their jobs and about the quality of the trucks we build and the foreign competition and domestic competition, we would have been wiped out.

Back in the early eighties we were losing so many jobs that Ford had to make a change and the UAW had to go along with the change. The result was the Employee Involvement program, and the new theme was cost savings and quality.

When I started running EI, the reaction was almost all negative. Folks said I was there to help the company, that I was a suck-ass, even though I've always considered myself a good union man. It was really touch and go in the first training sessions. But as we explained what we wanted, we got more people involved. When we started doing training on Saturdays, we would get maybe ten guys involved out of thirty. Now we get almost everybody to come back for another session. Maybe some are coming for an easy eight hours' pay. That's all right with me. It still gives us a chance to tell them what we think.

We don't try to brainwash anybody. We don't try to force anybody into anything. If you want to be a part of it, fine. If not, that's OK.

Our philosophy is that it's all right to make suggestions about your job as long as you don't hurt anybody. Don't come up with any ideas that are going to eliminate a job. The company is doing enough job elimination without us helping them.

One instance that happened when EI first started gave the program a bad name. The Instrument Panel line came in on a Saturday, and the people on the line decided to relocate the stock and change some things to make their jobs easier. They knew the shortcuts because they'd done the jobs. That Monday the company made the shortcuts they suggested and eliminated a job off that line. That is not Employee Involvement. If the company is going to eliminate a job, let them do it, not the EI leader.

Of course, it is naïve to think that helping to get better quality or stock won't affect jobs. I know that somewhere down the road what we are doing is going to make it easier for them to eliminate someone. But I don't know if I can prevent that. I do know that if things had continued the way they were, it is possible none of us would have a job.

Ford is going to eliminate people no matter what we do. They are looking for ways to eliminate supervisors. They would like to go to the team concept with twelve people on a team and no supervisor. That's what they are doing at the Flat Rock Mazda plant. And General Motors has it at the Poletown plant in Detroit.

If there is anything I can do to make a man walk out of this plant with some satisfaction that it is not going to be as hard coming back tomorrow, I'm going to do it. But I'll never knowingly do anything to damage anyone.

In our training sessions I tell people we should do what we can to make Ford viable because these are our jobs. If Ford can make more money, fine, as long as we all keep our jobs and we are not hurting anyone. Anything we can do to build a better truck, I am all for it.

The union has given me direct orders not to let anybody in EI meetings get involved in areas covered by union contract. If a man tells me he needs a fan in his work area, that's a health-and-safety issue, so I'll tell him to go see his union committeeman or I'll see his committeeman. If you have too much work, that is also between you and your committeeman because work standards is a contractual area.

In EI sessions we try to train people how to work together as a group. Once a month we do listening exercises with hourly and salaried people to show how a message can get distorted as it goes down the line and to teach them how to really listen and understand what people are trying to say.

Employee Involvement is about how well the foreman and the guy on the line can communicate. If you can get these two guys to talk and not harass each other, then you're getting somewhere. Then, if my job is overloaded, my foreman should be willing to say, "I need some help for this man." And if the foreman has a problem, the guy on the line ought to help him. I really don't see the logic in messing up a truck just to settle a dispute.

The people on the floor are willing to work with us, but I'm not sure middle management is. We haven't yet gotten the foreman to where he is communicating with the worker as a person, not as a robot doing a job. The biggest change has to come from management. If they want us as hourly people to be really involved in our jobs, they have to get more involved in theirs.

People are a little more reluctant now to fight Ford Motor Company than they were back in the late sixties or early seventies. Back then it didn't take much to create a walkout. We had several wildcat strikes. The only thing we ever got out of them was ten or twelve people fired.

Back then in the union, if you weren't real violent, you weren't recognized by the employees. A committeeman would get more votes for fighting with a foreman than he would for correcting problems on a job.

People then didn't have as much pride in their work. You would sometimes see sabotage. I saw it happen when I worked on the Frame line. We used to have a breakdown once a week for a half hour because some guy would stick a tool in the line. These days people take more pride in their job, and that extra half hour isn't going to make or break them. They care more about how the trucks turn out. You very seldom see somebody sabotage something to get time off the job.

The layoffs in 1980 made a big impact. People became afraid they were going to lose their jobs. Another factor might be age. People have more to lose now. When you are 40 or 50 years old, it is hard to go out and get a job.

If they shut down the truck plant, I don't know what my next job would be because I don't have a college education. I'm not going to stoop to the level where I would do anything the company wants me to do to keep my job, but I am willing to give and take.

People have mellowed a lot. They are not as violent. At one time, if a foreman and a worker got into it, they were ready to go to blows. You would stand there nose to nose, fighting with a foreman. Now people have the ability to communicate rather than fight. I just don't see the yelling and screaming like I used to.

Maybe it's because the union and the company can sit down and bargain better today. Maybe it's because the union is more skilled in handling situations and not letting things get to the point where a man has to walk off his job to get something settled. Maybe it is just better communication between the company and the union on how to deal with change.

The union has helped by making it known that we are not viable as a union if we don't build a good truck. The UAW is a powerful organization, and they survive with what we pay them in union dues. They know if they don't convince the workers that it is important to build the kinds of vehicles people will buy, workers will lose their jobs and they'll lose dues money. The union's strength could dwindle real quickly if it lost too many more people. They've already lost a lot.

I learned about the importance of job security at a young age. My daddy was a coal miner. In the coal mines you could be working today and then tomorrow there would be no mine. That's what happened to him. In 1951 the mine closed, so we left Kentucky and moved to Ohio to work on a vegetable farm. We never had any money. My dad made $44 a week working on that farm. My mother and my three brothers worked the farm, too. I started working it when I was 10.

My mother died when I was 12, and my dad remarried when I was 15. My dad kept working on the farm. He never worked in a factory until he was 60.

I came to the conclusion when I was in high school that I wanted to be able to live better than my dad did. I was the only one in the family who graduated from high school. But I couldn't go to college. I didn't have any money, and there were no scholarships.

After high school I worked as a truck driver, making $35 a week. That wasn't enough to get by on, so I got a job in a bicycle seat factory and got up to $1.50 an hour. After I got married in

1964, we moved to Detroit to try to earn more money. I started working at the Continental Can Company for $1.75 an hour.

One day somebody told me that Ford was hiring. Now I had tried to get a job at a Ford plant in Sandusky, Ohio, but they told me I was too light because I weighed only 140. My weight wasn't even mentioned at the Michigan Truck Plant. My first day on the job there, they had me hanging tires on school buses.

That first week I must have quit at least twenty times in my head. I wouldn't want to walk out in the middle of the day, so I would try to make it to quitting time. The next morning I always came back. It was the money. I was making about $3 an hour and working fifty-eight hours a week.

But I had to work hard. Every day, as soon as I got out of bed about 1:00 in the afternoon, I would start dreading coming to work. We started at 6:12 P.M. and worked until 4:42 A.M. After a while I got used to it, but I never looked forward to coming to work, except for Fridays, when I would get that check.

My wife and I worked our marriage out around the overtime. We knew that overtime was our chance to buy a house. I would get home after 5 A.M., and she would be up, and we would eat breakfast together before I went to sleep. That's when we saw each other. Our marriage has lasted twenty-two years, and we've never even had an argument. I'm real proud of that.

Over the years at the truck plant I've held a lot of jobs: inspector, repairman, utility man, assembler. I never liked to stay in one place. I wanted to get the feel of everything. About three years ago I saw they were looking for someone to head the Employee Involvement program. I didn't know anything about EI, but I applied for the job anyway. I was surprised when the joint steering committee of union and company officials picked me. I started the job on a Friday and didn't have the slightest idea what I was doing. That Monday they sent me to school to learn about the EI program.

When I first started, I had a lot of problems speaking in front of people. I had never done that before. So the company paid for me to take a Dale Carnegie course. It helped a lot.

Now I enjoy coming in and doing this job. It gives me a lot of satisfaction helping people. My parents always taught me to respect people and treat people fairly, and I've always been that way. Even if I don't like somebody, I'll do what I can for him. For example, if a guy is buying a truck built here and calls me, I'll follow that truck all the way out to the garage to make sure that everything is done right.

I am satisfied to be where I am at now. I never expected to move up this high. I like being able to meet the higher-up people in the UAW and Ford. I've met Douglas Fraser, who used to be president of the UAW, and Donald Ephlin and Stephen Yokich, who are UAW vice-presidents. I've also met Harold Poling, the Ford president. I like to listen to their philosophies. I've learned a lot about Ford and the UAW from them. If I didn't have this job, I would never know more than a small part of what goes on in an auto plant or in contract negotiations.

Ford's intentions in Employee Involvement were to get people to be more involved in their jobs and to learn how to do the jobs better from the people who do them every day.

In Japan people are taught that approach from the time they are young, and jobs are set up differently. They work in groups of ten to twelve people with very few supervisors. Ford has picked up parts of the concept from the Japanese, like SPC and quality circles.

SPC stands for statistical process control and means doing your job by statistics. The idea is to keep a chart on each job and keep track of defects. If defects go above what is the normal percentage, you know something is wrong.

One group kept a chart on bolts. One day they had twenty-five bad bolts and the next day they had thirty, and they should have been getting only two or three defective bolts per batch. So they used those charts to prove to the vendor that he was sending them bad stock.

Quality circles are a group of ten to fifteen people who sit down to discuss their problems. We had trouble getting the quality circles to work here. So Louis Callaway, Jr., the plant manager at the time, decided to get one person from each work zone to talk to everybody in that zone and ask what could be done to make the jobs better and get better quality. That guy became the zone leader. The company let him off the line once a week for a few hours and let him try to take care of problems, rather than the foreman or the supervisor.

The idea was to leave everything up to the workers in each zone. Let them choose the zone leader from within their group. Let them change leaders, give everybody an opportunity to be an EI leader. It started working better that way. The only problem we had was getting people to give everybody an opportunity. Sometimes one guy would really get into being the zone leader because you could get some good free time on the job, three or four hours a week to walk around, trying to help somebody who has a problem on the job.

The EI leaders would take responsibility for things like new floor mats. The company had done an ergonomics study, a study of how to work with less strain, and decided that floor mats would save your feet and Ford wouldn't have as many medical problems. So they gave us money in EI to pay for the floor mats with the requirement that people had to get involved with it. It became the EI leader's responsibility to find out who in his zone wanted them, where they wanted them, how much they cost and to make a report to the joint steering committee. The mats would get pretty expensive, but the money was always approved.

Sometimes we send the EI leaders away to solve a problem. For instance, we were getting bad radiator supports from Chicago. We had engineers talking to engineers for three years on these radiator supports, and nothing happened. So we sent three people off the line to Chicago. They went and talked to the people who were building those radiator supports and said, "Hey, can't you help us out a little bit? You are killing us at the truck plant." And you could see improvements after that.

The Ford Woodhaven Stamping Plant used to be one of the worst suppliers for body sides. The body sides they sent us were wavy. We started taking five guys a week to Woodhaven, and then the next week they would send five people over here, and we would show them how it affected us when they sent bad parts. You wouldn't believe how the quality of the side panels went up in just a year just because one hourly worker was talking to another hourly worker.

As a result of these things, warranty figures that come back from the dealers are much better now than they were a few years ago.

I am a firm believer that a person who works the job has the ability to correct the problems of that job better than any engineer. Very few of those engineers got their knowledge from experience. They got it from the book.

Bernard Clifford

Born July 12, 1948, in Bay City, Michigan
Hired July 28, 1972
Utility welder

WHEN I FIRST WAS HIRED, the plant was run really badly. The workers felt like they were not part of the process and that nobody gave a shit about them, and management reinforced that feeling. It was like a war between management and the workers. For one side to get the other to do something, they had to bring out the guns and hold them to their heads.

Now there is Employee Involvement, which is supposed to get the workers to feel like they are part of the production process, that they have some input. That's a real sound idea. It's just what I always thought should have been done all along.

I'm always a little leery of anything like EI at first. Management talks a good line, but to implement a change is another thing. When EI first started, nobody trusted management, so only a few people were involved in it, and most of them were suck-asses that nobody trusted. To get more involvement, management had each group pick its own EI leader, rather than have them appointed by the foreman. Some guys I worked with asked me to be their EI leader, and I was voted into the job.

EI has improved things. There is a lot less animosity between

UAW-Ford
Employee Development and Training Program
On The Road to [?] and Your Horizons

Bernard Clifford

workers and management. People feel more like they are a part of what is going on. They are not just tied to the machine. They are not peons. The EI program raises everyone's self-respect. I never had too much self-respect at work before I got involved with EI.

I'm also on the education committee for UAW Local 900. There's a lot of money spent for education. They have computer classes. They have a class for small-engine repair. There are orientation classes for people who want to go to college.

The union is working more with management now, and it is less of an adversary relationship. That's a gain because if it is "us against them," nothing gets done and people have a lot of bad feelings.

The adversary relationship worked all right in the past, but now we have to compete with the Japanese. They build a better product. They have better worker relations. The American companies were no longer successful with their old management program, so they either had to change or lose their business.

Now the company talks about a closer relationship between management and workers. They should implement more of what they talk about because there is still a lot of the old shit that goes on. There is still some hostility among workers. And there are still foremen who boss you around or write you up, who take an authoritarian position instead of talking to people like they are people, asking them their opinion and trying to work with them. There are still a lot of people, workers and management, who think the other side is a bunch of assholes and who have an attitude of "Fuck them."

Quality now is a lot better. Anytime you get people to be a little happier, they are going to do a better job. Most people want to do a good job. They like to feel they have tried and done their best even if they don't like the work. I hate the work, but I always try to do the best job I can.

I still think of this as a temporary job. It's been a temporary job for me for fourteen years. And if I stay here thirty years, it's still going to be a temporary job. I'll never give up on my dreams, no matter how much I think I have to stay in the plant and I don't have any choices. My dreams are too important.

I don't want to lose the idealism of the sixties. I'm more mature now, but my attitudes haven't changed much. I believe in the same things. Family is still real important to me. Having an awareness of what is going on around me and what I can contribute is important. Just enjoying life is important.

I made $35,000 last year. But money is kind of irrelevant because you always exist on what you get, no matter how much you make. If I made less money, I would live with it. If I make $40,000 this year, I'll spend $45,000. I'm always working to get out of debt, but I haven't succeeded yet.

In fifteen years I could retire, but by then the truck plant could be gone. I don't give a shit if they close it down or not. In some ways it would be a godsend for me. It would get me off my ass and make me do something I really want to do. I would like to have a job related to psychology, where I could work with people and help them deal with their lives.

Most people feel their job is their life. But my job is not important at all to me. It is just something I have to do to bring in money. I'd rather not work the overtime. An eight-hour day would be great; it would feel like a vacation after working ten hours a day for so many years.

The only time I think about the plant is when I'm there. When I'm outside, I divorce myself from it. I used to come home to my ex-wife and bitch a lot about how much I hated the plant. I wasted a lot of time bitching about something I had no control over. I finally realized that either you live with it or you quit. So now I live with it, and I try not to let it bother me.

I run big guns that weld together big pieces of copper and metal in the body. Welding the tailgates used to be a real bitch because I'd have to lift them up by myself. They weighed seventy-five pounds and I weigh 160, so it was a real workout. In 1985, because of EI, we finally got a hoist installed to lift the tailgates. We'd been bitching about it since 1978.

I'm a utility man, too, so I cover a job if they need somebody. I try never to work the same job two days in a row. I hate working the same job all the time. I get paid more for knowing all the jobs, but not much, about 10 or 15 cents an hour.

I used to be a relief man and work jobs for people taking breaks; but robots replaced a number of the welding jobs, and since I was a low-seniority relief man, I lost that job. Robots eliminated a lot of welding jobs, but they have created a few, too. Every day the robots mess up and miss welds. Sometimes they can reprogram the robot and correct the problem, but usually they have to wait until the line is down to fix it. So they need an extra man to do the welds they miss. I do that a lot.

My work is often boring, but I move around a lot, goof around, and talk to people to pass the time. There are a lot of interesting people in there to talk to. We talk about movies or politics or our families. That helps, plus now I'm clear that it is just a job. My attitude has changed. I'm a good worker, and I don't mind working. I have a good attendance record. I don't think about how bad it is, and it's not so bad.

I grew up in Midland, Michigan, and if I expected to work anyplace, it would have been at Dow Chemical, where my dad was a foreman. I never even knew that cars were made in Detroit, and I never once thought about working in an auto plant.

My dad got the job at Dow when I was 5, and we moved from Bay City and bought an old farm for about $2,000. We had a big house and fifty or sixty acres, one or two cows and pigs, and a horse. The closest neighbor was three-quarters of a mile away. The house was surrounded by woods.

I had three brothers and two sisters, and they were my only friends. My brothers and I were real close and always hung out together. I'm still real tight with them.

One of my brothers went to Vietnam. I lost a few of my friends there. I was really opposed to the war. I didn't feel I owed it to anybody to get my ass shot off for nothing. So I cheated and lied to get out of the draft. I did drugs before my physical. I put needle tracks in my arm to make them think I was a junkie. I took so much speed for three days that it made my blood pressure go up so high that they gave me a 1-Y and I never got retested.

There are a lot of Vietnam vets in the plant, and I envy the way they are all bound together by their experience. But none of them has ever given me any static about not going. They all say, "I don't blame you. That was the smart thing to do."

In 1972 I had just lost my job at Ypsilanti State Hospital as a child-care worker, and my wife was pregnant with my first daughter. I was out driving around, looking for work, one day and saw the truck plant and said, "What the hell?" At the time they hired new people every day, and I was one of the lucky ones.

My ambition was to do psychology. I was still in college, and I managed to finish my degree eventually, even though I kept working at the plant. But I haven't used it for anything. You can't make as much money with a bachelor's degree in psychology as you can in the truck plant. The truck plant is big money and a lot of benefits. The medical benefits have helped me a lot. They've paid for all the counseling and therapy I've had.

I had it made the first few months I worked in the plant. I hired in as an inspector's aide, and I worked only eight hours a day. It was real easy, and I got to go around and talk to people. But then they sent me to reality, to the Body Shop, and I got stuck in the grinding booth, doing a really nasty job. I had to put on the door hinges and grind all the places where there were burrs from the welding guns. I used an air-pressure grinder and heavy-duty sandpaper. The grinder threw sparks and a lot of dirt. I got metal in my eyes a few times. I finally got some good goggles, but it took me awhile because I didn't bitch enough.

I really hated it. While I was on that job, I did a lot of drugs, mostly speed. Speed gives you a lot of energy, and you don't feel depressed—until the next day, and then you have to do it again. Back then speed was pretty common with the younger guys. I was young and kind of stupid, and getting caught and getting fired never crossed my mind. I didn't advertise the fact that I did drugs. I didn't smoke dope because you can't smoke dope and do the job. But speed kept me going.

I was depressed an awful lot back then, but doing drugs just made things worse. I had a wife and a child, and I felt like a failure because I had gone to school for a long time and hadn't finished and my job was really lousy and boring and I wasn't too happy with my wife.

I really hated having to do the same thing over and over every day. And on the job I had, it was hard to talk to anyone. I was inside a booth, and the closest person to me on the line was the door hanger, who was outside the booth. To talk to him, I'd have to quit working and go outside. I did that a lot, even though it was impossible to catch up once I got behind. But I was desperate to talk to someone. Without conversation there wasn't anything but the job.

To pass the time, I would think about what I wanted to do for a living. Back then I thought somebody owed me a decent job that I liked, but I didn't feel I should have to make any kind of effort to get it. So I stuck it out, but only because I had a daughter and I had responsibilities and I figured it was better to stay than to just quit and not have anything.

My wife never seemed to understand how much I hated the plant. She liked the security of it and didn't seem to care too much that it was hell for me. Eventually we split up. I had married her when I was 20 and she was 18; we were both too young.

After about a year in the plant I finally got smart and quit doing speed and started going to therapy because I didn't feel like I was doing what I wanted in my life. The therapy has helped me adjust so that the job doesn't seem so bad.

My first wife and I had our first daughter after we'd been married about four years, then another daughter three years after that. It wasn't an easy thing to accept all that responsibility because I was real self-centered. But I did a fairly decent job even if I wasn't that well equipped for it emotionally.

We separated when Heather was 10 and Amber was 7. For four years I raised the kids by myself, with a lot of help from my girlfriend. Every morning I was exhausted, but I would get up at 4:30. Heather would get her sister off to school after I left for work. A neighbor was supposed to check on them, but she was real irresponsible and didn't do much. I would call home after I got to work to make sure they were up and had their lunches and were ready for school. A lot of times, when there wasn't school, they just stayed home by themselves. I would work my ten hours, come home, and take them to McDonald's. Now they're living with their mother in Washington, and I'm remarried. I miss them.

I hope my daughters are able to discover what they want to do in life. I never really knew what I wanted to do or how to get what I wanted. I've taught them it is important to enjoy life. I've taught them they don't have to go along with the way things are supposed to be and accept everything blindly.

I wouldn't want them to work in a factory. I've always told them: "Don't do work you don't want to do just for the money. It's not worth it."

Chapter Two

Breadwinners

The greatest benefit of working in the plant is
the money. The fringe benefit is the people you
meet.

> —*Calvin Rachal,*
> *Michigan Truck Plant worker*

Gary Shellenbarger

Born November 13, 1949, in Detroit
Hired August 21, 1970
Painter

I AM A PERFECT PERSON for factory work because it takes very little to entertain me. I've been programmed real well by TV. I grew up with TV.

My father and mother were divorced right before I was born. My mother raised me by herself until I was 7. She worked in a supermarket, and I spent a lot of time by myself at my grandmother's house. Television was just starting out then, and I watched it all: Howdy Doody, Captain Kangaroo, Milky the Clown, and Soupy Sales. I'd have lunch with Soupy. The TV was the friend I spent most of my time with.

In the early fifties my mother bought a house in Taylor, outside Detroit. It was a little burned-out shell of a house, but it sat on thirteen lots. Taylor was still just swamp and woods. The house had an outside toilet and no indoor plumbing. We carried in water from the fire hydrant.

Over the years my mother unloaded eleven of the lots and kept two of them. She made enough money to put some additions on the house and paid everything off. When I was 7, she remarried.

My stepfather's parents were from Croatia; my mom's parents

Melisa, Eric, Jennifer, Gary, and Judy Shellenbarger

were from Kentucky. My stepdad was an intelligent man, real
artistic and secure with himself, very sophisticated. He got a job
in Detroit as a lab technician. He never missed a day of work,
even though he'd stay up to read until two or three in the morning. He went to work, took classes two nights a week, figured out
how to fix everything around the house, and built some more
additions.

Two years after she remarried, my mother was able to quit
work and start a second family. I finally got a brother and a sister
so I had someone else to play with.

I remember when I started out in kindergarten, I felt as smart
as anybody. But right away I started being compared with other
students, so I started thinking of myself as not being as good as
them and started getting treated that way. I was held back in the
second grade because I was a slow learner.

By ninth grade I realized that I would need a good high school
record behind me if I was going to go to college. So I began taking
college prep classes. I did pretty well. I made the baseball and the
football teams. Being good at sports gave me a little bit of status. It
helped me keep up my interest and get through high school. I was

never a really dynamic student. I tolerated the learning, but there was no inner hunger or desire.

I pumped gas on weekends during the baseball and football seasons and after school between seasons. I saved up enough to buy a car, a '55 Mercury, for $55. I took it to the junior prom. Most of my friends worked and had cars.

I applied to Northern Michigan University because I loved the woods and they had forestry courses. They accepted me on probation, because I had gotten a D-minus in chemistry. That summer one of the teachers I was close to, who was a coach, told me, "You're not college material. You're going to end up working at Ford on the assembly line." I never really knew if that was his view of me or if he was issuing me a challenge.

I didn't get an athletic scholarship, and I had always counted on getting one. My mother offered to go back to work to help me pay for college. I didn't really want her to, and there was also a little fear in the back of my mind that I might not be able to maintain a C average and I would get kicked out and lose my draft deferment.

A friend of mine who worked with me at the gas station just quit one day and took a job at Fisher Body. He told me to apply. So I got on my sports coat, my gray pants, and my white shirt; that was the only way I knew how to apply for a job. I walked in the employment office, and there were all these people in blue jeans and T-shirts. I wasn't sure I was in the right place.

They asked me if I wanted hourly or salaried employment, and I said hourly. They asked if I had any plans to go to school, and I said yes, thinking what other kind of person would they want to hire except someone smart who was going to school, getting ahead. "Oh," the guy said, "well, that's part-time employment. We're not hiring part-time people right now."

I was really upset. I needed $1,000 for room and board at college, and I was only making $3 an hour at the gas station. So I went down to the draft induction center and signed up. I wanted to get the burden of military service off my back so I could get on with my life. I knew the GI Bill would handle the financial end of my education. I was going to be on easy street and have a good time going to college when I got done. I thought if I let my mother put me through school, I'd wash out, get drafted, go to Vietnam, get blown away, and it would all be a waste. So I decided to get it over with.

I went to Fort Knox for eight weeks of basic training. People told me not to volunteer for anything, but I did because almost everything I volunteered for meant I had to go for more training, and the more training I took, the more time I spent stateside and the better odds I had of getting through my two years. I burned up about a year that way, going to jump school, going to NCO [noncommissioned officers] school, getting trained for this and that.

I knew that the army was giving people who came home from Vietnam an early out. If they had six months or more of service time left, they served it stateside. I also had my eye on the dollar. I wanted to make as much money as I could, so I could have a little when I got home. So I volunteered for what I thought was the safest assignment, which was going out in the jungle on reconnaissance patrol every four days, with nothing to do in between. Just snoop and poop in the jungle with lots of artillery support. At least that's how the guy from this Airborne Ranger outfit described it. I added up the days I would have to spend in the jungle and the days I would be out, and I started thinking my odds were getting better all the time.

When I was a kid watching an army movie or when I heard older people talking about relatives or friends who got killed in the war, I thought it would never happen to me. And the first couple weeks in Vietnam it was just like in the movies. The enemy always died, and none of us did. But then one guy got shot, and the next week two more got ambushed. I went out in the jungle and picked up their bodies, and my whole attitude changed—from that gung ho, John Wayne, go-get-'em, shoot-'em-up idea to "I'm just going to do what I am supposed to do, stay away from the killing as much as possible." I didn't want to have to kill anybody. So I laid low. I wasn't going to be a hero. I wanted to get my six months over with and go home. And I managed to do it.

I had gone over there wholeheartedly. I believed in what I was doing. But then the United States just up and walked out of there. All of those lives were wasted, all that for nothing. Now I feel like they played with my life.

When I got out of the service in April 1970, I was married and had a child. I had the woman that I wanted and I had the military obligation out of the way, but now I had to support a family. I went to work at Farmer Jack supermarket for three months but was only making $100 a week. My wife had a job at K mart, and our two measly little incomes did not allow us to support ourselves.

We didn't have a house, so we stayed with her family a few weeks, then with my family a few weeks.

After I got laid off at Farmer Jack, I heard they were opening a new Ford parts plant down on Pennsylvania Avenue. So I went down there and filled out the application, and the guy asked the same questions. I told him, "Look, I'm married, I have a child, I have responsibilities. I have to have a good job, and I plan on going to school part-time on the GI Bill. What other kind of person do you want working for you?"

He checked with his boss and came back and told me: "Sorry, I can't touch anybody who's going to school." It made me wonder whatever happened to "Honesty is the best policy."

I walked out of there not sure if I'd ever get a job. I drove all the way to Saline and applied at the Ford plastics plant. I filled out two applications there, the hourly and the salary, but they weren't hiring.

Finally I ran into a neighbor whose husband worked at the Michigan Truck Plant, and he gave me a referral card. I went down there, filled out the application, and took a physical. I told them I had no plans to go to school. Then I asked the guy, "How come you can't hire anyone who might be going to school?"

And he said, "Because it costs so much to train them and they leave right away."

I said, "Well, I would think you would want people interested in education, you would want smart people to work for you."

And he said, "It's a funny thing. We can't hire anyone who's going to school, but after you've worked here six months, if you decided to go to school on a part-time basis, we'll help pay for it."

I kept that in mind. I wasn't breathing a word that I was planning on going to school.

I remember the day I started work, the personnel manager told me, "You're going to make more money than I do, but the difference is that you're going to earn it." And I remember thinking: It's about time. I need it so desperately. See, I felt a lot of pressure because I wasn't providing for my family. I had all the responsibilities of a full member of the Establishment but not the income.

My first job was putting pop rivets on the back of the cab. I had to hustle, but I was able to keep up with it. That was a Friday, and we worked fifteen hours. The next day we worked nine. I loved it. The first week I took home $180 after taxes, and that was for only two days. When I got the paycheck, I raised my arms up and said, "Yahoo! I found it!" I finally had a good-paying job. I took the money and found an apartment for $150 a month. My wife was elated.

It had been a real strain not being able to support my family. I didn't blame myself, but I was very frustrated that I had been caught in that position, especially after I had blown a good job by telling the truth twice in a row. You see, I was the perfect example of the all-American boy. I had a good solid family life; I didn't see where I had done anything wrong. But now I'd finally made it. I'd finally learned how to get around the obstacles. Too bad I had to lie about my personal intentions, but I did what I needed to do to get the job.

I didn't miss a day of work. We signed a one-year lease on the apartment, and the overtime I was working let us immediately start saving to buy a house. It gave us all we needed. The first year I made about $6,000, but I started in August. The next year I made $12,500. In 1985 I made $54,000, but I worked all the overtime available. You see, I'm very materialistic. I'm a goal setter, and I'm a planner.

That first year I started working on my plans: I worked at Ford in the afternoon and got set up, applied for my VA loan, and found a house in a subdivision close to work. My situation had really changed: I was in. I was established.

In the factory I never took a side. I went there to do a job. I kept my sights on what I was going to do, what I went there for: the paycheck. Everything else was insignificant. The most important thing is that I would do for them what they wanted, and I was to get what I wanted. I wanted the money. If they are paying, then I'm staying. It's as simple as that.

I observed that the easier jobs paid the same as the harder ones, so I figured I wouldn't work harder than I had to. I would try to get the easier job. Intelligence didn't come into play unless you were on salary; you weren't really part of the decision-making process. The management made all the decisions; you had no responsibility.

I remember in high school the teachers always belittled factory workers and unskilled manual laborers. When I worked in the supermarket, I wore a white shirt, bow tie, and dress pants, and I worked with the public. Was that rewarding? No, because the pay was bad. What was rewarding to me was what I took to the bank. In the plant I don't have to deal with the public, I don't have to talk to this truck, I don't even have to talk to the guy next to me (I can hardly hear him anyway with all the rumble and roar). I can sit there and just program my body to do what I have to do to assemble the truck and let my mind drift anywhere I want to go. There is no pressure. And once I'm out the door, I don't give the plant another thought until I go back.

I found something I could do well enough, fit in, please the management, work the overtime. If the overtime hadn't been there, I would not have been as comfortable in the job. It was meeting my requirements, but I didn't want to stay there. I wanted more. I felt that college was a requirement of society, and I saw those salaried workers and figured I could start at the bottom, go to college, get a degree, and change sides. I could go on salary, become part of management, climb the ladder, and make some money.

So I started going to school at night. I still had high goals, and I set my sights on being a lawyer. I didn't know if I could do it, but I figured I would rather go for something that was worth something and fail than go for something that had a nice title and no financial reward.

I went to school part-time for over ten years. All that time I worked fifty to sixty hours a week and went to school two nights a week. I had very little social life. People told me I must have a boring life. I didn't see it as boring; what else was there? I didn't care about playing softball—I had played sports all through high school; I'd already done enough of that. I didn't need the social life, the recreational activities. I had my sights on a different goal.

I wasn't home much for my son and my two daughters when they were young, but I didn't think I was missing much. I wanted to have all my education out of the way and be very well established in my new career by the time they were in junior high school. I figured by that time I would be able to pay them back, be their father and their buddy, too, play baseball with them. So I swapped my time with them for the future.

Some people in my classes said they were going to college because they didn't want to work in the factory. I thought that was funny. Here I was going to college, working in the factory, driving a new car, and they were driving junk. I was living in a house, and they were renting an apartment. I had Blue Cross, and they were going to the clinic. I had three kids, I was supporting my wife, she was going to school, I was going to school, and we weren't hurting at all, and they were belittling the people who work in the factories. I didn't see what they were laughing at. I didn't see anything degrading about a hard, honest day's work. I didn't have any special skills or any special training, and I didn't need any scholastic requirements to do what I was doing. I just had enough desire to put in a hard day's work.

After I got my liberal arts requirements out of the way, I decided to major in accounting because I figured from there I could go into law school, or if I didn't get in, I could take the state CPA exam and go into tax law, and if I couldn't handle that, I could just settle for being an accountant. Later on I became a computer major, too. See, I was always thinking of how to market myself because you have to be prepared to do something if your job is not there anymore.

Around 1978 I was finishing up my accounting major. The courses were hard, and I was struggling with the overtime. I saw there was a promotion available to a foreman's job, so I took it. One of the reasons I took it was that I didn't really like the way things were being run and I wanted to change things. But I found out how little control a foreman really has. A salaried person is subjected to puppetism. You have instructions that come down from upper-echelon management, and you don't question them. You have very little input.

So I became molded into what they wanted. I kept the place moving, got along with people, kept them content, took care of their needs. I became their problem solver and got the job done and fit in. Whatever they wanted I gave them, wholeheartedly. The pay was not that much more, but I didn't have to put in the hours that the people on hourly were putting in to make the same amount.

I liked being on salary, but I was not an organization man. I was not devoted to the organization; my life did not revolve around my job. I just wanted to give them what they were paying for. I followed the rules, but I wanted to come home on my time and be with my family. For me, the job was a vehicle to attain my personal goals.

I had figured I could handle being on salary and going to school, but I was wrong. I lost two years of my college. Between 1978 and 1980 I passed one class. They would change my shift in the middle of my semester, and that would mean I would have to switch classes, and that didn't work out. Educationally I lost, and in 1980, when they eliminated a shift, I lost financially, too. I went back on hourly, but the work wasn't steady: I would work one week, take two off, work another week, take two more off. I couldn't afford to go to school anymore. I lost sight of it for a while. I got within ten classes of graduating, so close.

I still might finish the degree someday, become a CPA, go to law school for tax law or something, or I might develop a family business. These are still possibilities. But for now I'm taking care of my family. I'm programming them for the next five years. I owe each of them something: a set of skis, a computer, a new car.

I won't let my kids fail. I put carrots out for them. I'll buy them a new car if they get all As. I also tell them if they save $250 I'll add $250; if they save $1,000 I'll add $1,000, and then they'll have enough to get a car. So they have two ways to get what they want.

I have some regrets about the direction my life has taken, even though I still enjoy making the money and meeting my materialistic goals. The work is hard, and the money's not always going to be there. I tell my kids, "Look, everything I had and everything you see and count on me for will not be there for you. It's gone, that job is gone, society is changing, it's changing from a manufacturing and laboring society to a technological and information society. If you want to have control, as much control as possible over your life, you have to prepare yourself now. You have to learn the skills." A professional person or a skilled person takes their job with them. But a laboring person or an unskilled person, their job dictates to them where they live and how they live; they don't have the control.

My sister-in-law and her husband moved to California in 1980. He's got a lot of skills, and now he works for Northrop, making government aircraft. I sent the kids out there for the summer, and my son came back and said, "Dad, let's go live in California."

I said, "Look, son, I'd love to, but I'm not prepared to go out and work in that economy. My job does not go with me; it's here. I can't live anywhere I want to. Look around you. Everything that we have is because I gave it to you. I'm trading my life for a dollar. The more hours of my life that I give them, I get more dollars."

I've been taking some time off lately to spend more time with my kids. If I squander the time now, it's gone forever. I gave up all those years with them when they were young. Now I'm trying to give them as much time as I can. I coached a girls' softball team; I trained with my son for the wrestling team; we go motorcycling in the woods; we go hunting together.

We're buying a new house in Livonia, and the house payments will be $700 or $800, compared to $320 now. That's going to eat up a bunch of my spendable income. But I'm doing it to put my kids in the most comfortable educational environment to prepare for college. If I gear them right and motivate everyone right, my wildest dream is that someday we could have our own family accounting firm. I don't want to depend on Ford. After my kids graduate from college, if I prepare them properly, I'm home free.

Dee Mueller

Born August 25, 1954, in San Diego, California
Hired April 25, 1978
Assembler on the Final Line

WORKING IN THE PLANT is not much different from being a waitress. A waitress puts up with a lot of shit. I do, too. One time, when I was working at Wayne Assembly, a guy grabbed my ass, and I slapped him so hard my hand hurt.

I was raised not to take any shit, to stand up for what I think is right. I've never been pushed around. Even when I was little, I could take care of myself. My brothers used to kick my ass, and that's how I learned to fight.

I'm like one of the guys now. I can get into the groove of all the joking and playing around. There are a few guys in the plant now who come around and squeeze my ass. It doesn't bother me, because when I walk by them, I say, "OK, free feel for a free feel," and I goose them. I'm the only woman on my line, and if the guys are going to grab me, I'm going to grab them back.

When I worked in the Body Shop a few years ago, I was the only female. But there was no problem. At parties the wives and I would have a good time. It was like they thought: She's not that bad. It made me feel good when they'd say, "We don't worry about our husbands if they're with you."

Dee Mueller

I wear my purple tennis shoes at work, so that people will know when I walk by. I told the assistant manager I just wanted to blind people. One time I wore my pajama top to work. I just do it to have fun.

Once in the Body Shop somebody told me what I was wearing was distracting the men. I had a bathing suit on under my coveralls. So I told this guy who was complaining: "Look at these men in their coveralls. Their pants are all the way down, and I can see their underwear. You tell them to snap up, and I'll snap up." By the end of the shift they had all snapped up.

My union rep still tells me, "Don't be bending over. Why did you wear something like that?"

And I say, "Hey, I just wanted to wake you guys up."

I get along with everybody in the plant. The only guy who ever gave me any shit was my old foreman in the Body Shop. He didn't like me, and I didn't like him. Once this 100-pound tool I was using broke off its chain and fell right next to my foot. He ordered me to pick it up, and I told him, "You're out of your mind." He threw a drill at me, so I spit in his face. I went to Labor Relations, and they got somebody to pick it up and put it back on the chain.

When I first got put on the Chassis Line, this guy I didn't even know started bitching at me because I wasn't hooking up the wire right. When he got done, I said, "Wait a minute. Don't yell at me. I'm right next to you. Besides, that isn't even part of my job." And he apologized. When I know I'm right, I go for people's throats.

The people in the plant are the same as when I started. Everybody is there for the money. The only difference is that I don't need as much money now as I did then.

My mom is from Detroit, but she lived in California for a year or so, and while she was there, she got pregnant with me. I was raised mostly by my grandmother in Lincoln Park, outside Detroit. My mom was working, and she couldn't handle all five of us kids, so my brother and I lived with Grandma. I bounced back and forth. I went to school in Lincoln Park during the school year and lived with my mom in Detroit during the summer.

The only time the parents, grandparents, all us kids, and all of our kids have ever been together was for Christmas 1971 at Grandma's.

My mom was a waitress all her life, but she eventually moved into managing a banquet hall. It was a lot of work. We might not see her for days. She'd come home just long enough to take a shower and go right back. She was tough. She worked hard to get us everything we needed and then some.

I had always wanted to be a nurse, but my first job was as a carhop. One day I was sitting on the hood of a car, and my boss told me to get off it. I was off work and didn't have a uniform on, so nobody would even know I worked there. But he called me into the restaurant and embarrassed me, so I picked up a piece of pie and pushed it in his face and walked out.

I was a little fighter in high school, a rough kid. I was in the tenth grade a long time. Then I got pregnant, and back then you couldn't go to school pregnant. So I left school and got married. I was 17 when my daughter was born. I'd known my husband since I was 9 or 10. The marriage lasted eleven years, though we were separated a lot of it. We had one daughter and then my two sons, all eighteen months apart.

Times were rough when the kids were little. We were living in Flat Rock, and I was working off and on as a waitress at a bar. I got food stamps, and I even tried to go on ADC [Aid to Dependent Children]. But I couldn't deal with those people. They wanted to know everything about you, and you had to wait a long time to get approved.

One time my son had really bad nosebleeds, and I had to take him to the hospital; but I didn't have insurance, and I wasn't approved for ADC, so they wouldn't treat him. I almost lost my mind, and I vowed I would get a job that would pay medical insurance.

I got the job at Ford only because I bugged the shit out of every unemployment office in the area. I had heard that one of the factories was hiring, so I just kept showing my face. I hired in at the truck plant and was put in the Body Shop. A lot of women got hired at the same time.

Once you have 90 days in, you have full union protection for your job. I made my ninety days by the skin of my teeth. They had me welding on the Bronco Line all day long. It was tough. I got little marks all over my body from the sparks. But I told myself I wasn't going to let the job depress me because I had too many mouths to feed. I stuck it out and got damned good at my job. The guy working next to me kept telling me, "Dee, nobody does this job like you." I could do it drunk, high, straight, or tired.

The year before I started at the plant I'd made maybe $5,000. I made $32,000 the first year at the plant. That was exciting to me. The more I made, the more I liked it.

One day, when I was working in the Body Shop, a guy came up to me and said, "When we all walk off, you're going with us."

I said, "I can't do that."

He said, "Yes, you can."

So I said OK. We all walked off, but I got nervous and went right back. They gave me probation for a year. I never got into any trouble after that.

I dated a foreman for two years. I was kind of pampered because of that. Nobody fussed with me because they knew I was going with him. He would make me work all the overtime. He'd say, "You're going to stay and sweep for an hour after this," and I'd say, "No, I ain't."

He'd say, "Yes, you are, because you need the money."

And I'd say, "Yeah, you're right."

I got laid off in 1981 and moved to Alpena. On New Year's Eve a fire broke out in our house and my two boys died. I experienced some real grief. I was really pissed off because I had worked all those years at Ford and had everything anybody could ever want. But it was all gone, and my boys were dead.

I still have a daughter. She wasn't with us when the fire broke out, thank God. She's in high school now and lives with her grandparents.

Getting up in the morning is the hardest part of the job for me. I get up about quarter to three. I can't just get up and go. I have to slap myself around, have coffee, cigarettes. My buddy picks me up at 4:00, then picks up three other people, and we drive to work. Some mornings I just fall back asleep. Sometimes we turn up the stereo, and I sit in the back seat jamming. Some mornings we smoke a joint.

When I get to work, I get a coffee and sit there and bullshit. Three out of five days I'll smoke a joint in the morning by myself while I'm on break. I've been smoking pot since I was 11. It gets me going in the morning. Everyone on the line knows I smoke joints, but I've never smoked a joint in the plant with anyone. Nobody's ever asked to join me.

On Fridays we cash our check and down a couple of beers. There's not a lot of drinking in the plant that I know of. I've seen a couple guys drink all day. Sometimes I want a little shot of it because I love to drink, but I usually avoid it.

Music helps me do the job. That's why I bring my stereo to work. I like all kinds of music, but at work I like to listen to the Rolling Stones. I grew up with the Stones and the Beatles. They've been pounded into my brain. But I'll also listen to blues and to the rap station and even country music sometimes. No matter how tired I get, how sore my muscles are, how much my fingers ache, if I hear a good song, nothing bothers me.

Our conversations in the plant are a little rough. We talk a lot about sex. We joke about feathers and whipped cream. We'll talk about anything and everything and crack all kinds of jokes.

Some days, if I've had a nightmare about my boys, I don't talk. It takes me five hours to even smile. A guy who works next to me will say, "I haven't seen your dimples all day." And the guys will start saying goofy things. They'll talk about the ocean because they know I love the ocean, and that puts me in a good mood.

I try to put the guys out of the mood they're in if things aren't right or their wife is really being a bitch. I come bebopping in, all smiles. I don't want to hear their shit for ten hours, so we make faces at each other. I try to be in a friendly mood for them because I can remember what it's like to be in a family.

I basically like my job. I like the money. I always show up. I like to take my mind off what's going on at home. The plant always has a way of doing that. Something's different every day. At breaks I roam through the Body Shop and bullshit. When I get out, I am very seldom in a bad mood.

From the time I started at the plant, my kids knew they were going to get whatever they wanted. I wanted them to have things that I never had, and I had the money. They didn't get everything, but they got a lot. It was nothing to go to the store and spend a couple hundred dollars.

I usually spend whatever I want. Visa and MasterCard are my best friends. If my daughter, Renee, wants something, she gets it. She called me up whining a couple weeks ago, and we went and spent $78 on a pair of tennis shoes. I might not be able to do that in a couple of months because I may not have this job, so I'm doing it while I can. If I see something I want, I buy it. I try to get my mom and my daughter what they want. And I usually have what I want, too.

I don't know how much longer I'll be in the plant, but I'm not worried about it. I'll stay here until they lay me off, and then I'll get another job. I'll do what I have to do.

Renee is smart. She isn't going to be dumb like me and get pregnant. She's not going to do the things I did. At least I hope not. She's got too much going. She wants to be a lab technician. Maybe in five or ten years she'll be wearing a suit and carrying a brief-case, or maybe she'll be a waitress or a mother. Whatever she decides to do, I'll back her. But I tell her, "Don't make me a grandmother until I'm 40."

It blows my mind to see the new robots they have in the Body Shop. They can do the job any man can do, maybe better. I can't wait to see robots on some other jobs. They'll take away my job, probably, and a lot of others, and the company will just keep adding more and more work onto the ones who are left. They're going to be working their balls off.

There's nothing stopping them from putting in so many robots that in five or ten years there's only going to be three people working in the whole place who are just there to make sure the machines work. I think that's what's going to happen.

It's a good change for the company because robots aren't going to screw up as much as humans do. They're going to be there every day, and they're going to do the same job no matter what. If a panel needs twenty-five welds, it will get twenty-five, not fifteen or nineteen. It's going to be done just the way it's supposed to be, on every truck. I think that's a good thing.

So people won't have jobs. The machines are going to be in; then we're going to be out. There's already rumors that we're all getting laid off again. If it happens, I'll miss the people that I work with, but I can get another job. There's just me now, so I'm not worried. But for these men who have families, it's going to be difficult.

I've lived in Flat Rock for a long time. Seeing all those Japanese people going around Flat Rock kills me. In protest one night we spray-painted the sign in front of the Mazda plant black. There's too many Japanese invading. They should be shipped home. We shouldn't have as many imports and exports. Keep it in the country. We'll take care of ours, and you take care of yours.

The plan is to bring them over and make them hire so many laid-off Ford workers. They also had to hire a certain number of Flat Rock residents for the Mazda plant. People are signing up because there are no options. If you can't get a plant job, you work at a gas station or store or rake leaves and shovel snow.

I got one of the applications for the Mazda plant in the mail, but I won't apply because I'm not working for any Japs. I don't understand how people could work for them. The more Japanese who come over, the less Americans are going to have because the Japs will work cheaper and harder. But if we go over there, we won't be treated as well as we treat them.

If I had anything to do with it, I'd ship everybody home: the Japs, the Arabs, all of them. Go back where you came from. Don't bring fifteen people from your country over here just to hang out or see what they can get into. They're taking our jobs, and that's not right.

If you come over here and have a family and want to stay and apply for citizenship, that's fine because that's what you have to do to survive. But these Mazda management people are already rich. We shouldn't even let them in the country. They don't come here to work hard and make a living and gain a little more freedom. They come here thinking we owe them something. But we don't owe anybody anything. We have to take care of what we have first, and we're not doing that.

America gets walked on too much. That's why everybody keeps coming. If we stood up for America like we did in the fifties, we wouldn't be in the shape we are in now. When people take us hostage, we should just go in and kick ass and blow them away.

Ljubisav Filkoski

Born October 10, 1941, in Yugoslavia
Hired October 28, 1969
Welder

EVERYBODY SAYS, "God bless America," but I say, "God bless Ford." I have a beautiful family, and they benefit from the money I make. But it's not easy. I really work for that money.

My father told me that no matter how much you work, even if it's only two hours a day, if you know why you are working, you are going to be better off than the man who works twenty-four hours a day and doesn't know why he's working. But I've turned out to be like the guy who works twenty-four hours a day.

For seventeen years I've worked at Ford ten hours a day. Every day the alarm goes off at 3:30 A.M. I wash my face and drink my Turkish coffee and read something. I leave at 4:00 and pick up a friend at a small restaurant, and we have a sandwich and go to the factory. He lost his driver's license, so I help him out. He has to start a half hour earlier than me.

As soon as I get inside the plant, I feel sick. I get a headache. Maybe I'm allergic to something there. Maybe it's just knowing I have to be there until 4:00 P.M. That's a long time. The line starts at 5:30. You just work, and if you don't, you won't have any money. When you come home some days, you are so tired that you can't even eat or take a shower.

71

Jagodica and Ljubisav Filkoski

Nothing has changed for me in seventeen years in the plant. I'm still working in the Body Shop, the same place I started out.

When I was growing up in Yugoslavia, my dream was always to go overseas, not because I hated communism or socialism or loved capitalism, but just to see the world. I wanted to find a French or German or English girl, get a broom, and clean, and that would be enough to make me the happiest man in the world. But I didn't make it out of Yugoslavia when I was young; I was too poor and had no connections.

When I was 10, my grandfather gave me an American dollar. I was the happiest kid in the world because one dollar was enough for me then. My hero was George Washington. I loved his picture on that dollar bill. Now I laugh about that.

I finished school and got married and had two kids. I found a pretty good job in the stock department of a factory that made refrigerators, freezers, and appliances. My wife worked in the same factory. The factory officials gave me an apartment to live in and said if I stayed on the job five years, the apartment would be mine. I had a pretty good life; in fact, I had a better life than I have now. But I didn't want to stay in Yugoslavia.

In 1967 I took my family to France to stay with a friend who was working for a group that helped people emigrate to the West. But the police arrested me. Somebody had said I was a spy for Yugoslavia. I spent three days in jail, and they sent me back to Yugoslavia. I was very disappointed. A few months later I finally found a way out. First we went to Rome for a year, and then, in December 1968, I came to the United States. I came to Detroit because there was family here.

When you start an assembly-line job in Yugoslavia, they give you three to six months of training. At Ford they give you two or three hours of training, and then you have to do the job. If you can't do it, then you have to quit.

After two or three years in the truck plant, working six days a week, ten hours a day, I was tired. I had been coming to work every day. I saw my friends get pink slips for coming in late to work or being absent. One day I decided to find out if they would give me a pink slip. I didn't care about my record. I wasn't in the army. If I had a good record, they would not give me another star or promote me from captain to major. And I didn't care if they called me a stupid worker.

So I started coming in late for work to find out what they would say to me. Each day for a week I came in later and later, but no one said anything to me. I felt like I was nothing, like they didn't care about me. The next week I didn't come to work at all for three days, and they still didn't say anything. The following week I didn't go in at all. Finally, when I came back, they called me into Labor Relations and asked where I had been and whether I had an excuse from a doctor. I said I didn't see the doctor because I wasn't really sick, just very, very tired from working so much overtime. They sent me back to the job and told me it was a serious offense and the next time they would get me. So I went back to working every day.

Ten or fifteen years ago there were maybe 300 or 400 people in the plant doing no work but making money. I remember back then people took extra breaks; almost everyone would go to the bathroom and take ten or twenty minutes two or three times a day. Or people went to First Aid to get aspirin for a headache. Now we make pretty good money, but we have to work for it.

We do quality work. I was an inspector in the Body Shop for two years. I looked for damage in the metal and didn't find much. I don't know why car buyers complain because American workers do a good job. Workers here are really very disciplined. There are very few people who don't come to work, or who come and do nothing, or who don't respect the boss or the supervisors.

Japanese cars aren't better than United States cars. No Japanese workers can do better spot welds than me.

No matter what my job is, I have to do the work. If I don't work, there is no production, and if there is no production, the company will go bankrupt. The people who own Ford are not going to lose money; we are going to lose money. And if they close the plant, where are we going to go?

The way I can help is just to do my job well. If I'm thinking about your job, I'm just spying on you and making trouble, looking for something you're doing wrong so I can tell my boss. I have no time for that. I don't know how to do two jobs at the same time. I can only do mine.

The EI program is not going to work because labor is not qualified to run the company. Labor is not educated enough and not smart enough to make the decisions for the whole plant.

*   *   *

The economy the last few years is killing people, and so people are really scared. If you lose your job, what are you going to do? If you have two or three kids, you can't get a job in a restaurant that pays $4 an hour. That's not enough to survive on. There is no way for you to find a job that pays $14 an hour, no matter how smart you are.

My brother and his wife are working in a factory in Yugoslavia. They have no money in the bank, but he's building a better house than mine. He has a month's vacation every year and travels all over Europe. When I get my vacation, I stay home. It costs too much to go anywhere.

Vacations are too short here. In Europe, in both the capitalist and socialist countries, there is more paid vacation time, though they make less money. Most Americans have never seen most of the places in their own country. They don't have the money or the time to go. You can't do anything with only two weeks' vacation.

Workers here make good money, but it's hard to save much with the prices so high. This is the richest country in the world, and we are the highest-paid workers in the world; but still, life costs too much and we don't have extra money. My brother makes $150 a month in Yugoslavia, but he saves $10 of it. I bring home $2,000 a month, but I spend $2,000. I pay the telephone bill, the utility bill, and the food bill, and I'm broke.

The Japanese autoworker gets less pay, but he doesn't pay $300 a month rent. He doesn't spend $150 a week on groceries. He doesn't pay $70 for shoes. Life is cheaper there.

Yugoslavian autoworkers work for 60 cents an hour. They make less than $4,000 a year. But that's pretty good money there, and the workers are happy. The company is happy, too, because they can sell the Yugo here for $4,000. America can't build a car for $4,000 because America pays you $14 an hour. Autoworkers are not to blame for the price of American cars—it's the system.

I wouldn't buy a Yugo. The engine is too small. The car has no power. It's like a motorcycle. I drive a Mercury Cougar, the best car in the world. I paid $16,000 for it. That's way too much.

My son grew up here but went back to Yugoslavia to go to school. He doesn't have a job, so I send him money. I want to bring him here if they'll let me. I'm hoping he can get a job, anything, even something for $2 an hour. I want him to finish college and become an electrician. I don't want him to work in the plant. The work is too hard. My father had no chance to help me, but I have a chance to help him.

I know I am never going to have my life the way I want it to be. That makes me very sad. I want to be free and independent, to travel, to have enough food to eat, enough clothes, to do smart things, to respect people and have people respect me.

I make good money, but my health is suffering. When I come home from work and take a shower, I can see scars from the sparks on my body. I have skin ulcers. The sparks that come off in welding are small metals that you can easily breathe in. If you work ten years and ten hours a day welding, do you expect to live long after you retire? No way. I guarantee that 90 percent of the workers in the Michigan Truck Plant are not going to make thirty years' seniority because of their health.

Chapter Three

Sages

Men will not get justice unless men also love it
and live it. We Americans have wasted infinities
of time and energy in the attempt to make a just
society without, at the same time, making the
members of that society just persons. We have
put our faith in arrangements rather than in ourselves. . . . To be a materialist is to think of men,
to deal with them, in external terms, as if they
were "things."

—Alexander Meiklejohn,
What Does America Mean?

Abson "Mac" McDaniel

Born October 18, 1922, in West Memphis, Arkansas
Hired November 9, 1967
Retired painter

I HAVE ALWAYS TRIED to treat people the way I want to be treated. I don't care what color you are or what position you hold; I'm a human being just like you. I never could figure out why it makes such a difference if you are black or white.

My hometown was a little place with mud streets and no pavement. We lived on one side of town, and the whites lived on the other. They could come to your side and raise hell, but you couldn't go to their side. If a white man and a white woman were coming down the street, you had to get off the street and let them walk by. When you got on the bus, you had to go to the back and stand. If you sat up front, any white man could jump up and whip you. Once I saw a bus driver beat up a boy who had sat down in the wrong place. There were thirty or forty black people sitting back there, and nobody raised a hand to stop him.

My father died when I was five. My mother took care of me, my brother, and my sister. She was always teaching me about what black people had to do to get along with white people.

People say you forget the way things were. You don't; you just try to forgive. I started watching "Roots" on TV, but I had to turn

Abson "Mac" McDaniel

it off because I got too angry and it made my blood pressure go up.

This world is big enough for all of us. There is enough food to go around. But some are starving while others have too much. If we joined together, we could all help one another to live. Colors don't mean a thing. We are all human beings.

A few years ago I walked into a bar in the suburb of Warren. I was all alone, and it was the middle of the day. When I walked in, everybody looked at me. The bartender walked right by and didn't wait on me. Finally, after a while, he came over and said, "Can I do something for you?"

I said, "I'd like to have a beer if you don't mind. You do sell beer here, don't you?"

He said, "Yeah. You ain't going to start anything, are you?"

I'll never forget that. It shocked me. I took one swig of beer, paid for it, and walked out.

I still don't understand it. We are all American citizens. So why do some people have advantages over others?

As a teenager I worked at a service station or the grocery store. I got paid about $11 a week, and that was a lot of money. Blacks couldn't get any real jobs. The women washed and ironed and scrubbed floors. The men cut grass or worked in the fields.

I worked at a fish market for a little while. I made enough to buy a shirt or a pair of pants and go to the movies once a week. We thought we were making a good living then.

A little money went a long way down South. You could buy a week's groceries for a dollar. We didn't have a phone bill or a gas bill or a light bill. All we had to buy was kerosene for the lamp. If the woodman didn't come by, we would go across the lake and get our own wood.

Now I'm just getting by. I make $500 to $600 a week. The car loan is $250 or $300 a month, and I spend $100 a week for groceries. The light bill and gas bill and phone bill are high. There's not much left for anything else.

If I had stayed in my hometown, I wouldn't have made it. Somebody probably would have killed me, or I would have killed somebody.

In May 1942 my sister got married, and her husband and kids went north. She wanted me to come with them, so I came to Flint in July. I got a job the day after I arrived at Buick Motor Division, and a couple weeks later I sent for my wife to join me. I was making 79 cents an hour; that was big bucks back then. We got a little apartment and later bought a house. After a year I was up to $1.14 an hour. I was on top back then. I was a young man, 20 years old, and I could look forward to something.

At Buick they were doing war production, making airplane parts. When V-J Day came, all the blacks either got laid off or got sent to work at the General Motors foundry nearby. There were no other jobs in Flint for blacks.

I put in fourteen years at the foundry. You couldn't see in the morning when you'd go in; there was so much dust and smoke. I was a furnace operator. You let the metal out the front, and you had to plug it with a steel stick with mud and clay on it. If you didn't open that hole up right, that steel would come over that trough and burn you. You had to be on your toes.

In 1946 we had a big strike in the foundry. There were a lot of scabs working who didn't belong to the union. They were getting better jobs in there than we were getting. I heard Walter Reuther speak, and he said we would keep the plant closed down until we got what we wanted. We didn't get much of a raise that first strike. We were out for over a hundred days, and we gained 14 or 15 cents an hour. But that wasn't the main issue. The issue was to get a union shop. The union meant a lot then.

In 1955 I got sick and had to go to a TB sanitarium for thirteen months. I had a clouded lung. The doctors were good, and they got me through with no operations, just bed rest.

I left General Motors in 1963, after I got into a fight with my supervisors. My first marriage was breaking up, and I couldn't concentrate on work. Some mornings I was bitter, and I'd go into work and take it out on somebody. My boss and I didn't get along. He might have been having a hard time, too.

I hated to lose my job at the plant. The next four years I worked at a nonunion machine shop in Warren and made $1.75 an hour with no benefits. In 1967 I found out they were hiring at the truck plant and got a job.

I got put in Underbody, where you stand under the cars and paint the bottoms as they roll by. It wasn't much different from the foundry. You couldn't breathe from the paint. They didn't have any masks or ventilation back then. The only thing I had was an old paper cap. Paint would always drip down on top of my head and right through that damn thing. I still had some hair back then. I think that helped burn it out.

Working in Underbody really messed up my shoulder. I went to the doctor and found out there is calcium in my shoulder. They wanted to operate but decided not to because there was only a fifty-fifty chance of it doing any good. If I lift my right arm too much, I can hardly get it back down or I can't turn over the next morning in the bed.

I finally got moved to the Prime Booth, where I painted the sides of the trucks. I liked that job a lot better—because I didn't have to stand under the trucks.

When I hired in at the truck plant, the union was better than it is now. We had some good committeemen. They worked on the line just like everyone else, and the union paid them. But lately everything has changed. Now the company is paying them, and they walk around all day. Some of them you never see.

It used to be if you classified for a job, that's the job you did. Now they take a man from one classification and throw him anywhere. He's got to go work there. They'll send him home if he doesn't do it. In the old days that didn't happen. It would be knocking some old man out of work. I've seen foremen tell workers, "I can do what I want to do, and I can put you in any job I want." That's wrong. And the committeeman is going along with them.

I used to be classified as a crane operator. Then I changed my classification and became a furnace operator. If they tried to make me work the crane, I could refuse it, and I had somebody to back me up. See, if they know you can do another job, they'll try to get you to do it. But if a man's not classified for that job, it's not his job, even if he volunteers to do it. In the past, if we ever saw a man doing a job he wasn't classified for, we would go tell the union man to stop him.

Now folks are working all this extra overtime because you get a pat on the back from the foreman, and the union should stop that shit. If it's not your classification, you aren't supposed to do it. It hurts me when I see it happening, but I can't go over there and tell the man he can't do that. So I just stand there and shake my head. The union representatives see it and don't say anything. They're the ones who are supposed to be your leaders. Sometimes it boils me so much I'll just be smoking inside, but not saying anything.

There has to be a change; this has got to stop. Seniority should mean something. If some youngster comes in and the big boss gives him my job, even though I'm qualified for it, then all the years I've put in at the plant don't mean a thing.

The people who sign up for the EI program are only hurting themselves. The company is going to get what they want out of them and then dump them. If they keep it up, we aren't going to have a union. Even now we don't have any real representatives. You have a problem, and they tell you they'll look over your papers and get back to you later, but they never do.

People don't see what's happening because these days people are not always looking ahead. They are looking for the easy money for themselves. They think they have a good thing going. They don't realize they're making it rougher for you.

If things keep going like they have been, there won't be many people working at the truck plant in ten years. Automation is going to cut a lot of men out of work. I wonder where the youngsters are going to get a job. We are supposed to be leaving a path for the younger people to follow, so they can have some security for themselves, but instead we're just looking out for ourselves.

Hillory Weber

Born October 11, 1929, in New Orleans, Louisiana
Hired February 27, 1953
Gun welder repairman

I BELIEVE IN GOD and that there is a Jesus Christ who died for my sins. But I also believe that Martin Luther King, Jr., was my Jesus Christ. He opened the doors of opportunity for me. There were no blacks in the skilled trades before King died. If King hadn't died, blacks would never have been airplane pilots, flight attendants, clerks, policemen, judges, attorneys, and candidates for president. King is my savior.

When I started at Wayne Assembly, everybody in the Body Shop and the Final Line was black, and the whites were in Trim, Cushion, and all the nice, soft, easy jobs. There were no black inspectors, no black security guards, no black supervisors.

When they opened the truck plant and I was transferred there in 1964, I went through the same thing again. In fact, one guy told me there would never be any blacks in skilled trades as long as he was there. He was wrong, of course, but there are still jobs they don't want blacks to have.

It is not much different up here from down South. Up here the white man makes you think you are as good as anyone else, but

Hillory Weber

he doesn't believe that himself. He'll tell you that, but he doesn't
live up to what he says.

My dad was an electrician. He had his own company. I'm the
youngest of four kids. My brother was in the trucking business.
My two sisters went to college. My mother was a housewife. My
dad didn't believe in his wife or daughters working.

My dad always told me, "Don't let one man have five things and
you're working right beside him and don't have any. Don't be a
fool." He also told me, "Don't ever keep anything in. If there's
anything bothering you, find somebody to talk to and get it out of
your system. Keeping it in could kill you." I do just that. I don't
care who you are, I'm going to tell you what's on my mind.

How I ended up in Detroit is quite a story. I had a job at Johns
Manville in New Orleans driving a fork truck. One day I was
driving down to the warehouse with a load of asbestos shingles,
and I saw a piece of paper blowing in the wind, so I picked it up. It
was a paycheck for a fork truck driver named Frank Boudreau.

The check was for $210. I looked in the hourly rate section, and it said $1.75 an hour. I was getting $1.10 an hour.

We had a lily-white union back then. I went to the union man and asked him why I was making less than Boudreau. He told me in plain English that a nigger is not supposed to make the same amount a white man does. That is the best thing he could have said to me because it made it clear to me what I had to do.

I felt there must be somewhere in the world where I would get paid what I deserved. I had a sister living in Michigan, so the following week I went into the office and asked for my vacation. I didn't know how to get to Michigan, and I couldn't even read a road map. But I got a map, and a man showed me how to get to Chicago. By the time I got there I knew how to read a map, so I got a U.S. map and drove all the way down Michigan Avenue to Detroit. When I got to Wayne, I saw the Wayne Assembly Plant and a help wanted sign. I didn't know what that meant. So I drove up to the security guard and asked him if they were hiring. He said they needed a hi-lo driver.

The guard made a phone call, and a little old gray-haired man came to the gate and brought me into the plant. He asked me if I'd ever driven a hi-lo before. I told him I'd driven a fork truck. I didn't know they were the same thing. He put me on the worst hi-lo he could find. I checked the oil and water and gas and got on the hi-lo and made every move he wanted me to make. He told me to start work that same day at 10 o'clock. It was Wednesday of the following week before they brought me an application and told me to sign it. No physical examination, no job history; all I did was sign my name and give them my Social Security number.

I applied to be an electrician, but I never got the job because I was black. The company told me I had to have a journeyman's card and ten years' experience. I already had the ten years' experience and a letter of recommendation from Johns Manville. I went to UAW Solidarity House, but they told me before I could get a journeyman's card I had to have an electrician's job at Ford. I went back to Labor Relations, and the man there told me I had to have the card. I was getting the runaround from both UAW and Ford just because I'm black. I'm convinced that's the reason.

Now I'm an electrical contractor on the side. I only take jobs at my convenience. I love the work. I just wish I had gotten that electrician's job in the plant.

*   *   *

Working in an automobile factory back when I started was hell. In some places it is still hell.

In the sixties the truck plant was worse than the state penitentiary. They were hard on people. They brought them in one day and fired them the next, even though they were supposed to give people three days to learn the job. They were so hard up for people that they went to Milan state penitentiary and got inmates to work. They brought them by school bus from the prison to the plant and bused them back at night. The rumor is that the prison quit the arrangement because the inmates preferred to be in the state penitentiary rather than work at the Michigan Truck Plant.

I make a good living at Ford, but I have caught hell to do it. Ford caused my arthritis because I had to work in a damp, wet place. Ford is also responsible for my high blood pressure and for ruining my marriage. My wife and I couldn't get along because of the pressure I was getting at work. I would work overtime and get accused of being out with some woman when really I was working extra hours trying to survive and make a better life for my kids.

I want to sue Ford Motor Company because they took all my young life. I'm quite sure they have made more off me than I've made off them.

I've been penalized a lot for things I didn't do. If I wasn't a strong person, I would have folded up. I'm not saying I'm an angel. I've been in the woods a very long time. I know the games they play. I know all the tricks.

I was disliked because I spoke up for myself. The reason I spoke up was that I was the most important person in the world. It was me they were mistreating.

I was given thirty days off twelve times for things I didn't do, things they blamed on me but couldn't prove. I remember one time I asked the foreman if I could go to the bathroom. He told me to go ahead, and then I got time off for being off the job without permission. What would you call that? Is that hate, or jealousy, or what? I never could figure that one out.

After working thirty-three years, I'm just beginning to have peace of mind. It's a good feeling to know that nobody can fire you unless you fire yourself by stealing or fighting, which by company policy earns you an automatic discharge.

When I first started, union reps did their job. The leadership really cared. The committeeman stayed in the plant all day, so that when you really needed him, he was there. They had a paging intercom, and you could pick up the mike and call him. And he always came. He couldn't escape because everyone in the plant had heard you page him. The union eventually stopped that. They told the company they didn't like to be paged because they might be in a meeting or out to lunch and if they didn't come when they were paged, that would show everybody in the plant they weren't there.

Now the only time you see a committeeman is when there's an election. Then he'll come around asking if you have any problems. At other times he's not in the plant enough to see whether a man has problems. Now the foreman calls the committeeman and meets with him before the committeeman goes to the man on the floor who's complaining. That's wrong. The committeeman should find out for himself what's going on from the guy on the line.

Ten years from now I don't think there is going to be a union because the company is already running the union. The union is just there, and the company does anything they want anyway.

People put up with it because they don't care like they used to. They'll say, "We can't stop progress." I say, "Together you stand, divided you fall." To me everything is divided.

Employee Involvement is for the company. It's to eliminate manpower. EI is educating the company about things that you're capable of doing that the company didn't know about. If you tell them how to do a man's job faster or better, that's taking the job away from him.

Also, they're combining jobs. For instance, my job as a gun welder repairman is to be responsible for all the spot welder guns. I rebuild the guns, change the tips, and keep the guns in good working condition. In ten years there will be no gun welder repairman. It will be part of the electrician's job.

I also repair the guns on the robot. A lot of people are pleased about robots because the robots are doing jobs they don't have to do. But that robot doesn't pay taxes. It doesn't take breaks. It's hurting the economy by eliminating jobs. You won't have Social Security because there won't be anybody putting money into it. In time there are going to be more people retired than working. So the bottom is going to fall out.

Soon the automobile will be made out of plastic. The body will be molded and come out one solid piece except for the hood and the trunk. Then they won't need the skills they use now, and there won't be any jobs.

* * *

In the old days everybody cared for people. You could walk down the street with a pocketful of money and nobody would bother you. You didn't have to worry about somebody breaking in your house. If you got into a fight, it was a fistfight, no guns or knives.

The economy has changed a lot of things. If a man has a job, he doesn't need to steal. If he doesn't have a job and he's got a family, he's got to support his family, so he's got to do wrong.

I don't understand people who don't want to give minorities an equal opportunity to make a living. What do they expect a guy to do? If he has no money and no job, how is he going to survive? If you give me a good job, you don't have to worry about me because I can take care of my family just like you. But without a job, how am I going to keep up my own property and pay my bills? Don't say that I'm dumb, that I'm not qualified. I don't want anyone to give me anything. Just put the opportunity there for me.

The poor blacks and the poor whites are the damn fools. The rich man doesn't give a damn about whether the poor are black or white. With the rich man money is the only thing that's important. With the poor, ignorant people it's the color of the skin. The poor man is watching the other poor bastard. He doesn't want him to have more than him. Some poor whites want to be the superior race.

For some white people it doesn't matter what color you are. All they want to do is work and go home and be left alone. Those guys are the good guys. But others always wonder why a guy who's sweeping the floor is driving a Cadillac. Well, it's because he has saved his money. He might be eating pork and beans and hominy grits. That shouldn't bother anyone. If you take care of your own affairs, you'll be too busy to worry about what someone else is doing.

Al Commons

Born September 19, 1924, in Hamtramck, Michigan
Hired June 12, 1964
Inspector

THE SEEDS FOR THE DEMISE of the automobile industry were sown when the assembly line was born. It's a very unnatural system of work and a waste of human talent. It is very demeaning. But it's very profitable.

Management's approach is that the simpler the work, the easier it is to train workers and the easier they are to replace. You can't keep that from sinking into a person's self-esteem. You begin to feel that way about yourself. You become uncooperative and feel you are in the system only for what you can get out of it. In time you become a self-seeker. You lose interest in your product, and you become alienated from your labor. You begin to think of yourself just in terms of a paycheck on Friday. You don't build self-esteem in an automobile plant.

Even though it gives us a certain amount of financial freedom, we are prisoners of the assembly line. You're tied to a machine, and you're just another cog. You have to do the same thing over and over again, all day long.

The tendency should exist today for a worker to become more important to management, but it is the other way around. Man-

Al Commons

agement is still trying to reduce work to a repetitive operation so that there is as little as possible for a worker to learn. Otherwise, he grows too important to the overall scheme.

I used to enjoy changing jobs because of the diversification and the wider range of application it gave me an opportunity for. Now I resent changing jobs because there is too much to learn in job change. Yet my value to management hasn't changed. They still feel they can replace me anytime they want to.

If you show initiative, aggressiveness, or cooperation, you are working against yourself because they'll take more advantage of you. That's what the assembly line for profit is designed for. It is built right into the system, and there is no way to avoid it. If you become too good at your job, they know they can't get anyone to replace you, and so they don't want to move you. You have become your own enemy. Management doesn't want to understand this. But I understand their position: They have to try to get as much production out of us in as little time as possible. That's their objective under the profit system. Quality suffers under that sort of system. The quality we do achieve is haphazard.

The automobile industry could have been molded differently had our union approached the negotiating strategy with management a little differently. The big change came in 1949, when Walter Reuther first put his idea of a pension plan on the negotiating table at the same time there was a wildcat strike at the Rouge Plant over assembly-line speedups. Management refused to negotiate until the strike was settled, and after that they refused to talk about the pension plan. That's when Henry Ford really spanked Reuther and convinced him to lay off work standards. The company said, "We'll take care of work standards, and you can have what you want at the negotiating table, within reason."

The union didn't want any more wildcat strikes or problems with work standards because that's when management got tough at the negotiating table. You wouldn't get your pie in the sky if you messed around with work standards too much. So the union backed off on work standards completely. That's also when the stopwatches started sprouting up like dandelions. That's when regimentation increased.

The union now is not concerned enough about work standards. There's the illusion of concern because there are work standards representatives in our plants, but they are powerless. They might be able to get a little bit of relief for someone who's overloaded. But management doesn't hire anyone to take care of that overload; they simply divvy it up among the rest of the workers.

The union has simply become a wages-and-benefits negotiator. Their purpose is to guide a contract, that's all. The union has very little power over the factory floor. And that's a tremendous erosion of the role of the union. Freedoms that have been won for workers through the years are being lost. Eventually the worker will be under the complete control of management.

We still have the power of seniority. Management will never breach the contract when it comes to benefits and wages. But management breaches the contract every day when it comes to work standards and in some areas of health and safety.

The union does not want militancy in the plants because then it affects the hierarchy and the union loses control. Union representatives have lost touch with the workers. Once they get elected to a job, they don't want to face the assembly line again. Every two years at our UAW conventions a resolution is put on the floor that union representatives have to come back and work in the factories for three or four months a year. They can never get that resolution to pass. Once people leave the factory, they don't want to come back. In time I wouldn't be surprised if we started appointing our committeemen instead of electing them.

When the union negotiates, they don't look to the future. They are more concerned with elections and with satisfying the people paying dues now. Had they been more concerned with the future years ago, maybe the ranks wouldn't be so depleted now.

There is a trade-off. Workers can buy more things now. On the other hand, they're losing the relaxed relationship that we used to have in the workshop years ago. Work regimentation has become more severe. There is high stress to produce and more tension as the automobile becomes more complex.

Since the invasion of foreign imports, management has gotten very concerned about the future. Since they are not a monopoly anymore, they realize that much of their problem stems from the animosity they've engendered between themselves and the unions through the years. Now they're trying to reduce that adversary relationship, and the union hierarchy is cooperating with them.

We're trying to develop the philosophy that we're both in this together. But that won't save the automobile industry because there is still one great big difference, which is stressed by management every day and in all their activities: We are the workers and they are the managers, and that will never change. The only thing that would change that feeling is if we changed positions every six months, and that's not going to happen.

If I could design things, I would reduce the division between management and labor. The industry would not have a president making over a million dollars a year. Income would be more even. The gap between the company president and the lowest man in his system would be narrowed. The difference between what the skilled trades and assembly-line workers make wouldn't be as great. There would be more interchangeability rather than such emphasis on specialization. Everyone would have a greater feeling of contributing and a greater share of importance.

The need for unionism in such a plant would be lessened. What made unions necessary was the hard-nosed attitude of management forty to forty-five years ago. Management is beginning to understand that now, and that's why they've created the EI system; but there still have to be an awful lot of changes in how management feels toward labor.

Employee Involvement is an illusion, because we keep losing more people each year as management streamlines the work force and increases production. Retooling does not compensate for all the work added onto the remaining people when people are cut. That work load has to be shared by the remaining people. So that increases the regimentation. I'm doing much, much more work today after twenty-two years in the plant than I did when I first hired in, and I thought it was stressful then. The EI program is just a little bit of sugar to help the medicine go down.

My dad was an autoworker. He worked as a welder in a supplier plant called Midland Steel, which built frames for automobiles and trucks. I remember him with cold applications over his eyes because he'd caught welding flashes. He was always coming home tired and dirty.

He was in one of the very first plants in Detroit that had a sit-down strike. I believe it was in 1937, and they stayed inside the plant for two or three weeks. That's how they won their first contract. I remember my mother taking him sandwiches and coffee; she was part of the women's brigade.

After that he was a very loyal union supporter. He felt that the union was the backbone of his sense of freedom at work. It's the only way they could get anything accomplished for themselves. I don't think he ever missed a meeting. If they didn't attend a union meeting, they were fined half a dollar, which was a considerable amount in those days.

Also, if the union recommended a vote for a certain politician, my dad would say, "That's my man." Today we don't follow that credo very much; we like to choose our own people. But in those days whoever the union hierarchy would recommend the members would vote for.

My mother stayed at home and raised children for a few years, and during the war she went into the automobile factories. She was a Rosie the Riveter. She stayed on after the war and was a union steward for three or four years. Eventually the factory merged with some other company. So she accepted severance pay after eleven or twelve years and retired.

My dad eventually rose to the rank of general foreman, but

when his health declined in his middle 60s, he took a janitor's job to pass the time until retirement. He worked until he was 68. He got to collect on his pension for two years before he died.

I'm not sure my parents enjoyed their retirement. They hadn't prepared for it. Very few people back then did. It just suddenly fell on them, and he was already 68, with the regimen of many, many years of work in his system. The adjustment was difficult. He didn't go fishing or go to the library or enjoy a play or relax. I heard him say before he died that he had felt better when he was working.

I enlisted in the navy when I was 17, a few weeks before Pearl Harbor, and served until six weeks after V-J Day. I spent two years on convoy patrol work in the North Atlantic. Then I was transferred to the Pacific and went through most of the island-hopping campaigns.

It was a real eye-opener for a young man to travel all over the world, even if the conditions weren't the best. It was my first introduction to Jim Crow. Having been raised in Hamtramck, I accepted black people. I didn't realize the scope of racism. In the service I was surprised to see how racist attitudes restricted blacks to certain minor roles.

Also, going in, I was very much a champion of the United States, the free-enterprise system, and capitalism. I felt America was second to none. We produced the best automobiles, the best airplanes, the best ships. But as I traveled, I saw things that surprised me. I remember examining some equipment the Germans had produced and being surprised at how clever they were. And I was amazed at some of the technology I saw on the Japanese ships.

I thought then that America was truly the defender of peace and democracy and that our system should prevail all over the world. But now I think differently. We cannot go all over the world and tell people how to live. It is up to them to determine for themselves what they want. We shouldn't impose our system on them. I'm not a hawk. I don't think there is a military solution to every problem in the world today.

We have developed the military-industrial complex that President Eisenhower warned against. It is very much in control and enmeshed. There is a sort of business relationship with the armament industry. With our nuclear arsenal we are on the brink of being able to eliminate in just a half hour's time everything that has evolved through the centuries.

Our foreign policy is in disarray. We should be favoring democracy, yet we play ball with dictatorships in other countries that have bountiful resources and cheaper labor. The automobile industry is beginning to look toward these labor markets itself. It undermines our unionism in this country because there is always the specter of moving a factory or eliminating it completely because you can get cheaper labor somewhere else.

I came out of the service in 1945. I got my first job at a small supplier plant that manufactured steering gears for the Big Three. I think my first rate was 95 cents an hour. I can remember taking home a little over $50. There was a week's vacation and no hospitalization. There was no pension plan. There were no paid holidays. The benefits those days were virtually nonexistent because all the contracts with the automobile industry were in their infancy. So there was very little you were leaving behind if you left a job you didn't like. Jobs were plentiful because the companies were just opening up to consumer production after the war and there was a lot of overtime. Between age 21 and 30 I must have had at least a dozen jobs, all with the automobile industry.

When I got married in 1950, I was working for Champion Spark Plug. If I had stayed there, I would have retired years ago. But my wife encouraged me to take advantage of the GI Bill and go to school. So I enrolled in college, but I only stayed for nine months. Marriage and going to school just didn't work out too well. I quit and went to work for Burroughs Corporation.

At Burroughs my work was a lot more refined and sophisticated than what I eventually wound up doing with Ford. It was quality control work. We had a contract with the air force and built the computer that was on Alan Shepard's first flight into space. I was testing electrical circuits, subjecting electrical components to stress, testing computers, simulating problems the computers might encounter in the field.

In 1964 Burroughs's contract with the air force was coming to an end, and they were laying off people. I thought a layoff might be pending for me, so I started looking for a job, and when I got the chance at Ford, I took it.

*   *   *

Despite my parents, I came into the factory with the same concept most of the public had about unionism, which is that the unions controlled all the activities in an industrial plant. The prevalent idea then was that the union had too much muscle. Everyone knew about the pie-in-the-sky benefits packages that Reuther was reaping for his autoworkers. And every three years people would see the prices of cars go up right after the union negotiated a new contract.

The first reaction to sticker shock is that autoworkers are responsible because of the money we make. Of course, there is a connection between the price of an automobile and the pay we receive, but no one can honestly say we don't earn every penny.

There are people who wouldn't do that kind of work for any amount of money. That was proven during the late sixties and early seventies, when we couldn't find enough people to work in the auto plants. They'd come in and work a week or two and quit. We couldn't keep people despite the best benefits package and best industrial wage in the world.

I hired in at Ford as an inspector, and I was disappointed at the kind of work I had to do. One of the first jobs they put me on was testing brakes. We had to handle three great big heavy fixtures, suspended by balancers you had to jockey into position on every brake as it came through. It was tiring having to maneuver that big heavy piece of test machinery. I can remember breaking in three or four people on the job through the years. Some would stay a week and quit. Their expectations as inspectors were much higher, and they thought the work was beneath them. But if you live in Michigan, you're a captive of the auto industry. It's very difficult to escape if you need a job.

Ford was my first job on a heavy assembly line, and I was shocked at the way employees were treated. The way foremen talked to people, you soon realized that you were a serf and the foreman was your master. Management's attitude and the submissiveness employees had to demonstrate to keep their jobs made me realize the importance of unionism.

In those days ex-athletes, especially prizefighters, were highly valued as foremen in automobile plants, especially at Ford. They were big barroom brawlers, bouncers, scrappers, and fighters, people who could bully people and command respect because of their size.

At that time the union could help you if you got into trouble, but the union couldn't defend you if your foreman wanted to become punitive against you for getting the union on him. Your days in hell were numbered if he wanted to take it out on you. He could wipe you out completely if he wanted to. He could put you on a job that had a tremendous work overload. Unless you were one of the best assemblers in the place, you couldn't maintain the pace. The foreman would purposely pick people to demonstrate that the job could be done, but these people didn't have to face doing the job day after day. If you had to do it for years, you would become dejected and want to quit no matter what the monetary rewards were. There were people on medical leave all the time just because they didn't want to come in and face those jobs.

The movement now is to robotize as much as possible because assembly-line work is very stressful, demeaning, and a waste of human talent. But a robot cannot replace a human being. A robot has to be programmed and run by another human being. It has no control over itself like a human being does. There are movements on the assembly line that a robot cannot possibly duplicate.

I've noticed through the years, as our production output and work load have increased, that people have developed such an assembly-line finesse and have improved themselves in managing their stock and their tools to such a degree that we would probably have to go through a thousand people in society to find one person who can do the work that well, whereas perhaps twenty to thirty years ago one out of twenty-five might have fit the bill.

Eventually we are going to be building automobiles that are particularly adapted to being built by a robot. Before, our engineers and designers could let their imaginations run wild, knowing that a human being could make whatever they wanted built. Robots cannot, so they are going to have to compromise their imagination and only design things a robot can execute. The product is going to be designed to fit the machine rather than the machine designed to fit the product.

Some people in the factory if left to themselves would be hard put to make a living. They don't have the skills. They realize that if their job at the truck plant disappears, they will never have another opportunity like it. That's why some of them take as much advantage of it as they can.

An income such as what we have at the plant now is a very unusual blip on the economic screen. We are some of the best-paid industrial workers in the world, and we have an opportunity to augment that with a lot of overtime at premium rates. People can make $40,000 a year working the overtime, and we have skilled tradesmen making $50,000 to $55,000.

But management has complete control of the cost-profit equation. Now management is reducing labor costs by reducing employment. At one time we were producing thirty-six units an hour with about eleven hundred people. Today we are producing forty-six units an hour with the same number of people. The union can bargain for an increase in wages every three years, but management always has final control over how many people are going to be earning that money.

I can't justify the kind of money the skilled trades make. I can't justify what we make in our industry when so many people are out of work. We should be sharing the work with people who do not have jobs. The gap between the poor and the people who have adequate resources to exist is much too big.

I get very angry with people who cannot understand the plight of the poor. They think they are lazy and won't get off their butts. It's very wrong for us to feel this way because in some instances people cannot get jobs. They do not have the brains or are handicapped in some way.

A man who has two or three children and no job must feel terrible in this competitive society. His kids are always seeing other kids with new bikes, other families with new automobiles. I think that contributes a lot to men just floating off and leaving their families. They can't take it anymore. They feel that maybe the family would be better off without them.

People at the plant are all on a treadmill. After we've spent ten hours in the factory and another hour to an hour and a half on the road, we have to squeeze every activity into the time left over. It doesn't leave us much time for our personal enjoyment and our families. We are neglecting a large area of our lives that is essential for a well-rounded human being. We can provide for our financial needs adequately, but we are denying another area of our humanity that should be nourished.

I know I need bread on my table and decent shelter, and I need an automobile; but I know there is more to life than just that. Because if that's all there is, it's not worth it.

If I could have gone on salary years ago, I would have because I have the same kind of impetus as all Americans: Get ahead if you can. But I was denied that opportunity, and looking back, I think I'm much better off because of it.

Working in the plant contributes to family stress. The fracture point comes when the man has just spent ten or eleven hours on a job and he comes home tired and his wife is all revved up to go out for the evening and socialize. He's not in the mood to do that after spending so many hours on the assembly line. They live in different worlds.

When I was a kid, I remember our family getting together with families of men my dad worked with. A group of them used to get together on weekends in the summertime, get a barrel of beer, and go out to a park and have a picnic. Now the only socializing I do with co-workers is on a one-to-one basis. Not much family socializing takes place anymore.

Unionism traditionally brought out the common bond between working people. Spiritualism or belief in a supreme deity does the same thing. Now I find that fellowship at church, worshiping every Sunday with people I've known a long time.

We're all competing with each other materialistically so much that people have gotten withdrawn. They are more conscious of how their home compares with your home, their car with your car. That tends to destroy the free-and-easy relationships between people. There is so much competitive zeal that I think we're losing the fellowship among ourselves. Our free-enterprise system sharpens our appetite for competition and the feeling that we want to be first in every race, and some of us can't be.

A lot of young people face a fearsome future. They're not going to have the opportunity to get the kinds of jobs we have that will let them provide for their families. I can remember coming out of the service when all you needed was $200 or $300 down and you could buy a three-bedroom house with $85 a month payments. Today buying a house is a frightening prospect for young people who want to get married. It might be our fault a little because we brought them up with such high expectations. When they go out on their own now, it is such a big step that they can't make it. A lot of them are forgoing marriage because of that. They don't want to face responsibility. I worry about that. We should be building a world that's safer and better for our kids, but we are making it more difficult.

My father, I'm sure, felt he was making a better world for me. I don't feel I'm making a better world for my daughter, but I don't know what to do about it. I'm caught in the stream like everybody else. I'm being swept along with the tide.

Harold Coleman

Born December 20, 1924, in Beckley, West Virginia
Hired September 4, 1964
Inspector

THE AUTOMOBILE INDUSTRY has lobbied for twenty-five years to eliminate every other decent form of transportation our country has ever known—trains, buses, streetcars. Now there are buses in the cities and a few subways in some places, but there is nothing like the mass transportation systems that used to carry people everywhere to their jobs from their homes. In the late forties you could get on a streetcar and get to any factory that made cars. Then the companies realized that the way to make millions of people need automobiles was to build plants way out in the boondocks, so that every worker has to buy a vehicle just to get to his job.

The biggest business expense on anybody's income tax is your automobile, because you need the vehicle to get to the job to earn the money to pay your taxes in the first place. But only the executives can write it off. I don't have the privilege of deducting my little old Tempo to go to a job thirty-five miles away.

The automobile has been the main thing keeping the economy going. But building quality cars isn't really good for the econ-

Harold Coleman

omy. If they built a car that would last and last and last, you wouldn't have to replace it and they wouldn't sell as many.

I know about quality because I have been an inspector in the truck plant since 1970. I've worked in every area: the Engine Department, Chassis Department, Frame, Trim. I see a lot that could be done better. But the company will not let quality stand in the way of productivity.

It's not the autoworker's attitude toward work, it's the circumstances he's working under which force him not to be quality-conscious. You're not permitted the time to do the job right in most cases. The theory is you can stop the line anywhere to improve quality. But it's not the practice. If what you're doing is so important that nothing else can be completed until it's done, then it's permissible. Otherwise, you can't.

The concept of quality is just a concept. They want quality, but they want it on their own terms and not in a way that would meet the needs of the human body.

To have the human body work like a machine—consistently, continuously, hour in, hour out, to produce a product—is inhuman. I take issue with the productivity, not with the factory itself. It's dehumanizing to work at such a pace that you can't even stop to have a cup of coffee or smoke a cigarette or go to the bathroom. You have no freedom from the production. It's true that you have relief men, but if someone gives you a break at 9:00, you're not supposed to need a drink of water or want a cup of coffee or go to the bathroom until you get another break four or five hours later. Meanwhile, you're constantly working from one unit to the next. It's like you are incarcerated from the minute you get there until it's time to leave.

When I started work at the truck plant, the only knowledge I had of assembly-line work was what I'd read or seen. The first few weeks I was there, I thought the world was going to end. Mentally I was prepared to adjust, but the physical exertion was so difficult that I thought I was being punished.

Working at the plant was a new experience for me because I had never worked in a factory of any kind. I grew up in a small town, and we had friends who lived on farms. So I learned from both environments.

My father was a coal miner most of his life and a member of the United Mine Workers. Once, when I was a child, my father took me to a lecture—it was the first public-speaking engagement I'd ever been to—and I saw John L. Lewis. He was a big, brawny guy, and I was captivated by him. He spoke of safety in the mines and a decent wage. He said a job is not enough; a worker must have some assurance of safety, too. But the mine, like any corporation, wanted to get their money and get their butt out. Human life is so cheap when it's someone else's.

I remember my father and other men in the community arguing about issues that apparently had been brought up at a union meeting, and how violent some of the opinions were. Those strong differences of opinion impressed me. I wondered how both sides could be part of the same thing and disagree so strongly.

When I was 19, I was drafted. There was a "hero magnetism" attached to the military at the time; the idea of the uniform, of coming home on furlough, was a romantic image that attracted you. When I was discharged after World War II, I used the GI Bill to go to school to get my license for the dry-cleaning profession. I came to Detroit because I had four friends from the service who lived here. I started a business, and I made my living in the dry-cleaning profession in Detroit until 1964.

I married in 1952, and we had two children, a son and then a daughter. I had in-laws who worked in the automobile industry, and we always talked about factory life and the union. For the well-being of my family, I decided to turn my job skills toward the automobile industry. I got recommended through my brother-in-law and was hired at the truck plant five months after it opened.

When I first hired in, I installed the glasses, latches, locks, and windshields. It was a lot of work, but at that time they only ran nineteen trucks an hour. It was timed so you had just enough time to do the work.

Over the years I've seen production increase. In 1969, when it went to twenty-five units an hour, people said it could never be done. But every time they increased production, it made way for new employees. The plant has about tripled in size since I started.

All the time this growth was taking place, the rumors persisted, as they still do, that next year they're going to close the plant.

In the plant, black and white workers have good relations. To the younger people who were babies during the civil rights struggles in the sixties, it's been like this all the time, black guys and white guys working together. Not only do they work together, but they go to each other's homes and invite each other to weddings and parties. I got a wedding invitation from a white co-worker, and I'd only known the guy a couple months. I even heard a black guy in the plant recently asking a white guy if there were any houses for sale on his street, and the white guy said he would get the phone numbers of the realties off the signs and give them to him. In the past that kind of thing wasn't common, and it wasn't spoken of in so casual a manner.

The EI program has opened some doors that will be beneficial in the long run. But the company controls what the employee will be involved with. To me, it's just another form of psychology that the company is using as opposed to its old brute-force days. Then it was cussing you out or firing you on the spot, or if they couldn't fire you because of the union, they'd suspend you for thirty days without pay or whatever they could get away with.

There's really nothing new about what they're doing. Salaried employees have always had the advantage of knowing when they were going to shut down for changeover or when we were going to work overtime. That information was always kept from the hourly employee until EI came about. So that, plus the opportunity to buy stock shares and discounts on automobiles, is something the company's been doing all along for salaried employees; they've just extended it to the hourly employees. It's not costing the company anything. I think they would balk if it cost them a dime.

The company instituted EI because the old way wasn't getting them the productivity or the quality they were after. They looked at Japan and other places to see how their competitors were manufacturing their products and how the employees were being treated, and they decided to change their strategy. They figured they could get more out of the workers if they treated them a little nicer.

The union seems to go after the same issues they went after in 1930: more pay; more time off; holiday pay. But the worker needs more than more pay. He needs a method of doing his job that's not so dehumanizing. He needs more control over what he's doing. And a man needs some assurance that he's going to have a job next week and the plant isn't going to close down. The union has to deal with a man's future.

Automation will make a difference in the company's payroll and help them make a product faster in certain departments. But automation has limited application for two reasons: first, the enormous cost of the equipment and of maintaining it; and second, limits on what the equipment can do. A machine can only do what it's designed to do. A computerized welding machine can only do welding. But one man could weld and paint. It's a lot of bull that automation can replace manpower. I cannot see a machine putting glass in a door, securing molding around a window, putting a doorknob or a latch on. I don't believe it.

Even if I'm completely wrong about this, and they eliminate another twenty thousand factory workers, where will they sell their product? It's the working class that buys their product. If they're waiting on the multimillionaires to buy their Tempo, they're up a creek. It's me that buys their Tempo, the guy that works on the line. And if they just make the big luxury car and sell it for $50,000, they're dealing with a limited clientele.

In ten years or so the automobile industry will be a world industry. Too many American companies have invested in foreign automobile manufacturing. You don't see the auto companies seriously lobbying in Congress to restrict Japanese products. They claim that our chief competition is the Japanese and that they are robbing us of our sales and our jobs. So why don't they get the import laws changed? It's because they want to have their cake and eat it, too.

I don't think there's such a thing anymore as an American product. Things may be assembled here, but the parts are made elsewhere. "Buy American" is just a slogan. It makes a statement about something you know nothing about. The guys in the plant believe it because it's easy to believe a concept and take the concept to be real. If you talk about it long enough and loud enough, it becomes real, but it's not a fact.

The big cities are fighting a losing battle. Places like New York, Detroit, Chicago are things of the past. It used to be necessary to have a center for everything to branch out from, but now everything is branching out, not around the corner, but around the world. We will have a world order, a world common market, a world corporation, a world automobile industry.

Many people will be unable to find a niche in the new society. They will be left out—permanently. For the kids, it's going to be a waste machine, a terrific waste of human beings.

Unless this whole capitalist system turns around, which is very unlikely, things will probably continue pretty much as they are, with a few corporations controlling all of the wealth.

One of my favorite books is *For Whom the Bell Tolls* because its hero was revolting against a corrupt government. But the book raises the questions: What are you going to replace it with? Do you have something better?

Chapter Four
The Pressured

All I'm asking for is a little respect.

—*Otis Redding, "Respect"*

Sheryl Jackson

Born June 29, 1952, in Detroit
Hired July 21, 1977
Assembler on the Engine Line

I GREW UP in the projects in Detroit, and my mom was on welfare. I remember when I was in junior high, they took us on a tour of an auto plant, and I decided that's where I wanted to work. Before that I had always wanted to be a singer or a seamstress.

After I got married and got a job at Wayne Assembly, I joined the middle class. My husband and I were both working at Ford, and we had financial security. His mother was wealthy. We owned a fish market and a record shop. We were going to move out to the suburbs, get a big trailer home, and travel the world. But all those plans weren't worth the price for me. I finally left my husband because I got tired of him being mean to me. He had served in Vietnam and had seen his buddy get killed, and he would fly off the handle for no reason. Once he even pointed a gun at me. I finally decided I didn't have to live with that. I didn't have to be punished for Vietnam.

Even after the divorce I maintained a comfortable life-style. I stayed in the middle class until they kicked me out the door in February 1980. I was really hurt the way they laid me off. "Here's

111

Sheryl Jackson

your pink slip. Just get out; we don't need you anymore." That's how it was. They weren't nice about it.

In a way I was glad to get laid off because I wanted to be with my three kids. I had been working afternoons and didn't get to see them much. Plus I hated working in that place. I had paid my car off, and I wasn't worried because I knew I had ADC [Aid to Dependent Children] to fall back on. And I collected my unemployment for a year. But when that ran out, I had to get by on ADC and food stamps, and that was peanuts, about $500 a month. Out of that I had to pay my house note and the gas and lights.

Things were tight. I couldn't get my kids what they wanted for Christmas. I didn't go to church much because I couldn't afford nice clothes and I didn't have a car. But I read the Bible a lot, and that helped. It said, "Don't worry about what you are going to wear for tomorrow, what you are going to eat. I'll feed you and I'll clothe you." It was true. The only way to survive in this world is to be strong. You just have to keep going. Things may be tight now, but don't give up. There is always a brighter day.

I was laid off for six years. I never thought I'd get called back. I looked for other jobs. I took the post office test twice. I took a test for corrections officers twice, but they never called me. After three years with no job I met a lady who has a cleaning business. I started working with her. We would clean houses for rich white folks out in the suburbs for $25 a day. But the work wasn't steady.

I was one of about twenty-nine people who got called back in April 1986 to the truck plant. The first day back we had an orientation. We met all the supervisors, the superintendents, the plant managers. We had coffee and doughnuts, and they told us about the plant, and they had videos and pamphlets about all the chemicals they use. They let us ask questions. Then they took us on the line and showed us the work and we met the foremen. I couldn't believe how nice the people were. They smiled at you and said hi. It's like one big happy family at the truck plant. Everybody talks to everybody.

Now that I'm working, I feel like a human being again. I'm in the work force. I'm in the big leagues. I can take care of my own. I can walk around with my head up high.

If you're on ADC, people don't respect you. They figure all you want to do is sit around and wait for the check. Maybe some women do that, but not me. When I was collecting ADC, I didn't feel like they were giving me anything I didn't deserve. I felt I was getting back what I had put in from the years I was working and the money they took out of my paycheck for taxes. Now I'm back to work, and I can help somebody else. They take my taxes out and give the money to somebody who can use it.

I get angry about people working overtime. The plant has been on ten hours for a long time. That is a lot of work for one person. Why not split it up and let somebody else get some of that money? There are a lot of people out there who want work. They don't like sitting around their houses. They have family and kids, too. Eight hours is enough. Share some of that work. Let everybody have some of the goodies.

I have a friend who was working at an auto plant in the suburbs. She got laid off and never got called back. She is doing house-cleaning now.

I'm not greedy to work overtime. Just as long as I have a job, I'm happy. Working all that overtime, what kind of life is that? You don't have time to do anything. You are tired when you come home.

My job keeps me moving. I don't have time for anything. I can't even scratch my head. The only time I get for a cigarette is if someone is walking by and I say, "Light me a cigarette," and they stick it in my mouth. And I smoke it while I'm working. The drinking faucet is on the other side of the line, so I have to ask someone to take my cup and bring me some water.

Sometimes I trip over the cord of the gun I use. Or the gun falls down and the screw drops out of it and I already have stuff in my hands. I have to pick it up and put the gun between my legs and try to put the screw back in the gun with my hands. It's a mess. The lubricating grease soaks through your gloves about every two hours.

I do the best I can to keep up. It helps that guys talk to you and make the day go by. We talk about everything, sex mostly, because that's all they know. They're always telling me what they can do. And they talk about their families, what they're going to do on vacation, stuff like that.

Now that my foot's back in the door, I'm going to try to save some money, so when they kick me out again, I'll have something to fall back on. I just have to roll with the punches. What can I do? I can't make those people make me stay there.

I know it is not going to last long; but I have a stable life, and it is OK. My job as a mother is putting my kids on the right track and working. I'll make it somehow. As long as I can keep my house, a roof over our heads, and food in the refrigerator, we'll be all right.

My oldest daughter is getting ready to graduate from high school. What kind of job is she going to have? Computers and robots are taking over. I can't find a job, so what are my daughters going to do? They will probably end up on ADC, having babies, trying to find a husband to take care of them, unless they are smart and start a business of their own or get lucky. If I had the money, I would help them go to college, or if I got a sewing business going, they could help me with that. But other than that, all I can see them doing is working in a restaurant. I always worked, and I want them to have a job and do something. I don't care what it is, as long as it is honest money.

My best advice to my kids is never give up, keep on searching for your dreams. Don't just go for anything, and don't be in a hurry. Be selective.

Lance Whitis

Born January 12, 1958, in Detroit
Hired July 9, 1976
Assembler on the Final Line

WHEN I WAS GROWING UP, I didn't really know what I was going to do with my life. I got kicked out of high school for smoking in the bathroom, so I went to Ford, and I've been there ever since. All my friends from high school and the neighborhood got jobs at factories, but I'm the only one that hung in. The others got laid off or quit because they couldn't take the hassle of the foreman arguing at them. Being in the plant is like being in the service. You have to take orders, and most people can't stand taking orders. So my friends that used to be in the factory are out on the street selling dope. They make $400 a day, and they don't want to work. But I'm not the kind of guy who can steal or rob. I'd rather work the hard way to get my money.

When I got hired at the plant, I thought it was a guaranteed job because everybody needs cars. I didn't know they were going to lay off people. Now I know the whole thing is going to fold. This is the last generation.

I have to hang on to building trucks. That's the only thing I have now. If I get fired or laid off, I don't have the skills to do anything else. I didn't sign up for the apprenticeship program

Lance Whitis

because I'm slow in reading and math. I don't know what I'd do if they got rid of me.

I'm the number one worker in the family now. I live with my mom and my sister. I'm still messing up a little bit, but I'm trying to get it together. I am in the hole with bills and income taxes. I've attended a number of programs that have helped me clean up my act. I'm just trying to hold on to my job.

They are trying to fire people. They don't care if you have fifteen or twenty years in. They are really tightening up on attendance. The other day they wrote up a guy for missing one day after he had perfect attendance for a year and a half. This guy had sixteen or seventeen years in. I don't think it's right to mess like that with people who come in every day.

I've got just a few months under ten years in, but I'm on probation for attendance. I'm under a different contract from the people who have ten years in, and that's not fair. If you've got ten years in, they have to accept your doctor's note, but if you're under ten years and you miss work, a review board decides if your doctor's note is a valid excuse. I think the union sold us out with that contract. How can you split a contract so that the rules are different if you have less than ten years?

My foreman knows I'm close to ten years, so he hassles me every day. He tells me I'm missing bolts, and I know I haven't missed anything. They are trying to mess with me so I'll quit or take a day off and they can fire me. It's not right.

I was fired from the truck plant a couple months ago. I was walking down the street, and the police picked me up and took me to jail and locked me up for twenty-four hours. I already had served thirty days' probation at work, so I knew that if I missed a day, I would be fired. Sure enough, I came in the next day and they fired me. The committeeman got me back the same day, but they had me waiting six or seven hours in the Labor Relations office, making me sweat. I went before a review board and had to talk to the plant manager. He told me there were plenty of people outside who wanted my job. He said it was up to me if I wanted to work.

My committeeman gave up a lot of things to get me back. If anyone else was defending me, I would have been fired. Afterward, he took me aside and said, "Hey, I got a son your age, and I know how it is to be on the street. It's hard for a black man trying to survive." He made me feel good because he cared.

Now I'm scared when I walk down the street to go to the store and I see a police car. I run home because I know that if I get stopped by the police and they put me in jail, I'll get fired again, and this time they won't be able to get me back.

When I first hired in, you could miss three or four days and they wouldn't say anything. You could give the foreman a hassle and tell him how you really felt. You could tell him to leave you alone. You could walk off the job. You can't do any of that now. You have to be careful how you talk to the foreman. If you miss one truck, they'll hassle you about it. They are cracking down. I used to be glad to come into work, but not anymore.

They have these EI meetings and say the Japanese are kicking ass and that's why we need to tighten up. But I think we are doing a good job already. I know I do my job. That's what I get paid for. I don't come in to mess around.

The management tries to make us think they care about the workers. We even have little TV monitors up in the plant so you can see the Dow Jones Average and how much profit we're making. They do things to try to geek us up. But it doesn't fool me because I know all they want is production out the door.

They don't care who they put on the hard jobs as long as the line is running. They don't care if you are 50 or 100, as long as you work. I feel sorry for some of the old people on the line. They really are busting their ass. I think they put them there to get them frustrated so they will take time off or quit.

It's hard having perfect attendance when you don't have a car to get to work. I have to depend on somebody else to bring me back and forth. The guy who takes me now has only missed eighteen days in eighteen years. He's dependable. He's the best ride I've ever had. He cares what happens to me, and that makes a big difference. It's hard to find people who really care.

Most people at the plant don't care. Everybody is out for themselves. When I worked at Wayne Assembly, we stuck together. If we were smoking a joint and somebody saw the foreman coming, he'd tell everyone. At the truck plant the workers tell you, "Hey, man, don't do that because I don't like it, and I'm going to tell on you." Everybody is trying to get the best job and kissing ass.

If you stay on the line and don't say anything, the time goes by slowly. Some of the guys I work with now don't say much. I think they have money bet on me that I'm not going to make my ten years.

Yaser Awadallah

Born January 26, 1946, in Palestine
Hired May 25, 1972
Shock installer

I WAS BORN two years before the Israelis took over our country. As we grew up, we learned that we had a native country and we had lost it. We lived on the West Bank until 1956, when we moved to Jordan, where my father had a job selling windows. My father died in 1964, and I took his place working to support my family. My mother came here in 1970 with all my brothers and sisters. She got me my work papers, and I came here in 1971.

I'm not political. I am a factory man. After ten hours of work I don't want to go to any meetings. I come home and go to sleep. And I am not against any religions. You have yours, and I have mine. That's your business. But I feel like the company and some of the people at the plant don't like Arabs. The company should not discriminate against whites, blacks, Arabs, or anyone because we all do the same work for them and get the same pay.

Arabs who have been working here many years are citizens of the United States just like everyone else. But people give us a hard time. They say, "Why don't you go back to your country, camel jockey?" I reply that the United States is a free country. I am a citizen, and the same laws that protect you protect me. I respect

Yaser Awadallah

this country. I don't hate it. If I hated it, I would go back. I'm not a camel jockey, but I am proud that my ancestors rode camels two thousand years ago. Don't tell me to go back to my country. Why don't you go to my country to see how we live?

Rich people are the cause of all the trouble. They always search for money and power. That's what causes the problems everywhere, not the differences between people. I'm not against Jews. I have Jewish friends, and I believe Jews and Arabs are cousins. If you look back two thousand years, we are related.

The problem is not between people, but between governments. Those of us who work on the line are just trying to make a living. We don't come to the plant to fight. We have to get along because we work together ten hours a day. I see the people I work with more than I see my family.

At the plant everybody tries hard to do a good job. Quality has gotten a lot better. People are doing such a good job that you see the repairmen standing around doing nothing. My job now is to install the back shocks. If they are bad, I switch to a new set. I don't let bad shocks go on a truck.

We do good work, but if you work too fast, they try to put more work on you. That's not right. We are not slaves. We are human beings. We work hard, but I am not working for my boss. I work for Ford Motor Company. They pay me. I go there to work by the rules, by the contract.

They should follow the rules. There is too much favoritism about who gets the easy job. It's not right that the general foreman can tell a supervisor to put pressure on one guy or let another guy switch jobs because he is his friend. He shouldn't get special treatment just because he drinks beer or goes fishing or hunting with the supervisor. The supervisor doesn't pay him.

I don't like it when a woman comes and takes away an easy job from a man just because the supervisor or general foreman likes her. It happened to me. I was working as a utility man, and they posted a new utility job on the line. I applied for it, and Labor Relations approved me for the job. But the general foreman wanted to give the job to this woman he had been dating. So he started pushing me hard. Finally I told him, "You can do whatever you want to do with her in your house, but this is not a whorehouse. She has six months and doesn't know anything. I got over five years, and I know the whole job." I eventually got the job, but after a while they made her a supervisor.

They give women too much freedom in this country. The women work in the plants just like men, but they can't do the same jobs men do. A woman's job should be to take care of the home. That's what my wife does.

I have a bad back. I first hurt it in 1974, when I was lifting tailgates. I would get terrible pains and go home and soak in a hot tub. I didn't want to take off work. We didn't have enough money with the house payment and bills to afford for me to go on sick leave. So I kept working.

On the job I have now, I have to lift forty-pound boxes of stock. One day I picked up a box and it slipped. I tried to catch it and hurt my back again. So I went to my doctor, and he said I had to take a month off. The company accepted that. But then a friend told me to go see a back specialist. He did an X ray, and it showed I had a slipped disk.

When the company got that report, they sent me to their medical department. They started questioning me like detectives, checked me out, and said I should go back to work with no restrictions.

They forced me to go back to a different job. They put me on the Chassis Line, where I had to bend a lot. One day my back got very bad. When I would bend, I couldn't get up right away. I would start to lose my balance, and my legs would hurt. So I told them I wanted to go to First Aid. They made me wait awhile, and then they told me that a plant doctor had told the boss not to bring me to First Aid because my record showed there was nothing wrong with my back. I was very angry. I went to see a guy from Labor Relations, and he started talking to me like he didn't care about me. They sent me for a second opinion, and the third-party doctor found I had a slipped disk and said I could work, but no bending, no twisting, and no lifting anything over twenty-five pounds.

I got my lawyer to meet with the company's lawyer. I told him I wasn't asking for money. I get paid $35,000 to $40,000 a year, and that's enough. I just wanted him to tell the company to leave me alone and not give me a hard time. So my lawyer told them, and now they leave me alone.

I work in the Frame Line now. To pass the time, I sing in Arabic, or I talk to myself about what I'm going to do if I get a little money, how I might open a business or something. That's my dream. I don't have an education, and I don't speak English very well, so I can't go to college or learn how to run computers.

I never bother anybody at work. Sometimes I work the whole ten hours and don't say a word. I just do my job, and that's it. On my job at least nobody hounds me. That's what causes the most pressure. Most people just want to be left alone.

I don't want to be a foreman or a supervisor. Those jobs make you too nervous. I've seen a lot of people get heart attacks on those jobs. I know one foreman who had a lot of pressure put on him because his line was not running good. They blamed him rather than try to find out what the cause was. He couldn't take it. They ended up transferring him.

I don't like the overtime. I work it only because I don't have the right to say no. The human being is only equipped to work eight hours. They should bring back the second shift and let somebody else work the other eight hours.

A lot of people have gotten laid off and lost their houses, and now they're on welfare. And when there is no work here, people start to shoot each other. Murder, rape, robbery, and stealing—

every day you hear about someone who goes in a bank or a party store and kills. I am scared to leave my house because somebody might break in.

I don't need the overtime pay. We don't spend much money. We have two cars; we pay insurance; we pay bills; we pay our rent. We don't buy a lot of expensive junk for our house. I don't go to bars. We don't travel much. We don't bowl. We save our money because we care about our son. I want him to have a better life than mine. My father died and didn't leave anything, and I had to work hard to take care of my five young sisters and brothers. I don't want to do that to my son. I want to give him a chance. I hope he grows up to be a doctor or an engineer. I will not let him work in the factory—no way.

Debbie Lynn Listman

Born November 3, 1957, in Ypsilanti, Michigan
Hired May 11, 1976
Installs windshield washer bottles

A WOMAN AT THE TRUCK PLANT always has to be on her toes. You have to watch what you do and what you say. You don't want to give anyone the wrong impression or lead anybody on. You get harassment. I mean, men will be men—or is that, boys will be boys?

I don't like to be touched. I've had guys pat me on the butt, and I've turned around and threatened them. I've told them, "You do not touch me. I'll give you one warning, and if you do it again, I'll try my best to get you fired because I'm not here to be a plaything for you. I'm here, same as you are, to make a living and support my kids and give them things I never had. I'm just here to do my job, to put in my eight hours."

My foreman knows I don't want to be touched, but he'll come by and pinch me on the leg or touch me somewhere. I don't like it, but what can I do? If I was to do something physical or start complaining that he's pinching me, he would stop, but then I'd get worse harassment later. So as long as he doesn't pat me on the butt, I don't say anything. I think if I said something to him, he'd just laugh anyway. Every time I say anything he's got something

Debbie Lynn Listman

dirty to say, some stupid stuff. I don't appreciate that. But I think he talks worse to other women in the plant.

I've never been confronted with sex from a supervisor. They've never harassed me to the point where if I don't give them something, they threaten my job.

When I was first hired at Wayne Assembly and walked onto the plant floor, there were all these men howling and whistling at me. I was afraid they were going to attack me. I wanted to tell them to knock it off. After putting up with it for weeks, I found out from somebody about a tunnel under the plant that I could walk through to get to my job. That way I didn't have to walk past all the howlers.

I eventually found out that men in the plant do that stuff just to relieve tension. They don't see women too often at work, so when they see one walk by, they get it out of their system.

There's a difference between the older men and the younger men. The older men come right out and make dirty jokes or tell you how they feel about you: "Hi, baby, I think you're gorgeous" or "Come on, I'm in love with you!" But the younger men just say hi. I like that better.

There are a few men working around me who don't like women being in the factory. They think women ought to be home taking care of babies. People have said to me, "You should stay home and raise your kids." I feel the same way sometimes, but the reality is you have to work. You need two people working to make ends meet these days.

I feel uncomfortable working around men who think I don't have a right to be there. I'd like to talk to them, but I can't. So I just go in and do my job and try to ignore how they feel. But you can't ignore it. It makes the job harder psychologically.

I would like to make friends with some of the men, but I don't know how. You need friends in there. I want to get into a union position someday, so I try to be friendly with everybody. I try to have a positive attitude with people, and if they give me back something negative, I just brush it off. But I don't want people to take my being friendly the wrong way. I just want to carry on a conversation, but it always turns around somehow.

For instance, I like to go outside and get fresh air. And I like to have someone to go out there with to talk to. But then that person thinks I like them. During lunch a bunch of people might go into someone's car and talk. It might not be the kind of conversation I like to have, but at least it's someone to talk to. But then you can't go outside with them anymore because they think it means something. I don't lead them on. But people talk. They say, "She's been going outside with so-and-so."

I've heard stories of women getting it on with someone in a car or truck in the parking lot. I don't know if those stories are true or if they're just rumors that get started, like the stories I've heard about me in the parking lot.

When I leave the plant, I don't bring it home. I don't discuss how my day was. I like to forget my days. I'm just there working, and that's it.

I come from a family of factory workers. My mother is from West Virginia. Her father was a coal miner and died young. After he died, my grandmother and her kids moved up here. My grandmother worked at Wayne Assembly for a little while. My grandfather was a supervisor for General Motors. My great-uncles work in the steel mills. My brother works for GM, too.

I was very young when my mom started working. I remember her getting up in the morning to go to work at the plant. She worked nine years for Ford at the plant in Saline and got a medical retirement because of a heart problem. We didn't really see enough of her. We had an older woman as a sitter. She took care of the house and of me, my four brothers, and one sister.

A lot of my friends had a lot more than what we had. I've had to work since I was 14. I never had a summer off.

When I started at Wayne Assembly, I was 18 and had three weeks of high school left. At the time I didn't really have any idea of what I wanted to do. I just knew I wanted to go to college. My grandmother, who knew the vice-president of the union local, told me that Ford would pay for my school. So I signed up for afternoons.

That first night was something. I never hurt so bad in my entire life. I went home and lay down in my bed and started crying. My mother came in and rubbed my feet and told me, "This won't last. It'll go away. It's just muscles you haven't used." She comforted me. She knew how I felt.

My mom was proud I had gotten the job. She figured I'd be secure financially. And she was right. When I got that first paycheck, I didn't know what I was going to do with all that money. It was the most I'd ever made.

For a while I took some college classes, but it was rough. We would get off work at 4:30 and I had an 8:00 class. It didn't seem to be practical to go to school and be too tired to understand what I was hearing. I did it for a couple of semesters and then quit. I figured I didn't need to go to school with all the money I could make in the plant.

I got laid off in April 1982, but it was only for four weeks. I was about the fourth woman called back after the layoffs in 1982. I was actually hoping I wouldn't get called back because it would have given me the opportunity to look for something else. See, I'm so used to what I'm doing and the money I'm making that I don't think I would just up and quit. I don't think I could find another job with that kind of money and benefits and vacation time. But if I was laid off, I would have to.

Since I survived the last recession, I believe I'll stay here through the next one. I have a feeling there's no way they're going to let me go. I think I'm being punished for the wild life-style I had in high school by being made to work in the factory all my life.

My job is to install water bottles. It's steady work. I've had harder and dirtier jobs. I've put in air conditioners. But they tend to keep the heavier jobs for the men.

With two kids and a husband and a house, I have a twenty-four-hour-a-day job. I get up at 5 A.M. because the plant is only five minutes from my house. Steve gets up at the same time, and he gets the children up and takes them to the sitter's at 6:30, and then he goes to work. We're lucky to have a sitter we feel comfortable with. She's in her early 40s and has two kids who are already out of school. We pay her $120 a week. I don't worry when I'm at work because I know she is taking good care of my kids.

After work I pick up the kids and get home after 5. My son, Justin, who's a year old, goes to bed at 7 or 8. So there's only a few hours I have with him. After he goes to sleep, I try to do what I can around the house, and I try to read a little bit—*National Geographic, Redbook, Health & Beauty*, and books on antiques. I take Sara, who's 3, upstairs with me, and we read something together or just talk, because that's the only time we have. I usually fall asleep around 9 or 10.

On weekends, if I'm not working Saturday, I do the laundry and the grocery shopping.

I feel bad that I don't have more time for the kids. When they get older, they'll understand that I was doing the best thing for them. I'm trying to save money for them so they won't have it so bad like I did. I'm in a credit union, and they take $50 a week out of my paycheck and put it into a savings account for their education. I never see it, and I never touch it.

I wouldn't want Sara to do the kind of work I do. If Justin could handle it, fine. I'd like Sara to have a good education and get married to the right person, to someone with enough money so she doesn't have to work.

I'm not proud to be an autoworker. I don't enjoy the job. The money is the only reason I stay there. It's the same as any job: You do the same thing for a while, and you get tired of it. The only way I keep my sanity sometimes is to tell myself that I'd probably get tired of any job.

They say EI is supposed to help you in relationships with the company. Give me a break. In one area I was working in, we got a new clock put up and some new picnic tables. I don't think too much of that. The idea is to get a better relationship with your foreman and let the company know the problems you're having. Well, I've told them some of the problems I'm having, and I've never seen anything resolved.

I don't like working ten hours. It's surprising how two extra hours really brings you down and tires you out. I'd rather see it cut to eight hours, add another shift, bring people back. It's crazy that people are out of work and we're working ten hours a day. Why not put in another shift? They'd be making more trucks and making more money. After all, they say there's a big demand for Broncos. But sometimes on the line I wonder where all these trucks are going to. I don't see a Ford truck on the road very often. It seems that with as many trucks and cars as I have made they'd be going down Michigan Avenue one after another.

I try to make the job more enjoyable by talking to people and listening to the radio. I love rock and roll. I used to play guitar and fool around with folk music. I find my radio real comforting at work. The music gets me through the day. I always sing. I boogie up and down the line, doing my job.

On bad days time goes by so slowly I think: Time's stopped; what's going on here? I psych myself by thinking about my kids, about what I could do if I work for a while, then take some time off and do something else. I think of trips I could take. I think about places I've gone to, like Hawaii. It's like going through labor; you think of something pleasant as you go through your pain.

Billie Jean Newsome

Born December 7, 1954, in Ypsilanti, Michigan
Hired March 12, 1977
Assembler on the Trim Line

I'M AN OPEN and down-to-earth person. That's how I want people to be to me—open. I can tell when people lie. When they do, I lay it on the line. I reverse what's in their mind.

A whole lot of white folks in the plant don't like Coleman Young. All the white people moved out and left Detroit for dead, and now there's a black mayor who built Detroit back up, and they say he's prejudiced. I tell them he's just doing his job.

One time this guy in Trim started making racial remarks to me. He said, "You people, you know my grandfather owned one of you."

And I said, "Oh, yeah, and guess what? This is the eighties, baby. Look, you're here and I'm here, and we're making the same money. Your granddaughter will probably be doing my house-keeping."

When I told some of the white guys in the plant that I have a housekeeper, they looked like they were in shock. It blew their mind that a black woman has a housekeeper. But I work ten hours, and there's too much for me to do. I'm too tired when I come home to cook dinner, so I have to hire someone.

Willie Gene and Billie Jean Newsome

Another time this same guy was getting down on me because I was black, so I whispered in his ear, "You know what, Jack? I work in the factory. My husband works in the factory. I got just as much as you, or more. So we might as well cut out the bullshitting. We might as well work together and be real people. Get that stuff out of your head." He looked at me funny, and ever since then he hasn't played that role.

They tease a lot of people, but I don't want them to tease me. There are enough problems in there. It's already rough, mentally and physically. We have to turn it around into something like love because we have to work together. The plant would be a better place to work with a more loving atmosphere. I just want to get rid of the prejudice and have everyone be as one.

When I first hired in at the plant in 1977, they had to hire black women because they were hiring white women. They put the women on hard jobs. I guess they wanted to see if we really wanted to work. I was working in Chassis, doing the splasher job. I had to shoot about fifteen screws in the mud splasher. I was hanging in on that job, probably messing up a couple of things, and they fired me before I got my ninety days in. They wanted to get rid of the women. They fired two white women and had to fire a black woman so it wouldn't look so bad. They called the white women back but not me.

The president of the union and Charlie Hoskins, the truck plant chairman, were furious because they didn't have any grounds for firing me. I had been doing a good job. So after three weeks they got me back to work, and I got paid for the whole three weeks.

Things would be a lot worse if there were no union. At least with the union you have a chance. If something happens, they can talk for you. They can get you back if you're fired. They defend you like a lawyer does. I don't mind paying my union dues as long as they do their job.

They're trying to get rid of the union. That's what Employee Involvement is all about. They're trying to say they don't have to have the union if they can get the employees and the foremen to have a good relationship. But I think the union should be there even if you have a better atmosphere.

I worked afternoons at the truck plant until 1980, when they laid off the afternoon shift. I was recalled two years later to Wayne Assembly. I kept getting laid off and called back. I would work sixty days, get laid off a year, work four months, get laid off again. Finally, in 1984, I was called back to the truck plant.

They put me in PEP [Protection Employment Program]. We were like plant-wide utility people who would fill in for absentees. We were supposed to be getting trained in different jobs. But I don't want to be doing different jobs. Once you get adjusted to one, it's aggravating to have to learn something new. If you can get settled in with one job, you can make it your second home because you know you're going to be there awhile. If you jump around from one job to another, you're all wound up in a ball.

Having people learn more than one job is slick. If someone's absent, they'll always have somebody else who knows the job. They can play chess with the jobs.

After a while they put me on the water shield job in the Trim

Department. I put sealer and waterproof paper on the passenger-side door and the tailgate. Until I got the hang of it, I got that sticky black sealer all over me every day.

I used to try to keep up with the guy working on the other side of the line doing the same job. But I finally realized he'd been doing the job for ten years, and it was natural to him. So I stopped running and started working at my own steady pace.

They laid me off again in January 1985. I was off a year and a month before I came back. They put me back on the sealer job. I didn't like it, and I didn't want to do it. After a week I started hollering at my committeeman. I told him I wanted to be trained for something else. He said, "OK, BJ, we'll see."

Now the committeeman and the general foreman always make deals. They negotiate, and you're in the middle. I told my committeeman, "I'm paying you out of my check every month, and I want my business taken care of right." But he was too slow, so I went over his head. They took me off the job; but it was only for a couple of days, and I got put right back on it. They were just playing games with me.

Finally I went up to the general foreman, and I said, "I want you to be honest with me. Am I going to be on this job as long as I'm here?"

He said, "I think so, BJ."

I said, "How come you didn't just tell me in the first place?"

At that point I started praying. I said, "God, you have to make things better because I'm tired of being a grimy monkey, with sealer all over the place." I hated to be nasty all the time. I hated having to wash that stuff out of my hair.

I don't wear coveralls on the job, so I would get sealer all over my clothes. Coveralls are too hot, and you lose your femininity wearing them. They make you look like a man. I'm already working like a man, and I don't want to dress like one.

The job was hard. Plus there was a problem with the sealer. When they ran the truck through the water test, it would leak. The supervisors would come over and ask me what the problem was. I would tell them I was doing the best I could, but most of the time the sealer had air in it and would bubble up and not stick. They told me to rub it down after I put it on to make sure it was sticking. But I told them, "When those trucks start coming, I can't nurse this job."

I didn't like having someone standing there watching me, like I wasn't doing my job, especially since I had just come back from a layoff. You don't know how long you will be there. They just use you when they can. Then they kick you back out.

In July 1986 they put in a new machine that makes my job easier. It loads the paper and puts a sticky chemical on it. I just pull out the paper and put it on the door. I don't have to grab the sealer gun and worry about that mess. It's fantastic.

Sometimes now I go down the line and check to see if there's been any water leakage. I want to do a good job. I own a Ford product myself. I used to buy other companies' cars, but now I have an '85 Lincoln. My husband, who works next door at the car plant, convinced me that since we work for Ford, we should buy Ford products. So I want to do a quality job. Plus I don't want anyone saying anything to me. If someone comes around and aggravates me, I get mad, and my whole day is ruined.

Now, if there's something wrong, they're not going to blame the machine they spent so much money on; they're going to blame the machine operator. They're not going to tell me if the sealer is really covering or not. They'll probably come back and tell me, "Take the tape and cover the holes," like it was my fault the tape is not covering the holes good enough.

I asked this engineer who was a sealer specialist if they had been getting any water leaks from the door since they added the new machine, and he said they had. But they don't say anything about it in the garage.

I don't think it's right to bring in all those machines because the machines can't buy cars. As long as the workers work and get paid, they will buy cars. But if you get computers and robots in there, who's going to buy them?

Ford doesn't have to pay wages to that computer. The computer doesn't have to go to the bathroom or take a break. Ford doesn't have to worry about the computer not coming in to work. Ford looks at making a profit, but they are not looking at who is going to buy the car. It isn't going to work. People have to have a job. They have to live. These computers can't come in here and take over. Where will people go?

My husband told me in his plant they put in a little robot in the Stock Department, but the employees tore it up because it knocked out a man's job. That's fantastic. They all stick together over there. They don't let their jobs get cut off.

*   *   *

My grandparents are from Alabama and Mississippi. My dad was a veteran and a construction worker. My mom did house-keeping. When I was 11, my dad had a stroke. He was in a convalescent home for seventeen years. Every Sunday my mom took us to see him.

My twin sister and I took my dad down South in 1981 to see his family. It was the first time I'd ever been there. I saw where my mom was raised. She had ten brothers and sisters, and they grew up in this shabby two-bedroom house out in the middle of the fields.

I've been working since I was 10 or 11. I was always baby-sitting or helping care for senior citizens in the projects. I never dreamed I would work in the auto plants.

People in the plant call me a Holy Roller now, because I'm saved. I go to church. I don't smoke or cuss in the plant. I'm not into the drug scene, and I don't drink anymore. That's a big change from the past.

When I worked afternoons at the truck plant, we would all go out and drink together. It was like a family. There wasn't any-thing anybody wouldn't do for you. If you wanted something, like weed, somebody would get it for you. Everybody was getting high back then. It was like a world inside of a world, like an under-ground world for ten hours. You would come in at 5 in the after-noon and get out at 5 in the morning, so you had to make the best of it, make it a party. We didn't have a whole lot of pride in our work back then. We were in there making money, getting high, and doing the job.

I used to take speed just to keep up with the work. I always took diet pills before I came in. I would share them with people in the plant because when I got high, I wanted everybody high with me. I would never smoke weed on the job because I would get para-noid. People who did smoke weed in the plant did it in the bath-rooms and lockers, not on the line.

I got saved because of my husband. I met him in 1982. I had just been called back to Wayne Assembly. I worked at the end of the line in the Cushion Department, feeding the line with parts. At the time I was still into getting high. I had my big radio next to me. I was sneaking in cognac with my Coke. I was smoking cigarettes. All the guys would rap with me. They called me the Devil.

But this one guy was different. He didn't say anything to me.

They called him the Preacher because he was always carrying his Bible around. They would scoff at him because he was always talking about the Lord.

Back then it was like a challenge to me when a man didn't pay attention to me. Out of respect for him, I turned down my radio, covered up my cognac, and put my cigarette out. I had been raised going to church, and I knew what I was doing was bad. I saw something different in him. It was like he had a halo over his head, so I didn't want to smoke in front of him.

At the time I was still partying. My daughter was staying with my mom, my cousin was staying at my apartment, and I was shacking up with this guy. One day I told the Preacher about my problems. He told me to get my family back together because I was not happy. It was good sound advice, and I followed it.

Eventually he took me to his church to be baptized. I had always wanted to live like that, but I had never met anyone who showed me how. He straightened everything out. He got me to bring my daughter home from my mom's to live with me. He loaned me $500 so I could buy some furniture on Christmas Eve and entertain my parents. Then I got laid off again. I was running out of money and was almost to the point of having to go on ADC when he asked me to marry him.

Now everything is different. I love it. No getting high, no partying, just living a good life. Since I've been saved, I see things more clearly. I don't worry about anything. I just see love. I love people better. What happened to me was just like a TV show. The Preacher and the Devil got married, and people at the plant still don't know what to make of it.

I'm happily married. If a guy tries to make time with me in the plant now, I reverse it. I ask him what he would think if his wife was making time on the job. So they leave me alone. I project a sister image, and we establish a buddy-buddy relationship. That's how I want it.

I'm glad to work at Ford because Ford is not prejudiced. Some people who work for Ford are, but Ford doesn't care who works as long as they do the work. Ford is good to people. Henry Ford gives money to help people, like the money he gave to Mayor Young to build the Renaissance Center. So we say since Ford helps others, Ford is blessed in return.

My biggest concern for my daughter is getting her an education. She wants to work in computer science. My husband and I tell her the factory isn't good, that she should get a job where she can work at her own pace. In the factory we have to work when the man says so. I want something different for her.

I was amazed in 1984 when I asked a friend of mine at the plant who she was voting for and she said Reagan. Just because they're working overtime and making money, these people think everything's OK. I don't understand these people at the factory who like Reagan. He's taking more from us all the time. He has too much power, and he's going to end up tearing this world up. But we don't worry because we're saved and we're going to be called up to heaven. Mankind is just going to destroy itself.

Chapter Five

Union Advocates

And so to our adversaries and to all those who
are preparing to dance on labor's grave, I have
just one word of advice: Don't waste money on
dancing shoes, because it ain't over yet! We're
coming back strong, and if you're in the market
for shoes, you better make them running shoes,
because before long we intend to have you on the
run.

> —*Owen Bieber,*
> *UAW president, on the eve*
> *of the 1987 contract talks*

Walter "Jeff" Washington

Born February 28, 1946 in Detroit
Hired March 16, 1964
President of UAW Local 900

I'M AFRAID we're going to have to fall on hard times to get people to start respecting unions again because too many people take unions for granted. A lot of upper-class and middle-class people call us factory rats. But us factory rats make good money and have some of the best benefits. And if it wasn't for us factory rats, this country's standard of living wouldn't be as good as it is.

It bothers me that people tear down the union and have lost all perspective on how we got the standard of living we have. It wasn't because the companies voluntarily gave workers anything or were good to people who were qualified. They don't care whether you're qualified. They care about you producing and for the cheapest rate they can get. They care about profits. We got our standard of living because the UAW fought for and won wage increases. And then even nonunion plants had to pay similar wages to keep their employees.

I remember, when I was in school, my dad worked in the plants, and so did the fathers of a lot of other kids in my class. When they went on strike, my English teacher thought it was a disgrace.

141

Walter "Jeff" Washington

Now teachers are in a union, too, trying to get themselves caught up to our wages and going on strike.

The public envies autoworkers making a good living without college degrees. Professional people hate unions because now you can't distinguish among middle-class people. One guy goes to school and gets a master's degree, and his neighbor, who didn't go to college, works at Wayne Assembly and makes as much money, drives the same type of car, and has the same swimming pool. The difference is his neighbor was willing to go on strike for months to get a new contract.

You go to a schoolteachers' meeting where they are talking about getting a raise, and half of them are driving imported cars. It's my dollar that pays their wages, and they want me to vote for a millage increase, so it angers me. When I ask them why they own a Toyota or a Honda, they say it's a high-quality car from Japan. I think we ought to start importing high-quality people from Japan to teach our kids so they won't be so dumb and high-quality barbers to cut our hair so we don't look so bad.

Sometimes we are our own worst enemies. Our own membership hasn't been educated by this union to know how they got what they got. A lot of our people don't even defend our union when it's attacked. Our neighbor wears a shirt and tie to work and puts down the union, and we agree with him. Instead, we should tell him that if it wasn't for the union, he wouldn't have his good wages or his nice house. It's a trickle-down effect. The barber, the grocery stores, the banks—everybody shares in the wealth of the union.

We're going to start having classes and seminars for our membership to educate them about union history and try to make them aware of how they got where they are. That's long overdue. We'll show them this movie about the days when people were getting hit over the head, having dogs put on them, and getting shot at and killed. When people leave after seeing that movie, they will have a different view of what the union is all about.

Our heroes today are the wrong people. Take Lee Iacocca. He should be called the father of concessions. He didn't save Chrysler. The workers saved Chrysler. He just took a stern position at the right moment. He went to Washington and got a little money with the help of the UAW and everybody else, and he came back and looked like the big folk hero. He doesn't talk about all those autoworkers who gave up their money, too.

I have pictures of Martin Luther King and Walter Reuther in my office because they stood for people and for what was right. I think anybody doing their people any good in this country has died some type of violent death. I love people like that. I cried at the funerals of John F. Kennedy, King and Reuther, and Nelson "Jack" Edwards of the UAW. Maybe it was just the era of the sixties that made me feel like that. There was the feeling then of hope for poor people, for black people, of trying to make some changes in this society. I still say there is hope, and as long as there is hope, there's always a chance for good.

I don't think kids today understand what the kids in my generation had to go through to make changes. I talk to my younger brother and his friends about the civil rights movement, and it's almost a joke to them. It's not anything they can feel. I preach to my son about those days, and it doesn't sink in. That pisses me off. Sometimes I think things have to go back to being real bad for people to understand why they have the things they have. It's a shame that people have to die or lose out or suffer in order for people to be awakened. But that is human nature: If there's no pain, there's no problem.

* * *

As president of Local 900 I represent a thousand workers at the truck plant and three thousand at the Wayne Assembly Plant, plus retirees. I'm also chairman of the Wayne Assembly Plant. I've got too much responsibility, to tell you the truth. The hardest part is trying to juggle all the duties.

I never thought I would be a union leader, even though my dad and grandfather were. My grandfather was financial secretary for the railroad porters. After the family moved to Detroit from Mississippi, my father went into the automobile plants in 1942. After the war, when blacks were just beginning to rise in the union, he ran for district committeeman in Local 900 and won. The local at that time represented the old Lincoln-Mercury Plant on Detroit's west side.

In 1958 my dad was fired because he led a walkout in the Paint Department to get the company to provide clean gloves. Back then they supplied used gloves, and they got so tight from the hardened paint that they cut off circulation in the hands.

My dad was never home when I was young. He came home at 11 at night and got up early and went back out again. He spent a lot of time on the road at conventions or meetings. Twice he was on the negotiating team for national contracts.

I went to all the Labor Day solidarity parades when I was young. I always thought it was exciting. I remember shaking Governor Soapy Williams's hand and riding in a horse-drawn wagon down Woodward. I still love the Labor Day parade. It's a joyful day, and I like to be around people who think like I do.

In 1959, we moved to Milan, fifty miles west of Detroit. My father was raised on a farm, and he had always wanted to go back. There were twelve of us kids, and he figured the only way you could feed them was to have a farm. I liked being raised in the country. My school was about twelve percent black, and the rest were mostly whites and Mexicans. It was a great experience because I got a chance to find out about different cultures and learn not to judge people on the color of their skin or the way they look.

My mother worked for the post office when we were living in Detroit, but in 1970 she went to work for the Ford plastics plant in Saline. All of us are Ford people. Four or five of my brothers and sisters worked for Ford. My wife also works at the Saline Plant.

My dad got me into the truck plant just after it started production in 1964. They were making chassis for buses and light trucks. I was 18 and weighed only 130 pounds, too light for a lot of the production jobs, so they put me on the cleanup crew on the afternoon shift. I had worked summers in a printing place, so I knew what cleanup was, and being a janitor in the plant was no big deal. But it was a big deal to get that check every week.

After a while I wanted to go on days because I had just started dating. So my foreman let me come in on day shift one Saturday to see what it was like. It was a hot day, maybe 98 degrees outside. It had to be 110 in the plant. They put me down there mopping up the sweat from the floors where these guys were wrestling all day with huge bus tires. When I got back that Monday, I told my foreman I didn't want to go on day shift.

Plant conditions were bad in the sixties. The line moved real fast. They had people in line outside; they could run out there and hire anybody they wanted. There was an atmosphere in the plant like a southern family: If you didn't belong to that clique, you would get screwed over. You were always trying to cut the foreman's throat, and he was cutting your throat.

After I was in the plant a year, my father and his political pals coaxed me into running for the union executive board, and I won. Since then I've only lost one election, and that was in 1968 against a guy who had been financial secretary for a long time.

Losing that election made me assess some of the things I had done wrong. I had gotten a big head; I didn't think I could be beaten. After I lost, I didn't run for two years. Being out of it those two years made me realize you can't get too cocky because you can always be voted out of office. That lesson has paid off. Now I always work hard in elections. I figure if I'm going to lose, let me lose working. I'll never lose sleeping.

The seniority system has caused some problems for the union. In the old days Ford, General Motors, and all the auto companies had big profits and didn't care about anybody. We got the seniority system instituted to protect older workers. But those older workers were a better breed of workers. Back then your father got you hired in the plant, and if there was a problem, the company didn't go get the union; they got your father to straighten you out. And he'd say, "Shape up, or I'll recommend they get rid of you because you're not going to ruin my good name."

But the seniority system got to the point where if I had seniority, I didn't have to worry about producing or about being laid off. When people were laid off, the antiunion folks convinced them that the union was at fault because it didn't believe in the merit system but only in seniority. Being qualified doesn't matter under the seniority system. I've seen people laid off who were model employees who came to work every day and produced.

The union has become overprotective of the wrong people, the habitual offenders. Instead of looking at the moral nature of the problem, we just enforce the contract because that's what people voted for. But I think we have to start looking more at the overall problem. In my opinion, if you come to work every day, you're entitled to a regular job. You shouldn't be displaced by some high-absentee worker with more seniority who doesn't give a damn. You can't disregard seniority, but find the high-absentee person some other job. Don't mess with the employee who's coming to work every day because when you do that, you're destroying the union. If you mess over the 95 percent of the people who come to work and do their job to enforce the rights of the other 5 percent, you don't have much left because that 5 percent doesn't support the union in the first place. Some of them beat your brains out every time they have a problem, but you can't even get them to vote for you.

Somewhere we have to draw a line, so that after the third or fourth time that somebody messes up the same way, we stop representing him. My system now is a one-shot deal. If you're a three- or four-time loser and you come to me and ask me to get you your job back, I'll get you one more chance, but that's it. After that I'm not going to fight anymore for you.

We have to start looking at the people who care about their job and start protecting those people.

If a guy can make a decent living and then get his retirement, that's all he wants. Somebody has to secure that for him. Without that guarantee, one day they could say, "We're shutting down your plant." Then a guy who's 50 or so and has twenty years in would be out of luck. Where the hell is he going to get a job making that kind of money and maintain the house he has?

The companies have got to start looking at taking care of the workers when they shut those plants down. They have to give workers a guaranteed retirement so they can live with dignity.

It would scare the shit out of me if somebody told me, "We're shutting down the truck plant, and I'm sorry, but you're gone." I have my home paid for, but my standard of living would change. I might not be able to do things I like to do. I'd have to get a job in a car wash or something. I'd survive, and others would, too, but these companies owe people more than to rob their youth from them and work them five and six days a week ten hours a day and then all of a sudden throw them out in the streets.

One of the biggest reasons we have so many people participating in the computer classes is the fear that their job might be cut. They want to be ready to go into the outside world. We had three hundred and twenty-seven people go through the preapprenticeship classes for skilled trades last year, so that they can compete for jobs. Ten years ago we might have gotten thirty or forty. People are interested in job security, and education in the trades and in technology is part of that. People appreciate those programs because they think the union is looking out for their future.

Technology is coming to the plant, and our people have to be ready for it. The more our people are educated and the more they can understand automation, the more they can understand why some things happen. We've put close to eleven hundred people through the computer classes. We have on-site college classes and are looking at offering an associate's degree.

The UAW-Ford training center helped a lot of people when they had the layoffs in 1980. They put a lot of people through the retraining program, taught people how to drive trucks, how to operate computers. I think that's the union's responsibility, to be able to take care of their own people. We're taking care of the ones we have left.

In the 1982 contract we got the GIS [Guaranteed Income Stream benefits program]. If you have fifteen years in and you get laid off, you get paid 50 percent of your salary until age 62. Of course, the company also has the right to put you to work somewhere else and pay you the difference.

We also look after people's health. We have a physical fitness center. We have the Employee Assistance Program to help people who have alcohol or drug or emotional or marriage problems. Some of these people with drug addiction are on their last legs, and we read the riot act to them and say, "Hey, clean up your act, or you won't have a job." We've saved a lot of jobs.

Plant environment has become a big issue: the cleanliness of the plant; the food in the cafeteria; oil on the floor; the dirt. Through the Employee Involvement program, we've gotten Astroturf on the floor, new paint on the walls, and other things to spruce up the plant. They said you couldn't talk about contractual things in EI, but when you got in there, you talked about everything you thought you could get. And you came out with something good for your people.

There's a different approach now in negotiations. You don't go in there and stand on top of the table and cuss. I don't want anyone to think I'm a company man because I'm far from that, but you have to be diplomatic. There's a new way of doing business, a change in attitudes. You sit down and negotiate. It's almost like ambassadors to other countries. You don't go in there and threaten to drop a bomb on them.

The main thing is learning about the people you negotiate with. Just a few kind words or a few thoughts about something personal means a lot to them. You break down those barriers of trying to screw them and them screwing you. That doesn't fly anymore. If a union rep takes that approach, all he can do is hurt the people he represents. The thing that's most important to me in negotiations is getting all I can get, however I can. If I get it, then I feel good.

There's got to be changes. Either you work with what you have to work with, or you won't get to work with it at all. If we struck the plant every time someone got fired, I don't think we'd be doing our people justice. You can get it done without so much fighting, without running your blood pressure up every time you have a problem. That's not doing yourself any good.

People said the poor quality of American cars was the reason Japanese cars started selling. I think it was the gas crunch. People said they were buying Japanese cars because of quality. Really they were buying them because they were cheap on gas.

I think it was a conspiracy that caused the oil crisis. The country had a lot to gain by the oil crisis. It was the start of big business putting unions in their place, breaking down the morale of people who believe in unions.

Walter Reuther told the auto companies in the fifties that they were going to have to come out with small cars. Ford did come out with those little Falcons and Comets, but they didn't really go all out promoting them because the big cars were selling.

Now the Japanese have invaded and are building plants. In order to compete, we have to cut the cost of making cars, too. So Japanese methods are being imitated. One thing the companies are pushing is mass relief. Instead of people taking breaks a few at a time, the whole line would shut down for breaks. That way they can eliminate all the relief people. At the Edison Plant in New Jersey, the other plant that makes Escorts, the union gave the company mass relief. I was told they saved $62 a car with that system, and they used that figure to try to get me to give in on that issue here. Whipsawing one local against another has become a popular tactic.

In 1983 I went to Japan on a fact-finding tour with our plant manager and some other officials. I learned a lot. In Japan they take the cream of the crop from the high schools and give them jobs in the auto plants or send them to college to learn management. You work your way up the system, and whoever produces the most gets promoted. The autoworkers work from 9 until 5:30 or 6 at night because it's prestigious to be coming home late from work. They carry briefcases, too; they might have their lunch in them, or welding tips.

It's not any big happy family affair over there like they project, with the workers loving the company and everybody pulling together. It's more of a peer-pressure system. People make sure you do your part because if you don't, they suffer.

When we were touring the Mazda Plant in Hiroshima, I saw this guy who was getting way behind on his job. He was running like hell trying to keep up, waving his tools. When break came, the other three lines took off, but everybody on his line had to work through the break to catch up. And they only get ten minutes of break twice a day anyway, compared with our six minutes every hour. That's peer pressure. The whole line lost break time because this guy couldn't keep up. How do you think they feel about that guy? Sure, the Japanese autoworkers have a job for life, but when they get through peer-pressuring your ass, you're going to quit.

They're going to import their concepts of teamwork and peer pressure here. Members of a team will control whoever isn't doing his job. The Japanese system is coming, and the UAW sees that; but we are trying to break into that system as gently as possible without hurting a lot of people. We don't want to do it overnight. That's why education is needed, so that people can understand why changes are being made.

Another place the companies are economizing is in the manufacturing of parts. Ford had a problem with engines recently that cost a lot of money. The problem was with tappets that Ford had installed by some little sweatshop down South. When the car gets out on the road and breaks down, people don't blame the little sweatshop—it's those no-good factory workers out there in Wayne, where they assemble the cars.

These parts vendors send this cheap stuff up here, and then they hire some temporaries or some mom-and-pop team for minimum wage to come in the plant and work on the line alongside people who are making union wages. We've been successful in chasing them out or at least making them go over to the salvage crib or somewhere else to do their work.

If the time's right, someday I would like to be vice-president of the UAW. But if they're crying for me to get out of here and retire, I'll get out. It isn't worth all the aggravation trying to do all those things and then retire and live only another year.

Despite all my responsibilities, I like taking time for my house and my hobbies. I built our house on land my father gave me in Milan. I went on midnight shift just to build it. I did it so I wouldn't have a house payment. There's so many more things you can do if you don't have a house payment tying you down, like hobbies. My hobby is building cars. I buy the parts from catalogs. I built a 1926 Ford, and my project now is building a 1932 Ford from the bottom up. It's going to be like an old Al Capone car.

I have two sons, and I would like to see them better off than me financially. My oldest son was talking about being an orthodontist, but now he's looking at the new Mazda plant in Flat Rock, looking at that money. But I think that would only be a short, temporary future for him.

Local 900's going to be around awhile. We just built a new union hall. When people see you're putting up a new local, it makes them feel there's a future. I named it after Nelson "Jack" Edwards because he was a man who rose from the bottom to be the first black vice-president of the UAW, and nobody has ever given him any recognition. He was a pioneer. He was a militant leader. He didn't bite his tongue.

"John Doe"

The name of the interviewee has been withheld at that individual's request.

I AGREED to do this interview because I once was an employee of the Michigan Truck Plant. The views expressed here are my own and not the views of the UAW.

If you have worked in an assembly plant, there is no union job you can't do. My job as an international rep is relaxing compared with the years I spent in the Michigan Truck Plant. I wouldn't take a million dollars to see those years again.

I call that plant the pressure cooker. You could feel yourself tightening up when you walked in the door. I used to get headaches working there. Eventually I was hospitalized with high blood pressure. When I moved from the plant in 1985 to the international union, my blood pressure went down so much my doctor took me off some medication to try to get it back up.

But being in the truck plant was a good learning experience, and I think I helped some people there. Some people thought that all union representatives would do was take a swipe at the problems. But I really care about their problems, to the point where I

151

take them home and try to figure out overnight how to solve them. I can't help it; that's just the way I operate.

Maybe I'm like my mother. She taught me that when you help people, even if they aren't appreciative, it makes you feel good that you did something for them. The most gratifying thing about my work, believe it or not, is just to have somebody say, "Thank you," because so few people do that for a plant union man.

My mother associates me with Walter Reuther because back in the old days, whenever you saw Martin Luther King, you usually saw Reuther with him. They weren't too sure about what he had done, but they knew that he was connected with the civil rights movement. They held the UAW in high esteem. Now here I am flying around the country representing the UAW. They don't know what I do, but they figure it has to be something important.

When you take a guy like me with a high school education, there is no other organization I could have improved in the way I did in the union. So I owe the union a lot.

The union is the only thing that gives working people like me the standard of living we have. If there hadn't been a UAW, there would be no need for the corporations to run to Taiwan because we would be making the same wage now as workers do there.

When I was growing up in Clarksdale, Mississippi, we were the first family to have a refrigerator out where we lived, and people came from all over the farms to see it. We were poor, but not as poor as some of our neighbors. My dad left my mother when I was 4, and my mom remarried. My stepfather was a tractor driver, and he was making $20 a week. That was good money in the late forties, compared with the sharecroppers we knew, who were picking cotton for $2 a day.

I remember one Saturday we were getting ready to go into town. That was a ritual in itself. We would put on our best clothes and get on the bus and go to an ice-cream parlor; it was great. I remember the people piling into our house and my mother showing off the refrigerator. When we saw the bus coming, my mother told everyone to leave. As we were going out the door, this woman ran up to her and said, "You can't leave yet. You've got to disconnect that thing. You can't leave that running."

My dad was a carpenter by trade and worked in the steel mills in Gary, Indiana, but he got arthritis and had to quit doing carpentry. He tells stories about his grandfather, who was an ex-slave.

His grandfather's feet used to swell and he would go to the place in the river where the water was moving the fastest and put his feet in and the swelling would go down. That was a long time before whirlpool baths.

My stepfather was reluctant to leave the South, but my mother insisted we come North. At the time a lot of people were coming to Detroit to work in the factories.

When we got here in 1949, we almost starved to death. My stepfather had relatives here, but they would have nothing to do with us. We were the country bumpkins, and they were on welfare. My stepfather went out every day to find jobs cutting grass or hauling trash for somebody. When he found work, he would bring home $2 or $3.

We were living in a two-room storefront on the east side. The store had moved out, and we didn't know who owned the building, so we just moved in. It was winter, and we had an oil stove that we had scrounged, and me, my mother, my aunt, and my stepfather slept huddled around it.

In later years I asked my mother why we never went on welfare. Did we have that much pride? My mother said it had nothing to do with pride; she just didn't know where to go and didn't want to ask anybody.

One day, after months of seeing my stepfather go out looking for work every day, he just walked in and mumbled, "I got a job." Now, my stepfather treats words as if they cost $10,000 apiece. We thought he meant that he had a job to do the next day cutting grass or something.

So the next morning my mother fixed him his lunch and asked him what he was going to do that day.

He said, "I don't know."

She said, "But you said you got a job."

He said, "I do, but I don't know what I'm going to do."

She said, "Are you going to cut grass or what?"

He said, "No, I work at Chevrolet."

Her face lit up. She said, "Why didn't you tell me?"

He said, "Well, I told you I had a job."

It was the greatest day I can remember. We got up and danced and tried to decide what we were going to buy first. Then we sat him down and made him tell us how he got the job.

He told us that he'd been showing up every morning at 5:30 at Chevrolet Gear and Axle and standing in line in hopes they were hiring. Every day the security guard would come and turn them away, and my stepfather would set off walking in search of a chore. So the day before, the guard yelled, "No jobs today," and waved the people away, but my stepfather didn't hear him.

Now, the security guard had seen him standing there day after day. He walked over to my stepfather and said, "Didn't you hear me say there were no jobs today?"

My stepfather replied, "I was just standing here, wondering which direction to take off in today to find work."

The guard said, "Do you have a car?"

My stepfather said no.

The guard said, "If you had a job, would you buy a Chevrolet?"

My stepfather said yes, and so the guard, who must have felt sorry for him, took him into the plant, and they hired him.

My stepfather's first paycheck was something like $75, and he had worked overtime. He had never seen a check before, and back then the General Motors paychecks and check stubs looked similar. He went to a check-cashing place and cashed the stub and kept the check. He brought all the cash home, and it was the most money we had ever seen. He said, "Doggone, that is too much money." He thought they had overpaid him by mistake.

About six weeks later they called him in at the plant and asked him if he had his first pay stub. He said yes and showed it to them. They laughed and said, "Not only are you an idiot, but the guy who cashed it is, too."

Well, my stepfather panicked. He thought he was going to lose his job. They didn't tell him anything more that day, so he worried all night. He was sweating. But it was just a joke to them.

He ended up working thirty years for GM. He never missed a day, even for a funeral. He hated to take off work on holidays; he said he'd rather be working than sitting around in the backyard complaining.

My dad considered himself active in the union because he had a friend who was a committeeman. He believed in the union. He never complained about paying his dues. I don't think he ever went to a union meeting, but if the union said to do something, he did it without question.

My mom was a hotel clerk for about twenty years, but after the hotel closed, she never worked again.

*   *   *

I went to elementary school and part of junior high in Hamtramck, in a mixed neighborhood. Then we moved to the west side, and it was all black.

When I got out of high school in 1959, it was in the middle of a recession, and there were no jobs. The only job I could find in the paper to apply for was in Dearborn. Back then blacks didn't work in Dearborn, but I didn't know that. The ad was for a delivery boy at a flower shop. I rode a bike over there and applied. They were so congenial and nice. They said, "No, son, we're not hiring, but give us your phone number, and the minute we are hiring we'll call you." I didn't get the message right away. I wasn't that swift.

I couldn't find work, so I joined the army. I got out of the service in April 1962. In September that year I got a job at the General Motors spring and bumper plant in Livonia. My stepfather's perfect work record smoothed the way.

I worked there three or four years and worked another year or so at Chrysler. My next job was with the gas company. I worked outside and didn't like that, especially in the cold weather. I remember in July 1969 I was breaking out an underground gas main and already dreading the next winter. I saw a group of people lined up, going into an abandoned bank building. I was curious, so I put down my tools and walked over. Back then you could walk right out of one factory and go to another and get a job, so I wasn't that concerned about walking away.

I asked somebody in line what they were doing, and he said the factories were hiring the hard-core unemployed. I said, "Well, that's me." So I went directly to the front of the line because I couldn't take much time off the job. I had a gas company uniform on, and I just cut right in, and nobody said a word to me.

So I told them, "Look, I need a job."

The guy said, "OK, where do you want to work? For Chrysler?"

I said, "No, I can't work for Chrysler, I got fired there not too long ago." My records were still fresh.

"GM?"

"No, I don't want to try that again."

"How about Ford?"

"I'll take it."

He said, "Did you ever hear of the Michigan Truck Plant?"

I said, "No."

"Do you know where Wayne, Michigan, is?"

"No."

So the guy gave me directions on a yellow slip and told me who to give the slip to, and away I went. I left my tools right there.

When I got to the truck plant, there was a trailer in the parking lot where they were hiring people. There was also a prison bus there, and I later found out that people in prison would come to work in the truck plant during the day and go back to the prison at night on the bus.

They took a group of us to the small-parts area in the back of the plant. A production manager rode in on a little electric cart, and he said, "The tall guy, can he paint?"

I was the tallest, 6-foot-2, and I said, "Yeah, I can paint," even though I couldn't.

He said, "Well, I want you in the Paint Shop, fall out of here." It was like the army.

It was total chaos in the plant in those days. You saw groups of people moving from the Labor Relations office into the plant. You saw groups of people coming back the other way. They would hire five people and ten would quit or get fired. I've often thought about that since: How could they keep track of what they were doing? I don't think they could. But they didn't need to then. The main thing was to keep the trucks rolling off the end of the line.

In those days the Big Three just jockeyed back and forth. There was nobody else to buy from. America was making money. Everybody was buying cars. You didn't have an import problem. No matter what the American companies built, people would buy it.

The way it worked in the Paint Shop then was that most whites started out in Prime and most blacks started out in Underbody. The whites got a head start. The order of progression was Underbody Booth, then the Prime Booth, which was a little cleaner, and finally Main Enamel.

In Underbody, instead of using regular paint, they would take all the scrap they could find and mix it up in one container and use the strongest thinner and the strongest chemicals they could find. I don't know the names of all those chemicals, but I know they made a lot of people sick. As the unit passed overhead, you would spray the underbody. The solution you were spraying was on hot trucks, and it would bubble up and drip down on your face. No matter how you covered yourself, it would get on your body, and the smell was almost unbearable. It went right through the overalls.

They put grease on the floors every night so the paint wouldn't stick. So you're slipping and sliding all day and spraying some paint chemical that's dripping down on you and you're sticky and hot. And a foreman is leaning into the booth, yelling at you that there were two units where you missed some spots. It's no wonder. Your eyes are burning, and you can't see anyway.

I didn't wear any protective "spacesuit" or headgear. I tried it one day, and it was too heavy, especially the helmet. I didn't want to be that hot for ten or twelve hours.

I went into the Underbody Booth with the understanding that I would stay there until they hired a new person and then go to the Prime Booth. That was the tradition. But in the first week I worked there I trained three people who all worked one day and quit. One guy was a cabdriver, and he said, "Hey, I can't do this. I'm going back outside to my cab."

Then they hired this guy from Texas who wore cowboy boots and western clothes. When I found out he was coming to paint, I was happy as hell. But sure enough, he went straight to the Prime Booth, and I was still in Underbody. I told the foreman, "You got a new hire, and they put him in the Prime Booth, and that's not the understanding."

He said, "We're just going to try him out in there a few days."

So I stayed there another week, and they hired in two more people and sent them to the Prime Booth. Finally I got the message. I decided to quit. But I wanted to quit at a time when I would hurt them. I wanted to get even. So I waited until a Friday, the highest absenteeism day. I was working day shift. This Friday two people quit. Quite a few others were absent. They did not have an extra person in the Paint Department. So I told the foreman, "I quit."

He said, "You can't quit."

I said, "Oh, yeah? I quit. I might not be able to do a lot of things, but I know I can quit." And I told them why.

They got the general foreman over. He told me he didn't want me to quit. I told him, "You said I would move out of here; but you hired four people, and I'm still in here. I'm not going to work in Underbody anymore." I started toward the front door, and I could hear the general foreman following me and chewing out the foreman for not keeping his word. Of course, the foreman was just following orders.

So the general foreman talked me into going back. He made all these promises. I would start at the Prime Booth and work there no more than two weeks and I'd be in Main Enamel. It was almost like I had a contract. And this time he kept his promises.

In Main Enamel there were twelve spray painters, six on each side of the booth. They would spray the colors. If someone was two work stations away from you, there were days when you could not see him. That's how thick the overspray was. That's why when a new painter complains today about overspray, the older guys don't give him much sympathy.

We also had heat problems. In July and August sometimes the heat would come on in the booth. And sometimes in the winter it would get extremely cold. The ovens that dry the paint on the trucks were on both sides of the paint booth. Sometimes the blowers would take the gas fumes from the ovens and pull them into the booth.

The Paint Department used to practically control the plant. When something went wrong, we were the only group of people who would insist that it be corrected right away. If the overspray got too bad, we would call the committeeman down and give him an ultimatum. We would give them thirteen minutes to correct the problem. So the committeeman would scurry along and get a foreman to call Maintenance. Maintenance would come down, and chances are they couldn't correct the problem. A lot of times we would have to show Maintenance what the problem was. We knew that when the overspray got real bad, it was because one of the overhead blowers had gotten plugged up and that had stopped the airflow.

If the problem wasn't fixed within our time limit, we would walk out of the booth and go home. That's unheard of now. Today, if anyone ever stops, they stand by the job until the problem is corrected. Back then management really hustled to meet our demands and keep us on the job because they couldn't replace us. Once we walked out, the whole plant would go down.

We stuck together in the Paint Shop back then. The relationship between whites and blacks was absolutely great. It was amazing. Ninety percent of the whites there were from Kentucky. The blacks were mostly from Alabama. It was a melting pot, but we got along very well. You see, when you have to work with people all day inside a confined area, you really learn about them, and you find out they're not so bad. There were blacks and whites who were absolutely inseparable. There were guys who wouldn't take a break unless they checked with their buddy's relief man to make sure he could go at the same time.

The relationship between management and some blacks was not as good. It seemed like when a guy put a tie on, all the things he used to think came back again.

Black and white workers don't get along as well now as they did then. I think things changed because some union politicians, to gain what they wanted, would constantly remind people of race. If two people were running for office and one happened to be black and one white, one would go down to the job and say to the people, "We have more whites here than blacks, so you should elect a white person." I have seen blacks do the same thing. It's got to have an effect when you pound into a guy's head that the blacks are taking over or the whites are taking over, when you go into a place where people are getting along and drive a wedge between them. I think that wedge is being driven by politicians and by the company a lot.

In the Paint Shop most people worked toward becoming utility people because a utility person has some free time and he can get out of the booth. We had a black guy in the Paint Shop who had painted twelve years and could not get a utility job. The company blamed it on poor attendance. Well, given conditions in the booth, you had to take a day off now and then. But in 1971 or 1972 we had a white employee with less than ninety days in the plant who became a utility man.

When that happened, we went as a group to the union and talked to them. They said they would do something about it. But after a couple of weeks we hadn't heard anything, so after work the spray painters went to the superintendent and told him we wanted that utility job. We didn't demand they take the job away from the other guy. We just said to make another position, which is something they did all the time.

They really fought that at first. Then they got scared because we told them we weren't going to work until this guy got a utility job. So they caved in, and the guy finally got out of the paint booth.

Being vocal at that meeting got me involved in union activity. After the meeting I was approached by my committeeman. I told him I didn't know anything about the union. He said, "Well, I see you have some influence in the spray booth. When I take days off, I'd like you to take my place."

So I got on the committee. He represented part of the Chassis Line, so I got to know a lot of people there. I wasn't thinking about running for a regular committee job; but I liked getting a day off from painting, and I figured I would work hard on those days because I didn't want the regular man coming back and people asking him who was the bum who took his place. I didn't know anything about the job, but I tried my best and tried to listen to people.

One of the main things I learned was how to write up grievances stemming from hearings. A hearing occurs when the company feels an hourly employee has committed some infraction. They take him into the Labor Relations office and the company's Labor Relations representative is like the judge and the committeeman is like his defense lawyer and the Labor Relations rep decides on punishment. Back then we were holding fourteen to fifteen attendance hearings a day as well as other hearings for work-related things like poor and careless workmanship. There were days when twenty hearings were held. These days if a committeeman holds two hearings a week, it is a lot.

When the regular committeeman had an especially rough day with hearings and there were a lot of grievances to write, he would take a day off. I would come in and get stuck writing a lot of grievances because they had to be filed within a few days. A lot of the old-timers in the plant, who hadn't had much schooling, were very impressed when they'd see me write fourteen grievances in a day. So that gave me a little bit of popularity outside the Spray Booth.

I still had no intention of running, but about that time, in 1973, we had a bad incident in the Paint Department—overspray and gas fumes to the point that several painters became ill and we had what they called the Big Walkout. Some of them are still talking about that. People got fired over it. Just about everybody got penalized in some way. People were not at all satisfied with the way they thought the regular committeeman handled it. So I was asked to run for committeeman. I won my election and served on the committee from 1973 until 1985.

It was a surprise to me when I got the position because I had only a high school education. I've taken some college courses as an adult, but I had never been in a position to know how I would act in a leadership role.

★   ★   ★

One of the hardest things about my job was to walk up to a person and see a real problem with work conditions that were absolutely terrible. For example, you see a guy trying to do the best job he can, jumping around like a Keystone Kop, trying to get that job done, and the company is saying there are no problems with the job as designed. And in fact, according to contractual language, the job is within a range where the employee can do it. We have lazy workers, but this guy is not one of them. So as a union representative I want to take action, but I know that if I do something like shutting the job down, I am going to get the employee fired because under the contract he is supposed to be able to do the job he has. So I have to stand there and tell him, "I sure would like to help you, but according to the book, this job can be done." What do you think that guy thinks about the union?

The contract language we use today for defining work standards was negotiated in 1949. When you think of the changes in production standards since 1949, I don't know why we are still living with inadequate language. It's because management keeps saying we have to have more production. And though the union has made other gains, we haven't won many victories in this area.

Work standards is a hot issue, especially in assembly plants. We're trying to come up with ways to deal with those problems at the bargaining table. The union is not just lying down and playing dead. In the face of everything that is happening, we're still taking the company on over work standards and using what tools we have. There are several plants where strikes have been authorized and several others that are close to striking. I was involved in a dispute at the Twin Cities plant in Minnesota with sixty-eight work standards grievances.

The company makes a big issue now of quality, and that's because the American consumer wants it. But I don't know how you get quality without slowing the work pace. I don't care how much you put quality in a person's mind, if you give them a job where they have to constantly run, then you're not going to get it. You have to slow the pace down some, which means less production and a little less profit.

Some of the things the company is doing now to improve quality are good, such as making people double-check themselves. If you put in a screw and you have the time, you check to make sure it's in right. But if you don't have the time, you can't even do that.

There are jobs at Ford assembly plants where the work pace and work load are so fast and so heavy that maybe when you start out in the morning, you think about doing the job right, but after you work four hours of a ten-hour day, the fatigue factor comes in, and you don't care how it goes in; you just want to get rid of the truck. So we have to look at that and do something about it at the bargaining table.

Another very difficult situation is when you have two hourly employees, one black and one white, and they call you to settle a strong difference of opinion. Once you hear what the problem is, you know right away who is right and who is wrong, but you really have to do a dance. I always tried to find some way to correct the problem or divert their minds from the question of who was right and who was wrong. Sometimes you might jump on the foreman and try to divert their attention to him because I'd rather them be angry at him than at me. If, despite your efforts, you are cornered, you have to tell the truth and walk away. Then the white guy calls you a rotten SOB, or the black guy calls you an Uncle Tom.

I always tried to smooth out any racial rough spots. When I got to be plant chairman, some people distrusted me because of my race. I had to win people over, let them know that their race was not important. The important thing was solving their problem. Once I'd done that, then that guy would relax. I might not be his favorite person, but he wouldn't mind me representing him.

The first thing that struck me when I got hired at the truck plant was that there were no women. It seems that Ford had decided that women would be detrimental to them in some way. They really had a fight to keep women out. The federal government had to pressure them to hire women.

In 1969 they had a camouflage attempt to show they were prepared to hire women. They took applications in the parking lot from about fifty women, including my wife. But those applications were never heard of again. They weren't even on file. When I became chairman, I tried to find them, and they weren't there anymore.

The first women came into the plant in 1972, and they had real problems. The company went out of its way to show women they were not welcome.

For instance, take a tire-hanging job, where you have to pick up the wheel of a truck, lift it up, and hang it on a hook, one right after another, ten to twelve hours a day. A lot of men can't do that job. So out of a group of five women ranging in size from fairly large down to petite, they would take the petite one and give her that job. There was no attempt to match the person with the job; in fact, there was a deliberate attempt not to, to provoke fights. Then, when you argued about it, the company would say, "Look, she gets the same paycheck as the guy that was on that job; she's got to be able to do any job."

One time I saw them fire fifteen women in an hour. We called the UAW civil rights department, and they sent two representatives to the plant. We did our homework, and we got them all back.

It was rough for women. They were the last hired, so they were the first to go when the layoffs started.

They also brought with them some unique problems, things that were new to us as union officials. For instance, I had never dealt with anybody who was pregnant and what that would mean for being able to perform a job. We had to educate ourselves. There was resistance within the union and with some of the workers. There are some people who really think that women belong at home.

The women didn't get much orientation, and that would cause problems sometimes. One time a woman on her first day in the plant was working on the merry-go-round, where they put lights and grilles and other parts on front ends, and a fellow came out of the garage area and told her, "You don't have to do that. That's not a part of the job."

She said, "That is what they told me to do."

He said, "Look, you sit down right here, and I'm going to go get somebody."

The line was running, and she sat down. He went back to his repair job. So she got fired. We got her back. The guy who told her to sit down is still at the plant today. I asked him why he did it, and I never did get a straight answer.

Things really changed at the plant in 1979. One entire shift of fifteen hundred people was laid off. After about a year sales bounced back a little, so we started back on a mandatory ten hours with voluntary additional overtime, but we never got back that other shift.

At first it was difficult to get people to work beyond ten hours because they had just seen fifteen hundred people hit the street, and they knew their extra hours were replacing other people's jobs. But as time went on, more and more volunteered to go twelve hours or longer. I think that's because we didn't educate people properly.

I wanted to know if people really gave a shit about the shift being gone, if they realized that accepting overtime would probably keep them from ever putting on another shift, because the company could see that they could get the same amount of production with a couple hours of overtime as they could with another shift. So I did a little personal survey. I talked to people who worked that extra overtime, and some of them were belligerent. Most people felt that refusing to work the voluntary overtime wouldn't help somebody get a job. The overall feeling was: We're not going to have a job very long, so whatever I can work I am going to do it.

We need to educate people about the union the way we used to. When I got hired into the plant, we had an orientation that I'll never forget. The union president rented a room at the Howard Johnson's and took fifty new hires and our wives to dinner. He had a speaker from the international who used to be a plant-level representative, someone in city government, a guy from the state legislature. They were all UAW people or their dads had been. They talked to us about their memories of when their fathers were on strike for months and their mothers went down and worked in the soup line and made soup for the strikers. And what the pay rate was back then, and how there was no break time. And what they went on strike for that's now in the contract, and how all these people suffered so our pay would be what it is today. They told us: "If the time comes for you to strike, remember we are counting on you to pave the way for the younger people coming to the plant so they can make some gains." They told us: "When the company says, 'Look what we are giving you,' remember that the company fought like hell and kept us out for months before they gave that up." I think 1969 was the last time we had orientations like that, and that's a shame. That's a necessary part of education.

The autoworker is a middle-class person now. Many are Republicans; they consider themselves men and women of means. We negotiated people right out of our own area of influence. They no longer feel they need us. Most people do not stop to think that the union is responsible for their standard of living. They think Henry Ford is.

Money is the reason some working people are setting themselves apart from other working people. You have a toolmaker in the plant making $70,000 a year, and he doesn't feel like he is a working person. He sits there and plays the stock market. He picks up the phone and calls his stockbroker or his financial planner from the plant.

I worked with these people every day, but I couldn't see the change coming until the 1980 election. I just took it for granted that working people were not going to vote for Reagan. I found out that I was one of the few people who were arguing against voting for him. I could not believe it.

One of the things that helped change people's attitudes in the plant was the Employee Involvement program. In 1980, when the company lost money, they were smart enough to admit they couldn't keep operating the same way. So they decided to cut costs, and they realized it was easier to join with the membership to cut costs than to hit them over the head. "We don't know where to cut," they said, "so tell us how to save money."

The company saw it would take a long time to get the union to abandon its adversary role and join in the new cooperative spirit. A lot of union representatives survived on confrontation because they thought that was what the membership wanted to see. So the company bypassed the union officials and went straight to the membership. They played on each individual's desire to be important. For so many years the company had treated each worker in the plant as just a number. Now they take a guy and ask him how things can improve. They tell him, "You are a part of this now. We are all in it together."

One group of workers at the truck plant told the company about a new glove on the market that costs less and fits better. You can grab small parts with it and still protect the hand. So the company made this whole group special in the plant. They took them down to headquarters, and a vice-president talked to them, and when they came back to the plant, their chests were out. The company figured: This is just great. We are saving money, and it didn't cost us anything; all we have to do is make these people feel good.

So people are going in and making suggestions. I saw a guy make a suggestion that cut his own job. He took himself right out of the picture.

And it is going further. The company cut out all the inspectors and found out it was a mistake. They were in trouble. They couldn't put the inspectors back on because the cost would go up, and it would be admitting they made a mistake. So they are using union employees to police other union employees. They have trained people through the EI program to make random quality checks in the plant and keep charts and graphs that are turned in to the company. Now they're just making quality checks, but tomorrow the company might be using the charts as evidence to discipline fellow workers.

Union representatives legitimately fear that the EI program is going to replace them. I have seen committeemen in the truck plant who took two weeks to argue with the company before they would agree to get a fan put up, and the EI leader is going down there with a clipboard saying, "Oh, you need a fan here," and getting it put in the next day. The union representative pulls his hair out because EI is taking his power away.

Automation has become a real threat to jobs. The truck plant is one of the few plants left that still has people painting. In the St. Louis Assembly Plant they already have a completely automated paint system. The only place you see a warm body is in the repair area. The unit comes down the line, and the colors are programmed into the robot. The arms are like a person's arms, but they can do more things. They can make a complete circle at the waist. It is amazing. It replaced dozens of people.

You are seeing automation now in every department. At Ford 70 percent of the welding is now done by automatic welders, and at Chrysler something like 90 percent.

Why do you think the company agreed to setting up a retraining program with the union? It's because they don't want sixty thousand Ford workers stumbling along the streets. Somebody looked down the road and said, "These people aren't going to be working in the plants, so we have to train them to do something else." The company has millions and millions of dollars in education and retraining.

Automation can't be stopped, but we could damn sure slow it down. What we are saying is if you want to automate your plants, then you have to do something to retrain people. So the company says, "Fine, we'll take that, it may cost us $10 million, but if you challenge us on automation and take us off our timetable, it'll cost $50 million."

*   *   *

The company is going to operate with fewer and fewer plants. They are closing down and consolidating parts depots, too. And even in plants that survive, they are finding ways to get more production out of fewer employees. You are going to see more of the kind of contract they recently negotiated at Chrysler's Jefferson Avenue Assembly Plant that forces the worker to vote yes on ratification. The other choice is to close the plant. The common-sense thing to do is vote to save your job. The only power the union has in that situation is to learn what the company wants. In the case of Jefferson Avenue Assembly, they wanted to combine job classifications, and that eliminates people.

Combining classifications is important to them because of efficiency. For example, the contract says you can only use the lowest-seniority spray painter if you want to loan him to another job. But the lowest guy really can't do the other job, so the company loses efficiency there. But if everybody is the same classification, you can always go to the top guy, the guy you really want. He is interchangeable.

In the new contracts the company wants to get what they call pay-for-knowledge. Pay-for-knowledge makes everybody interchangeable. It means that if you are willing to learn ten other jobs, you'll make a little more money than the guy who is unwilling to. So absenteeism won't affect any area so much because they have this interchangeable superhuman over there who they pay a few cents more. He is essentially a plant-wide utility man. If you learn how to drive a tug, put on bumpers, spray paint, work in the Body Shop, you become a valuable person.

If everybody is interchangeable, you need fewer people. If I'm working in this house and I have three other people with me and I can only vacuum and she can only wash dishes and he can only make beds, I need three people, but if I had one person that could do all of that, I would only need the one.

Twenty years from now you'll see about four hundred people in the Michigan Truck Plant working one shift, compared with fifteen hundred before 1979. In a two-shift plant you will see around eight hundred. Most of them will be skilled people, electricians, or whatever skills are necessary to keep the automation going. You will see a few backup people, and that is it.

I think the UAW will survive, but the only way it is going to survive is to do two things. First, we have to organize outside the auto industry. We are already headed in that direction. Second, the barriers to merging with unions outside the country are going to have to come down. I think you are going to see unions merging and becoming truly international unions. That will have to happen to deal with the company's master plan, which is to build everything in low-income countries and ship it back here and sell it.

The changes that are coming won't affect me because I got twenty years in. I'll be OK; the guys coming along after me won't.

The kids face a bleak future. You are going to see a lot of people walking the street. You are going to see a lot of work for $2 an hour, if there is anything for them to do. I don't see the crime rate going down; I see it going up. Something has to be done to develop new industries and to train people for new industries. The company's not going to do that, so we have to do that. If we don't, you won't be able to go to the store because somebody is going to take your money. People in this country are not going to stand idly by and starve to death. They are going to feed upon one another. It is happening already.

A kid is going to have to be a professional to make the kind of living that you make today in a factory. I look around at these young people, and they are not headed in that direction.

I think people at the turn of the century had the same fears because they figured the buggy shops were going to be gone and there would be no work for their sons. I think other industries will take the place of the auto industry if we work toward it and train people toward it. If things stay as they are now, I see chaos in twenty years, but somehow I think something might take the place of the auto industry. Computers are not the answer. What the answer is I don't know.

Jim Vernatter

Born September 1, 1941, in Pike County, Kentucky
Hired February 27, 1964
Health and Safety representative for UAW Local 900

MY JOB IS TO POLICE the plant and enforce OSHA [Occupational Safety and Health Administration] regulations. My goal is to serve the workers and do the best I can for them. I want people to leave there and be able to enjoy retirement. If you're dead from cancer or crippled from being injured, you can't very well enjoy it. And no matter how much money you make, if you leave there in bad health, it's useless.

I feel like I'm carrying on my father's fight. I grew up in the coalfields of Kentucky, and my dad was active in the United Mine Workers. I saw the struggles they went through, and I am trying to fight for the workers like he did. If I can accomplish one thing for someone every day, then I've done something worthwhile. I try to treat everybody the same. If I can't do that, I shouldn't be doing the job.

My job is a lot different from a regular union committee job because I can really take care of some problems. I've got a lot more leverage behind me. I've got the state, the federal government, the grievance procedure, and the international union.

The most frustrating part is how long it takes to get things

169

Jim Vernatter

done. For example, there was a job where a guy was lifting an eighty-five-pound tire up above shoulder level. The doctor and an engineer both looked at the job and agreed with me that he needed some help. The money was appropriated to put in a lifting device, but local management balked. I argued and argued for six months. Finally I found out it was the guy's foreman who was holding things up. He was opposed to it because it would slow down production. I told him I didn't care about that; I was concerned about the man's back. We finally got it installed, but there's no reason it should have taken six months.

An even more frustrating case is this guy who's been installing rear springs. Back when we were making buses at the plant, the springs weighed ninety pounds, so we had a hoist installed. Now the springs weigh thirty-five or forty pounds; but the guy who's on the job is small, and that's a lot of weight for him to be lifting all day. But he doesn't use the hoist because it takes too much time, and he would get behind. I told him, "Use the hoist, and if you don't have enough time to do the rest of the job, they've got to take something off it." It's aggravating because you can't get them to understand. They're scared to take the company on. They won't take a position.

I got the Health and Safety job in 1975. That first year I submitted over three thousand safety complaints to the company and filed over six hundred grievances. I put a lot of pressure on them. It cost them a lot of money and caused a lot of aggravation.

One day the company called me in to a meeting along with the vice-president of the union. They wanted to know what the problem was. I asked what they meant.

"Why are you stirring up so much trouble?" they said.

I said, "Well, I've got problems on the floor."

They said, "What would it take to get you to back off some?"

I played dumb, but I knew what was coming. I'd never been approached in that manner, but I had heard about it. The union VP was sitting there, Labor Relations people were there, and here the company was talking like this to me.

They said, "If we paid you twelve hours a day, would you back off some?"

I said no.

They said, "Will you take seven days a week pay?"

Now they were talking a lot of money, but I said I wouldn't take it.

They said, "Just what would it take?"

I said, "What it would take to get me to back off is for you take care of the problems. That's the only way that I'll back off."

The union VP and I left the meeting, and he told me, "Buddy, that's a lot of money."

I said, "My pride means more to me than all their money. If I had somebody get hurt on something that I knew needed to be fixed, I couldn't live with myself."

Now, unfortunately, not everyone's like that. You see trade-offs on grievances. The company knows how the union reps operate. It's like playing poker. If you play poker with a person long enough, you can read whether he's bluffing. That's how the company is. They try every way they can to go around you. Once they learn how they can work you, they've got you controlled, whether you realize it or not.

The union has done great things for working-class people. But somewhere along the line people within the union put more emphasis on personal gain. They got things done for themselves, their families, and their friends and put more emphasis on those people and on their own salaries than on the people the union is supposed to try to help. And so they became a lot less vocal.

I don't know why the union goes along with letting a company work people ten hours a day, six days a week, while a whole shift is laid off. The United Mine Workers at one time had a clause that if anybody was laid off, even one person, there was no overtime worked.

I think if the next contract said we don't need a union anymore, 30 percent of the people who are union members in the plant would agree.

The union is to blame for not educating its members. They don't realize where what they've got came from. We've gathered too many worldly goods—our boats, our cars, our motorcycles— so we're satisfied. Our members can't comprehend that people sacrificed—lost their homes, their jobs, and even their lives. They think everything they've got was a gift to them from Ford. We need to instill in people's minds that whatever you have today, it's like your health: It could be gone tomorrow.

It should be mandatory that workers attend union training sessions and membership meetings. Make people sit down and see the movies about the days of the hard struggles, when they were fighting on the overpass. If you see people with blood streaming down their faces, people lying on the ground shot, and don't have some compassion for them and what they've done for you, there's something wrong with your heart.

Part of the reason for the erosion of the union is the EI process. You can't jump into bed with the management that you fought for forty-odd years and struggled with to get anything you gained. EI is designed to weaken the union and get younger people more management-oriented.

Ford is not going to spend the kind of money they have spent on EI unless they can get back what they put out. Common sense tells you that. If EI is successful, you'll see fewer supervisors because hourly people will actually run the work zones. Each work group will have a leader who will function as a supervisor, making sure the operators have the tools and equipment to do their jobs and helping out if there's a problem. Yet he'll be classified as an hourly employee, and his pay rate will be lower than supervisors' today.

If the company succeeds in what they're doing and gets even more concessions than they've been getting, organized labor will never again be as strong in this country as it has been in the past, because the companies will never give unions another foothold. They won't yield to them. They learned one thing through strikes: that if you keep them out long enough, and they're hungry enough, they'll come back. And unfortunately they're right about a majority of people.

If the union's not careful, I'm afraid they'll get so weak they'll never get back again. And if the union ever goes, this country is going to be in real bad shape.

Another problem is that our international union leadership relies too much on legislation to do things we could do for ourselves. You need to have political leaders on your side, but too many politicians whose campaigns the union has contributed to have turned their backs on us when we need help—and we've supported these same people again.

The UAW labored for years to get people elected who support content legislation. But it ended up as a partisan squabble in Congress, and the content legislation they finally passed was watered down. And with so many Japanese transplants coming in, content legislation becomes less relevant. There are four Japanese firms in this country now, and the estimate is that six more will locate here by 1992, and five in Canada. People don't ask how many of those parts are going to be manufactured here. If all your parts come from overseas and all you do is assembly here, your work force keeps dwindling. So what good is content legislation then? I'm afraid we're going to lose thousands and thousands of jobs and never get them back.

The union was more vocal in the sixties. I was always very outspoken myself. One time there was a wildcat strike, and the union was trying to get us back to work, and I stood up at a meeting and told the union spokesman to stuff his contract. I shouldn't have said that because he was only doing his job—I realize that now—but because I was outspoken like that, people encouraged me to get more involved.

Around 1969 I ran for election committee and won. Then, in 1971, I got on the plant committee. It was a very difficult job at the time. Through politics I was led by some people into a group that became labeled as racists. And there probably was some racism there.

You can't serve a membership if you don't serve 100 percent of them. You can't select a group of people and say these are the ones I want to represent. But I was tagged with the racist label, and it took me a long time to overcome it.

What happened was that a group of us who were white resigned our positions as union officials to try to pressure the union president, who was black, into settlements prior to an election. We wanted to take over his job. But it didn't work, and we left him high and dry with no support. We were wrong to do that; the membership suffered because of internal politics.

After that we had a meeting with another caucus in the union. We wanted some people brought in, one of whom was black. And a guy said he didn't want any blacks brought in. So I got up and told them I could not be part of an organization like that. Word got around of what I had done, so when a vacancy in Health and Safety became available, the union president gave it to me.

Having had a handle put on me in the past, I was determined to prove myself. That was the only way I could get back people's respect, and that's what I've tried to do since then. I've come to one conclusion: If my record and actions don't speak for me, then I can't convince anyone any differently.

There has been progress in health and safety. We have made so many improvements in the plant, through the help of the international union and the state, that in 1986 I filed only a hundred and seventy-four safety complaints and one grievance.

I'm proud of what we have achieved to help the painters, who are exposed to more dangerous chemicals than anyone in the plant. In the past the paint booths weren't cleaned and kept in good repair, and there were severe problems with overspray—excess paint getting onto the painters. Nothing changed until we really put pressure on the company. We threatened strikes and constantly filed grievances and brought in the international union and the state health inspectors. Finally the company realized that the overspray not only endangered the employees but harmed product quality. If paint doesn't fall right and overspray gets on the truck, it affects the finish. Once they realized that, conditions for the painters improved, and so did the quality of the product.

Another accomplishment I'm proud of is how we've improved the welding booths in the Body Shop. For years those guys breathed the exhaust fumes coming from the welding, and galvanized steel is a very toxic metal. So we got the company to put a $40,000 welding device in there with an exhaust suction on the bottom to draw the fumes out. It took years of fighting because all they wanted to do was give us a cooling fan.

The OSHA law has helped make safety improvements possible. But under the Reagan administration the law has been weakened. There are 40 percent fewer compliance officers now than when Reagan took office. Without the officers to police the rules, there are fewer inspections.

The biggest danger facing people in our plant now is in skilled trades. Our tradesmen get in a habit of doing things their way. In 1986 Ford had six fatalities, and the Big Three combined had twenty-one. That compares with fifty fatalities in the previous ten years. The union is concerned about that, and rightly so. We've got to do something to put a stop to it.

Most of the deaths were due to not killing the power on power equipment. Even with all the bulletins and meetings and safety talks we have, some tradesmen still fail to follow proper procedures. They take shortcuts and risks to gain extra time to read a paper, take a break, or just catch up on their work. They want to pick up five minutes for themselves. But it only takes one mistake to kill you.

If we've talked to people and provided training and they still neglect to take precautions, I'm not against discipline. I would much rather have someone angry at me for getting disciplined than to have to tell his family about a fatality.

At the same time the union's putting pressure on the company to force management at all levels to enforce safety precautions. The company has set aside over $5 million for another round of safety training for their thirty-three thousand tradesmen. The national Ford people I've met with really want safety. But on the plant level, most management people put production first. They don't mind if you can interject safety as long as it doesn't interfere with production. That's the attitude of the supervisors and the foremen, and that has to change.

I was raised in the coalfields of Pike County in eastern Kentucky. My father and grandfather both worked in the mines. My dad was a miner for thirty-six years and died of black lung disease. I remember him coming home from work with grease and grime all over him. He could barely get in the door, he was so exhausted.

People in that area were so poorly educated that they couldn't manage their own money. The companies ran their own stores, and we did all our shopping there. Some miners would go for years without drawing a nickel's worth of pay because the store took everything they made. My dad worked for years and never had a payday. All he got was what he got from that store. We would get our necessities, our food, and even our coal for heating our houses through the store. They'd allow you so much money for school clothes and books. If you went on sick leave, they'd cut you back from $8 a day to $2.50. Most families had a lot of kids, and you couldn't feed them on $2.50 a day.

When we were growing up, we didn't have bicycles or anything like that. All we did was push a rubber tire around. We had a swimming hole, but girls weren't allowed because no one had a bathing suit. But it was a good life because there was less TV and more socializing with your neighbors. Even though it was rough and we wore a lot of patches on our clothes, we never went hungry. We had a lot of love in our family, and when you have that in a home, the other things are secondary.

What made people stick together back then was a common goal. But today people get their hands on money or material things, and they forget where they came from. It's "I've got mine and you get yours." That's what's hurting society all over the world. I don't see how someone can be in the union, much less be a union official, and not be concerned about the welfare of mankind. For me, that concern is in my blood. I was raised that way.

My dad took the oath for the union in an outhouse, with guards watching. He never had a union office, he was just a member, but that's how they swore them in. He was thrown in jail once for walking a picket line. The judge locked him up for thirty days, but come election time, my dad was out campaigning for him. When I asked him why, he said it was because the judge was a Democrat and he couldn't vote for a Republican.

My dad spoke often of a woman who led the miners and encouraged them to organize. I don't remember her name, but it really made me enthused to know a woman could take part.

John L. Lewis was United Mine Workers president. I doubt that you could find a miner with a bad word to say about him. He improved the working conditions and the pay rate. They eventually got hospitalization. John L. Lewis really fought for the workers. He shared their beliefs and their sorrows. I really looked up to him.

One of my brothers works for Volkswagen in personnel. Of the eight boys and four girls in our family, he's the only one who's turned out antiunion. The company's brainwashed him. It's the money he's gotten. We still get along, but we try to avoid talking about union matters.

After high school I got married and went back and forth from Kentucky to Michigan, looking for work. Finally we put everything we had, which wasn't much, in my 1951 Mercury and headed up here. We've been in Detroit ever since, except for one year, when I went back down there and drove a soft-drink truck.

I'm proud of my heritage. A lot of people who were born and raised in Michigan resent southerners who have moved here. But we came because we had to. There was no work down there.

When I first came to Detroit, I worked in a service station, six days a week, fifty-four hours a week, but I was only just getting by. So I quit and went into construction. I liked working outside. But I got laid off in 1964, and they were hiring at the truck plant. I decided to try Ford for a while. The work there was steady, and they had overtime, and that was an opportunity to make some extra money and maybe get a home. My plan was to stay until the overtime ran out and then go back to construction.

They gave me one of the worst jobs in the plant: putting in the fire wall pads. I'm 6-foot-2, and I had to bend under the instrument panel to get up under it. It wasn't easy, but I hung with it. After six months they put me on the afternoon shift as an inspector. That was a lot easier.

We were working twelve hours a day; there was no limit on overtime then. I kept waiting for the overtime to stop so I could go back to construction. But time kept slipping by. Next thing I knew I had three years in, five years, seven years, and then our children were born, and I had to take into consideration the benefit package. So that's how I stuck at Ford Motor Company. I've made a good living and met a lot of good friends. The work has been hard at times, but it's been worth it.

Working a lot of hours didn't cause many problems in my family life because I worked the night shift. Still, I didn't get to spend as much time with my kids as I wanted to. My wife was understanding and realized that my job came first. That helped. A lot of families couldn't cope with the overtime. The divorce rate in our plant was real high. People worked so long that when they did have time off, they were exhausted and didn't feel like doing much besides sleeping. That put real stress on some families.

I bought a house in Romulus in 1965 on a land contract and sank almost everything I made into it and paid it off in seven years. It's more than a nice house; it's a home. We've tried to teach our children that everything they want is not necessarily good for them. We've given them some luxuries, but we've tried to instill in them the value of managing money and saving for a rainy day.

I believe family life has broken down because so many married couples are both out of the home. They're working to get all these material things, and they leave children unattended. Children need you to be there to guide them; but all they're getting in some cases is material things, and that's not enough.

My son is going to work for Mazda in Flat Rock. The choice was strictly his. He likes the benefits he'll be getting there. With Mazda's retirement program, hospitalization, and other benefits, he'll be able to get married and have a better future for his family.

He went through five interviews, and he had to pass all five to get the job. The first was a two-hour test on math, reading comprehension, and following instructions. Next was a two-hour interview with two other people who threw different problems at him. Then there was a five-hour test where he worked with six other people to solve problems together. Then another two-hour preemployment physical, and another five-hour test where you work assembly in the plant and they watch how you work. Finally he got hired, and they selected him as a team leader, so he's going to Japan for thirty days to be trained and will come back to Flat Rock and be a leader.

During the physical they gave him a drug test, and they can do that anytime they want while he's working. And there will be no eating, smoking, or drinking anything on the assembly line.

I have no objections to the Japanese coming here and manufacturing. They're no different from Ford, General Motors, and Chrysler. They all go to Mexico and Brazil and Australia, anywhere they can get cheaper labor, and import parts back in. Mazda's going to do the same thing. Certain parts will be made in Japan and shipped here for assembly. But at least they're going to give twenty-five hundred to three thousand people a job.

There's no reason for people in the richest country in the world to live in the conditions they do. Hundreds and thousands of people are without food, shelter, clothing, and proper medical care. And there's no reason for that to be tolerated, not when corporations are making billions of dollars of profits. This country is going to pay dearly one of these days for what's going on. I really believe that.

The majority of the people in Detroit are on welfare, but not at their own choosing. The public thinks they're a bunch of deadbeats, but if there were jobs available, most of them would work. They don't want to bring their kids up in those surroundings. But until we start putting money into training and providing work for them, they'll never come out of it.

It's up to us as citizens to provide the services needed. I don't like higher taxes, but unless we get jobs for our young people, the crime rate and the drug problem are going to get worse. And we cannot keep letting outsiders steal our manufacturers away to southern states or wherever else they want to go because they get tax breaks. We have to do everything in our power to keep industry in our state. It may mean raising taxes, but if there's no jobs, you aren't going to pay any taxes.

Jobs are going to the nonunion states. What is left here for young people? Unless something is done, our children may have to go somewhere else to get a job at $6.50 an hour. I feel sorry for the young people coming up now. There's nothing there for them. They can't buy a home or raise a family for $6.50 or $7 an hour.

The only good I could see coming out of this is if the working class could see what they're up against with the corporations and come together in a common cause. Until we get the working class to realize that they're in this struggle together, that they have to change things to have something for your children and their children, we won't get anywhere. If we could educate people and get them to participate at the polls, you'd see some changes.

I believe the day will come when the working class will be so depressed and downtrodden that they'll unite. Right now the politicians and the money people are pushing them back, but you can only push people so far, and then they rebel. If enough people are put against the wall and suffer the way some people are suffering today, it could happen. There's just not enough who are hurting yet.

The love of money is holding us back. Recently I asked this guy in the plant if he would be willing to give up $1.50 an hour to get back the second shift. And he said no. I said, "That's the problem. All you think about is yourself."

Larry Poole

Born September 29, 1950, in Detroit
Hired May 24, 1972
Bargaining committee representative for UAW Local 900

WHAT INSPIRED ME to become a union representative was the way some of the foremen treated people. They had this almighty attitude: "I'm God, and you do this and that, and if you don't, we're going to take you and hang you." I watched my co-workers go through that, and I thought something had to be done.

When I was first getting involved, the union didn't accept anything from management. We raised hell whether they agreed with us or disagreed. We thought that was the way to keep the company on their toes. We did a lot of things just to prove a point. Looking back, I think we should have exercised a little more intelligence and diplomacy—things we acquired later through experience. Don't get me wrong. I'm not saying we were a bunch of raving idiots. We were reactors to what the people wanted, and we had a lot of people in the plant back then who were gutsy. But what is right politically is not always the best thing to do.

I got elected to the bargaining committee in 1975, and I've been active in that capacity ever since. I represent the people in the plant in their labor disputes. I'm also part of the negotiating team for the local contract.

Larry Poole

Over the years my job as a union rep has gotten harder because people have changed and their problems have intensified because of the cutbacks. People complain more about having too much work to do. Also, I think the attitude of some of the people has changed.

The fear of being laid off and the plant shutting down has taken a lot of the fight out of the membership. A lot of things people used to stand up and take a position on, they don't anymore. It's because of the economic climate. They keep telling the people all the time, "Poor quality, poor quality, we're going to lose the plant." People got a little taste of the hard times back in 1980 through 1982, and now they tend to be a little bit cooperative. The attitude is: "Well, I'll go along with this because I have to have a job."

When the militancy declined, it became hard to represent the people. The company will look at me and say, "There is not a problem. You are the guy stirring up the problem." And a lot of the time that is true because I go and complain for people when I think they ought to be complaining.

It makes my job harder when people don't complain because the company's primary concern is production. Their only threat to production is the people, not Larry Poole, and if the people are not willing to take a position, then I can yell, I can sit down and meet with management, I can write a thousand grievances, but it doesn't mean anything to the company. It was a lot easier to get things done when more people were willing to stand up for their rights along with me. Fortunately, there are still some members who will stand up and fight.

We in the union advocate that if a job is overloaded, the best way to prove it is to let it go down the line. Now some people have more of a tendency to run and get it. They are afraid to let stuff go because they might get written up and disciplined. There's that fear even though few people get disciplined with time off anymore. The company can't run people out like they used to because they have cut down right to the bone. They don't have the extra people they used to have.

Problems people face in the plant today include some of the same old things such as line speed, overloaded jobs, harassment, and layoffs. They are also concerned about reductions in classifications. Some of the more preferred jobs—like materials handler, hi-lo driver, truck driver—are being eliminated. That is not necessarily due to technology. The company, trying to be more competitive, is cutting costs in indirect labor. They figure it doesn't take away from the personnel needed for production to eliminate people who feed stock to the lines and work in an indirect way with production.

Since the plant went to one shift in 1980, there has been about a 15 to 20 percent reduction in maintenance area jobs, about a 15 to 20 percent reduction in the Stock Department, and about a 30 to 35 percent reduction in Quality Control people.

The union has to look at it realistically. If they don't need the people, we can't legitimately argue for them to keep paying people who have nothing to do. But our priority is keeping as many people employed as we can and preserving preferred jobs for the older, higher-seniority workers.

Since we went to one shift, we've lost somewhere between 20 and 25 percent of production jobs on the remaining shift. At the same time we've had an increase in production. We are putting out more work with fewer people. We have fewer repairmen repairing defects and fewer inspectors catching defects. It's a difficult task to improve quality with increased production and loss of manpower.

I was the oldest of five kids—three boys and two girls. I grew up in a series of places on the west side of Detroit. We moved ten or twelve times before I was 16. We were poor. My father and mother were separated, and I was raised primarily by my mother, uncles, and grandparents. At times we all lived together, and other times it was just me and my mother. But I spent a lot of time with my father, who also played a major role in my upbringing.

I finished high school but never went to college. I kept saying I was going to take classes and improve my education, but I never got around to it because I was so involved with the union. I regret that sometimes.

I want my kids to get the kind of quality education I never had and be able to do something constructive with their lives. That's why we moved to the suburbs, because the school system is better out here. If they have the same type of education I had, they are not going to be able to survive in today's job market, where you need a college degree.

When I was in high school, I worked at Danny's Supermarket on the midnight shift until it started interfering with my schooling. I got off work at 8 A.M., and when I went to school at 9, I was bobbing and weaving.

I got hired at a Chrysler Plant, Detroit Universal, in 1967. It was a small plant that made drive shafts and universal joints. I went to high school in the morning and worked from 3:30 to midnight. At Danny's I had been making about $1.70 an hour. The first week at Chrysler I brought home about $110 for 40 hours. Sometimes I would work a Saturday and bring home about $130.

I quit Chrysler in 1970. I had relatives in the construction business in Atlanta, and I went there. It didn't really interest me, and I only stayed about three months. I came back and started working at the Michigan Truck Plant later that year. I worked there about three or four months and quit because I couldn't get along with the foreman. I came back again two years later to stay. Had I known I would have been coming back, I never would have left in 1970.

When I first hired in, it was chaotic. The line moved fast, everything had to be perfect, and if you missed something, the foremen harassed you. You worked six days a week. There were no restrictions on overtime then, so you might work eleven or twelve hours. You didn't even have time to spend the money you made. A lot of times I would go to the bank and I would have two or three paychecks to cash. I could cash one check, and it would last me a month.

Back then the black workers and the white workers were all being harassed. Race wasn't really a factor on the line. There was a sense of working together. Sometimes you would see new black hires get worse jobs than whites, but it depended on which area of the plant they were placed in and who their foremen were.

When Louis Callaway, Jr., became plant manager, there was a definite change. He was the first black to run the plant and the first to realize that the plant was in trouble and attitudes had to change.

Callaway got a lot of respect from blacks and whites in the plant. Callaway was more open. You didn't have to go through the chain of command to reach him; you could talk to him as easily as you could to an ordinary supervisor. He spent a lot of time on the floor, and he was fair. He tried to improve the atmosphere in the plant and make the grass look a little greener.

When I first started, there were no women at the plant. Management's attitude was that women shouldn't be working there. They put them on jobs they knew they couldn't do. The company's position was that they got equal pay and should do exactly the same thing the men do.

I remember once they needed people on a tire job and on the shock jobs—muscle jobs—and they put these three women there. We went down there, and these women were standing there with tears in their eyes, trying to lift forty-pound tires. The superintendent just said, "I turned in a requisite for three people and this is what personnel sent me. Those are the jobs they have to do." They fired those women because they couldn't do the job. We filed grievances, and the women filed civil rights discrimination complaints, and all three of them eventually got their jobs back.

They also harassed women sexually. They would put them on hard jobs, and the foreman would tell them, "Hey, if you go out with me or do this with me, things are going to be better." There was a lot of that going on in the plant.

Today there are very few women in the truck plant. The company uses a little bit more discretion now on what jobs they place women in, but you still have isolated incidents where a woman is placed on a job she physically can't do and we have to go through the hassles and the arguing and get her reassigned.

Back then, on the afternoon shift, when you were working ten or twelve hours a night, there was very little time you had to spend with your family. You came home at 5 or 5:30 in the morning. If your spouse didn't work, maybe that's when you would have a few hours for some communicating before you would go to sleep. When you got up, it was time to go back to work. I'm sure many spouses felt like they didn't have a companion.

The plant was a community, like a city within a city. With so much overtime a lot of people became wrapped up in the plant. The plant was home, and your real home became your second home.

I've been fortunate because my wife has a lot of sensitivity to me. We have a very solid relationship. Sometimes I come home pretty screwed up after a day at the plant, and she understands that. If I snap at her or I don't want to be bothered, she knows how to respond. But the plant takes away a lot. I'm sure I could contribute more to the relationship if it weren't for the hours and the nature of my job.

The Employee Involvement concept came along when management decided they wanted people more involved in the process of obtaining quality, of being competitive through cutting costs. Years ago we in the union used to go to the company and advocate listening to the people. But that was when times were good, and even though we had problems on the job with quality, the company didn't want to listen to the people then. Now that the company wants to eliminate and cut back and increase profits, they want the people to help.

Because of EI, some people now feel they are a part of the process, a part of the company's survival. They think: This is what we have to do, and if we don't do it, we aren't going to make it. They've got them thinking just like the company. There are a lot of things going on where they should rebel a little bit and take the company on. But some people have become part of the problem along with the company.

I think the concept of EI will eliminate the union or at least seriously decrease union participation. It will cause the hourly work force to be completely gobbled up and controlled by management. A lot of the benefits they gained through having a union are going to be lost.

There is very little I as a local union representative can do about the course of the union as a whole. Someday maybe I'll get an opportunity to be a part of the international union and spark more change. I'd like to go back and pick up some of the militancy that we used to have years ago.

I would like the union to remain a strong force in the retention of jobs lost due to technology and offer more security to the workers. We can't stop technology, so we should come up with better ways where it is not so profitable to replace human beings with robots and machinery. We should make the company obligated to place people in other jobs or make them pay people if their jobs are lost to technology and plant closings until they can put them in other jobs within the company with no wage and seniority loss.

Foreign competition won't bring an end to the auto industry in the United States, but there will be a huge overcapacity. Everybody wants to sell cars in the United States because that's where the big bucks are. If there are content laws, then the foreign companies will just do more building here. Content laws are not the key. The foreign manufacturer will still get a bigger piece of the U.S. market. There will be more layoffs because there is not going to be a need for Ford, General Motors, and Chrysler to keep making so many cars and trucks. A fair-trade agreement that will increase U.S. sales abroad is one answer.

More and more, people lack confidence in the union, and the union is slowly losing a lot of power. The union is only as strong as the people. The big auto companies know that many people don't stand behind the union, so they can be a lot more successful in some things they try to do.

I am all for the union. The union is under a lot of heavy criticism, and the union deserves some of it. I disagree with some of the things that the union has done, but a lot of people have forgotten the importance of the union. They talk about some of the things that we gave up in concessions. I think we gave up a little bit more than we should have, but had it not been for the union, we would have given it all up. It was a hard fight for the union to retain some things, and the company is constantly trying to take back things we fought hard for and gave up a lot of money for in strikes. But we won some things—we've gotten profit sharing, some wage increases, and some increased job security.

There are times in my job when it doesn't seem like we're getting anything. You are not winning your arguments, and the company is not giving in. But there is some gratification in just the purpose of the labor movement. I like trying to do something constructive, being one of the leaders in the struggle. I guess it is in my blood. If the union is to survive, people like myself and some of the others from the so-called dying breed have got to continue to hang in there.

Chapter Six

The Disenchanted

When truth is buried underground, it grows, it
chokes, it gathers such an explosive force that
on the day it bursts out, it blows up everything
with it.

—Emile Zola, "J'Accuse," L'Aurore,
January 13, 1898

Jerry Conrad

Born September 8, 1939, in Webster Springs, West Virginia
Hired October 27, 1966
Relief man on the Trim Line

I'M NOT A COMPANY MAN. I don't give a damn about this company, and they don't give a damn about me. I'm just surviving like everybody else. I have ten more years to go before I can retire, and I hope and pray to God I get out of here.

When I leave the plant, I leave the plant. My wife always says, "How was your work today?" I might have gotten into a fight with the foreman, but I'll say it was OK. I never talk about work. When I walk out that door, I don't think about it anymore.

I don't want my son or daughter working in the damn auto plants. I don't want them to have anything to do with the auto industry. It's too uncertain. I tell them they are going to graduate if they have to go to school until they are twenty-five. I tell them, "Look at me. I never finished high school, I'm a damn factory rat, and I'll always be a factory rat."

Fifteen years from now all the plants will be automated, and there aren't going to be any jobs. It's going to be all big arms going around and guys standing there pushing buttons. We are a dying breed. It is obvious. Production work is a dying art. My sister tells me that I'm a professional. She says, "Jack Nicklaus couldn't go

Jerry Conrad

out there and make a truck." Well, maybe I am a professional, but if so, I'm one of the last ones.

Sure, I'm happy that I took this job. It got me this house, it got me a car. That's everybody's dream, right? A house and a car and money in the bank, which I don't have.

The best thing about working in the auto industry is the money and benefits. I made $44,000 last year. But the dollar isn't what it used to be. I have to run home and put my paycheck in the bank to cover the check I wrote last week. Of course, I have more things now than I used to. I have a Thunderbird and a Mustang. And I have eight years of payments left on my house.

I've seen some guys retire with no money, and I've wondered how a man could have worked thirty years and not have any money in the bank. But I really understand now that I'm raising kids again. I took custody of my two teenagers from my second marriage recently. I'm glad I did—they are good kids, and I love them—but it puts more of a strain on my new wife and me.

Sometimes I'll have a bad day and take it out on my wife or the kids. As soon as I do, I'll say to myself, "Dumb-ass, why did you do that?" and I'll apologize. I want them to know I love them. My daddy never told me that, even though I know he does love me.

I never really had a boyhood because I worked all the time. I had to work in the hayfields all summer long. I hated it. My dad worked me like a dog. I might have weighed ninety to ninety-five pounds, and he would put a hundred-pound sack of feed on my shoulder and make me carry it to the feed house. I didn't dare fall down because it would fall down on top of me. I love him now, but I didn't then.

The guy I looked up to was a boozehound who played the guitar and ran with women. He was my big hero. I remember in the early fifties he got a bus ticket from Ford Motor Company to come to Michigan. But he cashed it in and got drunk on it. I couldn't believe it. Here that guy could be retired now. Instead, he drank himself to death.

At that time coal mines were really booming. They called us the billion-dollar coal state. There was plenty of work then, and they couldn't get anybody to work up North. So Ford had to start a recruitment drive to get the hillbillies. They sent down representatives and put bulletins in the paper for "good-paying jobs with good benefits" and got all these hillbillies to come up. There are so many Kentuckians who came to work in this plant and other plants that they call Ypsilanti "Ypsitucky." They would bring up a nephew or a brother, and before you know it, half of Michigan is hillbillies.

The town I grew up in is a little bitty coal-mining town in the central part of West Virginia. These days there's nobody left there but old people and old farmers. When a kid gets to be 18, he's gone. There is nothing to do except work in the coal mine, and nobody wants to do that. A lot of them join the service. That's what I did.

I joined the navy in 1956, when I was 17. I had no idea what I wanted to do. I thought I might make a career in the navy, but after four years I wanted out. When I got out, my parents had moved to Florida. I moved down there, got married, had a couple of kids, and got a divorce. There wasn't any good work in Florida for an unskilled laborer.

I had an uncle who lived in Detroit who had worked at Great Lakes Steel. My mother called him to see if he could get me a job. I came up and went to the unemployment office to apply to Great Lakes, and a guy came by and asked if I'd rather work for Ford. I said, "Who pays the most?" He said Ford. I said, "Where do I sign?" I went to work at the truck plant that night. It was a madhouse. People were running and falling on top of each other. The first day I was scared to death and almost got fired. There were about thirty guys hired the same day I was, and I'm the only one left.

I couldn't believe the money I was making. We were bringing home $300 a week. I hadn't been grossing $100 a week down in Florida, and that was working three jobs.

Before 1973 we could work as much as we wanted. I was working eleven to eleven and a half hours a day and eight hours on Saturday, week in and week out. We started at 6 in the evening and got off at 4 or 5 or 5:30 in the morning.

Absenteeism was ridiculous. Some guys would go out for lunch and not come back at all. They fired guys for missing work. I never got fired because I always made sure someone covered for me, but I took my time off. I had to; the schedule was too much. Hell, I wasn't made to work like that. And I was single then. The plant was 90 percent single guys, but a lot of the guys were rebelling against that schedule.

We'd always send one guy during the last break before 2 A.M. and he'd get a couple cases of beer and we'd all sit in the parking lot of the union hall after work and drink beer until the wee hours of the morning. That's all you did back then. You ate, slept, and worked.

We got paid on Thursday night. Five or six of us guys would get together before the line started on Thursday and make bets on who had the most money in their pocket. The one who had the least had to buy. Sometimes I had three or four payroll checks in my pocket I hadn't cashed yet. That's what kind of money was rolling in.

I didn't even know what a union was when I came here. Florida is mostly a scab state; there aren't many unions there, and the ones they have are small. I liked having the union here, especially when I got fired in 1967.

One day I took a truck radio from Line One and took it back to my line to listen to the baseball game. They were watching me, and I didn't know it. They called it attempted theft.

I was out all through Christmas with no pay or benefits. It was rough. I was married again and had two children, and we had a very small Christmas that year. After about three months off I started having my doubts that I would get my job back, so I got a job with a trucking company. Finally, after five months off, the union got me back. I was making good money with the trucking company, but I didn't want to lose my seniority at the truck plant, so I went back.

In the old days there was a lot of stealing at the plant. One of our plant chairmen was accused of taking over a half million dollars in stolen goods. They said he had this scheme to take alternators out of the plant. He'd supposedly take a pallet and bribe the guard $100 or $200 but he would make $500 or $1000 on it. Westland police arrested him and charged him with theft, but he was never convicted. He no longer works at the plant.

There's not as much stealing going on now because too many people got fired for it. One guy got fired for trying to take a damn squirt can out under his overalls, an oilcan you can buy for $1.98. Why would a guy get fired for $1.98?

I watched my foreman get a kid fired once. It was quitting time, and this kid, who was no more than 19, tried to take something out under his coveralls. I saw my foreman get on the phone and call the guard. The next day I asked the foreman, "Does that make you a big man now? I thought you were more of a man than that." It was really none of his business, but it made him look good. That guy is still a damn lying foreman, and that's all he'll ever be, a production foreman.

The union has changed. When I hired in, the union was really anticompany. That plant chairman who the company sued for stealing the alternators was great. He hated authority. He would put out bulletins that said, "Watch that big fat-ass guard up there; he is watching you." If an assembler was pushing a broom, he'd break the broom because it wasn't in his job classification. I respected that plant chairman for having some balls against the company.

But the union has mellowed on that stuff now. They go along with that EI bullshit. EI is just a bunch of psychology. It benefits the company more than it does the hourly guy. Some guys participate in it just to get an hour off the line. That's tempting, but I don't get involved. Just leave me over on the side, and I'll do my thing and good-bye. I'm a relief man, so I don't work the first hour, I take two hours for lunch and break, and I'm done an hour before quitting time, so I can't bitch. They don't say anything, so I just do my job and don't say anything to them.

I used to be in the union clique, but I got tired of all the politics. I got fed up when I saw these friends of my committeeman complaining that their jobs were overloaded, and that same day they had some work taken off their jobs. So I called my committeeman's attention to this one guy I know who stays in the hole all day long running. He's a big dummy, and he won't say anything for himself, so I screamed and raised hell. But the committeeman just laughed at me because I'm not in his clique. That's just not right. He was elected to represent the people, not just his friends. I'll never vote for that guy again.

I'm against women working in the plant. They want a man's money, but they don't want to do a man's job. That's why so many of them were fired and quit. This one woman, they took her to Line One, and she couldn't do the job. She sat there and cried for five working days. If I was the foreman, I would say, "Hey, you can't do it, hit the street." But they won't make them do the work. But they will send guys to the office for poor and careless workmanship or for refusing a job.

Now they are going to put these women into skilled trades. It's part of the affirmative action program. I don't think it's right. Anyone over 45 can't apply. That pisses me off. I got twenty years in, and I can't apply for the skilled trades job. That's age discrimination to me. There's no woman who has more than ten years in the place, and they are giving them an apprentice job over me with twenty years. But that's what it says in the contract, so there is nothing you can do about it. I'm one of the guys who ratified the contract, right?

Women do get harassed at the plant. When the women first hired in, our general foreman got in trouble for hassling them. He told one woman to date his brother or she'd be fired. Instead, she went to the plant manager the next day and almost got him fired.

The truck plant is making gobs of money now because we're putting out a world-class unit and they are not paying a second shift. They've overloaded the jobs. The best thing for quality would be to slow down the line so people could do their jobs better.

Meanwhile, the politicians are letting these Japanese imports in. They're getting their kickbacks and we're getting shit. It's a damn rip-off. The politicians are getting richer, and we are busting our butts trying to make a buck. I'm a registered Democrat, I always vote Democrat, but I have no sympathies with the son of a guns. I know they are getting kickbacks for these imports.

The foreign companies are getting smart. They're bringing

their auto plants over here, but they are still selling a foreign-made product. It turns me right off. I don't blame the people who work there; a guy has to work.

If I saw someone with a broken-down foreign car on the road and it was raining snowballs, I wouldn't stop to help them. Not here in the Detroit area, no way in hell. I was at a picnic at my wife's uncle's house the other day. He was driving a damn Toyota. He is making American bucks and buys a foreign product, and I resent that.

I remember it used to be you wouldn't even buy another American company's car. Some guy was telling me he had to park across the street because he had a Chrysler car and worked in a Ford plant. If he parked in the lot, he'd find his tires flat and his windows busted out. Now I got a friend on Line One and he went out last week and bought a General Motors truck for $18,000, and I said, "I hope it blows up on you." I couldn't believe that. The guy is biting the hand that feeds him. He could have gotten the same pickup here a lot cheaper. But he didn't like the Ford product.

I remember back in 1980 when this TV newsman was reporting on the big recession live from the parking lot of the Michigan Truck Plant. He was talking about how foreign orders are killing Detroit and how the truck plant went down to one shift, and all the time he's on TV he's backed up against this repairman's Toyota pickup. Boy, did we give that repairman hell. About a week later he traded in the Toyota and got a Ford pickup.

Betty Foote

Born June 6, 1936, in Idlewild, Michigan
Hired June 15, 1976
General assembler

I LOVE THE PEOPLE in the plants because they are so colorful. They are Richard Pryor- and Eddie Murphy-type people. They're really comical, and they can be uplifting.

People in the auto plants are really honest inside the plant. Because we work close together, we talk about our lives and share our problems. We find out we all have similar concerns: house notes and marriages and neighborhoods and children and drugs. If I didn't hear about those concerns from people I work with, I would be like other black people who think their kids are the only ones doing bad things because that's what's reported in the newspapers. But it doesn't have anything to do with color. We're all just people, and we all have similar problems.

But when you get outside of the plant, there's a different attitude. We all make the same money, but the attitude still is: I don't really want you coming to live next door to me.

The supposed concern for workers' happiness now with the EI program is a real joke. Ten years ago they didn't have EI, and they weren't talking about management-employee relationships. But

Betty Foote

all they are doing now is talking about it. It looks good on paper; but it is not effective, and they don't want it to be.

When you read that American autoworkers don't care, that is a lie. Workers' attitudes have changed; they want to see good products put out. And they want to call management's attention to any problems with the cars. But management is still the same. They don't care. You can tell them, "Look, this bolt doesn't fit in here," and they'll say, "Well, just put it in anyway." It embarrasses me to even tell them anything anymore because they look at me like: Well, so what? Just do it. We're just trying to get these cars out of here.

What's going on is no fault of the workers. American workers aren't shiftless. When you work in the plants, you understand why nobody wants to buy an American-made car. You see with your own eyes that all management wants is to get it out that door. You can't stop the line if there's a problem. Don't let anybody tell you that. If you stop the line, you're going to go right out on the street.

They showed us this movie about health and safety, and I learned a lot about some of the chemicals I work with. But what a joke! The film said that the rubber gloves I used when I was wiping cabs are not good enough because the solution leaks through and gets on your skin. Now suppose I had said, "Well, look, I cannot do this job because these rubber gloves are not the proper thing to use." They would have said, "Well, that's all we have. What you want us to do?" And if I'd called a union rep, he would have said, "Well, Betty, just use them tonight, and maybe tomorrow they'll have some more gloves."

Relations between workers and management haven't changed. The foremen are ridiculous. They really need to be retrained. They'll put you on a job, and they won't even show you the basics of the job. You have to ask another employee how to do it because the foremen don't know. But if I miss something, the foreman will say, "Well, baby, the inspector says that you missed that." Of course, I missed it. I don't even know what the hell I'm looking for. I'm just doing it by trial and error.

They shouldn't have any supervisors. Just let the employees run the department because at least they respect each other. The product would still get out, and you wouldn't get harassed by a dumb supervisor who makes unnecessary remarks and rules because he's trying to make you think he knows the job. An employee who works on a machine every day knows what he's doing. He doesn't need a supervisor to tell him.

When I first started at Wayne Assembly, there was a foreman who didn't want women in his department. He liked to shake his fingers in my face. I told him I didn't read sign language. I went to Labor Relations, and they came right down and told him to stop shaking his fingers in my face. There was no need for me to call a union rep.

In the paint booth when I started, we never saw our committeeman. I got into a little trouble because I got up at a meeting once and said our committeeman never came in the booth. They told me to keep my mouth shut. They still dislike me. I guess I talk too much. I tell the truth. I'm not going to lie, and if you don't know how to scheme and connive to get a problem solved in the plant, you're not going to get it solved.

I'm not sure if we need the union. It depends on how fair management is. Some small companies have good management. But the auto companies will lie and say one day they're not going to move the plant, and the next day the plant is closing up and shutting down. So I guess I'm happy the union's around.

The jobs haven't gotten harder over the years, but we have more work, and we're working faster. If they eliminate eighteen jobs off my line, the people who stay will be running to do the extra work. Me, I don't run. I'm too old to start that.

Nobody feels secure anymore because of robots. People are afraid their jobs will be eliminated. Automation means job elimination. That's the bottom line.

They're giving people an opportunity to go to school, so they can get trained to operate or repair the new machines. The classes are from 4 to 6 in the afternoon, so the day shift people can go to school after they get off and the night people have to come in two hours early. But you still have to work ten hours on top of going to school, and that's a big load. I tried to take some brushup classes in spelling and stuff like that, but I was nodding off all the time. I couldn't concentrate.

My dad and mom were born in Ohio, in a little town called Paulding, which had both white and black farmers. My older brothers and sisters were all born in Fort Wayne, Indiana. My dad used to go up north hunting and eventually decided to move up there, to a town called Idlewild. He was a builder and worked in a plant in Muskegon, about sixty miles away.

My mom died when I was 2. My dad remarried, to a really nice lady who wasn't much older than my oldest brother. He kind of raised her along with us. My dad didn't have any problem raising us. He could cook and wash and iron. He and my mom had six kids, plus he had one by my stepmom and she had two of her own.

At Christmas we had to go out in the woods and cut down our own tree. We couldn't afford tree lights, but we would make some flour paste, bring some construction paper home from school, and make little rings and decorate the tree. For a long time we didn't have electricity. We had kerosene lamps, and the lampshade cost a nickel. You had to guard it with your life when you cleaned it so it wouldn't break. A nickel was hard to come by.

We didn't have TV. We had to do our schoolwork before dark because my dad didn't want our eyes to be ruined reading by the kerosene lamp. At night we all sat in front of the radio and listened to school lessons they would broadcast. Everybody wanted to be top dog in school, so you studied.

Idlewild was a big resort for blacks. Count Basie, Della Reese, the Four Tops, all the big names used to perform there, and we got to know them all. We worked at the restaurants and the hotels they stayed at. I remember how the club owners would open up their drapes and put boxes on the outside so us kids could stand on them and watch the show.

We didn't even know what dope was. It wasn't acceptable. Anything that went against family values would cause you to be ostracized. If I had a girlfriend who got pregnant, I couldn't run around with her anymore. And if anyone got pregnant, she would get married.

I had big dreams because I met all these black lawyers, doctors, and politicians who were on vacation. They really helped me out later. The name Idlewild opened a lot of doors, because in any city there were people who had been to Idlewild.

When I got out of high school, I went to Chicago and got a job as a cashier at a clothing store. In 1961 I moved to Detroit, and the next year I married one of the businessmen I used to work for in Idlewild. He died four months later. My second marriage was another tragedy. He was a talented fellow, but he loved his liquor. I was no competition for the bottle, so we split up.

I moved back up north in 1968. By 1971 I had two daughters and was working for the school system as a librarian and a secretary, bringing home $126 every two weeks. I had a girlfriend in Detroit who told me the plants were hiring, so I came back down. A guy who was a hunting buddy of my dad got me a job at the truck plant.

At first the language at the plant frightened me. I had never been in an atmosphere like that, with all the joking. People called each other such bad names that I expected a fight any minute, every day. But there never was. They even would swear at the foreman and say, "Get out of here, motherfucker, I'm going to kick your ass," and he wouldn't get mad.

Some of the men were hard on me at first. They'd say things like "Oh, you're in nice shape for being an old lady." Or they might say, "We're going to take a leak." It took me a whole week to realize they weren't going to take a piss in front of me. They were just feeling me out.

I was going to quit after that first week. I was so tired. My hands were aching, and my whole body was a wreck. But when I got my first check, it was over $400 and I told myself, "Maybe I don't hurt as bad as I thought I did." The work didn't get any easier, but the money was decent, and I figured it would enable me to do some things I wanted to do, so I just hung in there, and now I've been there ten years.

The people at the plant are really good people, black and white, young and old. When my hands would hurt, someone would say, "Now, Betty, your hands are going to ache for a little while, but you'll get over it." Or they would say, "Betty, take a cigarette break, and we'll cover for you."

I painted with an air gun for three years, ten hours a day plus Saturdays, and all the time I had pain in my neck and shoulders and hands. They kept calling it tendonitis and giving me cortisone shots. But that didn't help. I finally found out that I had carpal tunnel syndrome and that any repetitive work, squeezing or pulling or pushing, would make it develop again.

Once I was properly diagnosed, they took me off the spray-painting job, and I worked with restrictions. I just floated around. For a few weeks I would wipe off cabs. Then I'd go out to the garage. I never had anything I could say was my job. I liked the variety, and I made friends in other departments.

I was laid off in 1980. For three years I was mostly laid off, but every year we would work for a few months. In 1983 I got permanently placed at Wayne Assembly and eventually got a job I could do without any pain: assembling brake lines.

I started coming in fifteen minutes early to build up some stock so I wouldn't have to do it the last hour. My foreman knew I was coming in early for my own benefit, but he told his bosses I had all this extra time, so they added an air gun to my job, despite my restriction. They said, "Either you do the job, or we don't have a job for you." So I did the job until I just couldn't hold the gun anymore. Then they sent me to the hospital, and the hospital told them my hands had become worse. But they wouldn't move me to another job. Finally, in 1984, I had an operation. After the operation they still didn't have a job that fit my restrictions. So they put me on medical leave.

To me being on medical is a form of punishment. They don't care that you hurt. They just want to keep you out on medical so long you'll do anything to come back. A lot of people on medical eventually go back and drop their restrictions.

I don't know whether I want to work anymore or not. Anything

I do, my hands hurt. I can't even wring a cloth sometimes because they're so sore and swollen. My hands are always going to hurt.

Nobody in management really cares whether you are sick or not feeling well. They care more about the truck than they do about the person. In my opinion, the company doctors have ruined a lot of people's health. They tell you you can do the job no matter how sick you are.

When I started at the truck plant, I wasn't used to leaving my kids. Up north I would drop them off at school, go to my job, and pick them up after work. We were always together. But here I couldn't do that. I arranged for my next-door neighbor to watch to make sure they got off to school. A couple times I had to leave them in the house by themselves, and I worried all day long till I got back home. Those were the worst days of my life.

Finally I hired my neighbor. I bought food for her family and paid her $55 a week. I took my kids over there after dinner, and she gave them baths and put their pajamas on. They would sleep there, and I would pick them up every day after I came home. I didn't like it, but what could I do? I had to get up at 4 A.M., and that was too early to get them up and take them to somebody else's house.

Other people in the plant had the same problems. Kids were getting themselves up and being left at home or being watched by neighbors. That's like breaking up your family. And for some people it really was the breakdown of their family.

When you work ten hours a day, you don't have time for your kids. When you get up, they're in bed, and when you come home, you're ready to go to bed. So on the weekends you let them have their way. You feel guilty, so you cater to them. I'd buy them pizza or fast food because that's what they wanted. Sometimes we would go downtown and stay at a nice hotel all weekend or go to Toronto and do whatever they wanted. They loved it.

A single parent who has to work can't get any help with child care. You cannot just go out in the streets and get a baby-sitter. You don't know who you're getting. But if I ask a child-care agency to send me a professional so my kids don't have to hang out in the streets, they won't do it because I make too much money, even though those are services I would pay for.

I can understand why kids get out of hand when parents have to work. It's because nobody wants to help you until it's too late. That's where the guns and things come in because your kids don't have any supervision while you're at work. And when you get home, you're so damn tired that you don't go in and search anybody's room.

In the plant they have women's lib mixed up. They think women want to be men. But we don't want to be men. We just want equal pay. We should all get paid the same because we are all autoworkers, but don't be ridiculous and pretend I can lift something I can't.

The women in the plant would like a law that they don't have to work more than forty hours. The men are the only ones who like ten-hour days. They're so geared to that check that a paycheck for eight hours would look ridiculous to them. I like the pay, too, but I want to be with my kids. The pay isn't worth it. Give me the eight hours, and let me go home and rest. Let me work some normal hours.

Working ten hours a day for years and years and years and years, and working every other Saturday, all you do is work and sleep. You're like a zombie. If your kids ask you something, you don't want any arguments, so you say yes to whatever they ask. Then, when they do it and you come to your right mind, you say, "God, did I tell you you could do that?" You're hardly even aware of what's happening with your kids.

When you talk to the union about working ten hours, they say, "Well, this is what the company and the UAW agreed to do." But I'm the one who works. Maybe I don't want to work that long.

To work ten hours, you have to be geeked up somehow. You have to be a really strong person not to take drugs. If you don't get on an inventive high, or a musical high, or do something to keep yourself happy at work, you are going to resort to drugs or booze or something.

We need shorter hours. Just have three shifts and let everybody get a little bit of money. Then you wouldn't have carpal tunnel syndromes and neck problems and back problems and all these health problems that people have. My doctor said ten hours is too long for anybody to work.

Jim Stephens

Born August 7, 1951, in Ashland, Kentucky
Hired August 25, 1971
Painter

THE BEST THING ABOUT working in the auto industry is that I've been able to give my kids a good education, nice clothes on their backs, and the basics. I want them to remember me as a halfway decent father who worked hard and tried to give them all they needed.

I've been painting in the plant for over fourteen years. It's a job. I'm not really thrilled with it, but it could be worse. I paint the finish around the door, the doorjambs, and the back of the tailgate, and put a coat on the outside of the cab. I work for two and a half hours and get a half hour break. In the old days you used to have big skips in the line. Now we get skips only if something breaks down. And the line runs faster.

When I first hired in at the plant, I weighed about 120. I had never worked in a factory and didn't know what the hell to expect. My first job was in the Body Shop, drilling holes in the tailgates. I had to lift the tailgates up on a platform and then put them on the truck. I lasted about three days before the foreman told me I just didn't have enough muscle to do the job.

Next they put me in Trim. My job was hooking up the choke

Jim Stephens

cable, putting knobs on, tightening them down, and putting in the heater hose. I couldn't do that job either. I was really trying because I really needed the job, but I kept getting in the hole. I had blisters on my thumb from trying to press the heater hoses together. The general foreman was a guy from the South like me, and he said, "Boy, I ain't never seen a hillbilly that couldn't do a job on this." He really cut me down.

I said, "I don't know what to say, man, I've never been on a job I couldn't do."

They transferred me to the Paint Department and made me a sander. Every once in a while I'd go back to Trim and talk to the guy who broke me in. He could do the job and sit down and smoke and drink coffee in between without getting in the hole.

I was doing OK sanding. But this other hillbilly foreman started getting on my back. I was leaving spots of dirt no bigger than a pinhead, and he would constantly get on my case about it. One day he came down really hard. I almost had my ninety days in, but I just couldn't take it anymore, so I said, "Man, why don't you just get off my back and let me do the damn job? I'm trying my best."

And he said, "You know, I've fired guys in here who had eighty-nine days in. If you don't do the job better tomorrow, within four hours I'm going to have to let you go." He called in a union committeeman, and he told me to just do the best I could. I did, and I made it. I got my ninety days in, and my probation was over.

After I got my ninety days, I asked if I could become a spray painter because they get four breaks a day. They kept putting somebody else in there, but finally they gave me a try. I didn't know the first thing about painting, but I made it.

In the early seventies we were having problems in the paint booths with the overspray. The union talked to us, but they couldn't tell us to walk out. We had to make our own stand. I remember, as we were walking out, everybody on the Chassis Line going, "All right!" We shut the whole plant down when we walked out; if it's not painted, they can't work on it down the line.

Everybody walked out and went to the union hall. The union told us to come in every day, and every day we came in and walked out. And the day shift did the same thing in support of us. We all stuck together. I think it lasted for three days.

We got the international union to come in. As far as I'm concerned, they sold us out. International said everything was OK, so we went back to work. But the conditions were no different. The company gave every one of us a hearing, and we all got disciplined. Three guys got fired, but the union eventually got them all back. I got a week off without pay.

Now the union is even worse than then. It seems like they don't care anymore. Every time the union tries to do something, the company says, "We're competing now, and if we don't have good quality, we're going to shut the plant." They're always saying that, but they haven't shut it yet. In fact, those suckers are selling like crazy.

I think the change came when they laid off the whole second shift. That's when a lot of people started worrying about their jobs. Now people are putting in more effort because they're afraid. The quality has gone up as a result. We're doing a hell of a job.

Things in the Paint Department are worse now than they used to be. They had a meeting recently and told us that we are subject to a lot of health hazards, that paint thinner soaking through your skin could cause tumors. I thought: Damn, that's a hell of a time to tell us, after fifteen years in there, and all the time the thinner is on our hands and soaking through our skin.

In the old days on the afternoon shift everybody got along real good. We cut up a little bit sometimes. We would do things like paint our boots. Most of the guys I worked with then are gone now. A couple of guys from Tennessee worked there awhile and then went back South. A lot got laid off.

For a while I would just get out of work, come home, take a shower, and hit the bed, and before I knew it, it was time to go to work again. That was kind of boring. Working ten hours a day, you never look forward to anything because your day is shot. There's no going out to talk to other people. So I started drinking with some guys after the shift was over.

I hadn't been much of a drinker before that; in fact, I can remember getting sick on four beers. But these guys could drink a case, and hanging around with them, I got better at drinking. We'd hang around after work in the parking lot, talking and drinking, from 4 until 8, when the bars would open up. Then we'd go shoot some pool, go home and catch a couple hours of sleep, and go back to work. That was before we all had kids. My wife didn't like it much, but I did it anyway.

Eventually drinking got to be a real problem for me. I missed a lot of work because of it. One time they fired me for bad attendance, but the union got me back. I got busted for drunk driving four times. The third time I went to jail for thirty days.

I'd say 70 percent of the plant has a drinking problem. They don't fire many people for drinking anymore, because people usually wait until they get off work to drink. I used to go out in the parking lot all the time to have a beer, but now I just go out there once in a while.

I don't think I'm going to see another five years in the truck plant. According to the contract, if you have fifteen years in and you lose your job to automation, they'll put you in another department or another plant. But it might not stay in the contract the next time. I doubt I'll see retirement.

They're going to automate the whole truck plant, and ten, fifteen years from now, there won't be anybody there. It's going to be all machines. I heard General Motors has a plant like that now—all automated. They have one guy there to turn the lights on.

My son watches the news with me sometimes, and they'll show these robots, and I'll tell him, "See there, son, one of these days Daddy won't have a job on account of that." I tell him that when I was growing up, things were pretty rough, but they weren't as hard as they are now. I tell him robots are going to take over a lot of jobs, and he's got to have an education and know-how to get a job. I try to stress to him: Keep going to school; get the best grades you can. I want to get him through college and into something that has to do with technology so he can provide for his family. I got him a computer, and he messes around with it. But he really doesn't know how to work it. I don't know how to work it, and neither does my wife.

I signed up to take computer classes through work, but I wasn't one of the people who got in. I'll take another shot at it. But I don't know if they'll let me in because I don't have a high school education.

With all this technology and everybody getting laid off, jobs are getting scarce. You can't have all these people not working. You'll just keep having more thefts and murders. Something's got to happen. I think there's going to be a revolution in this country. One of these days the people are going to get together against the government.

Yvonne Sumpter

Born January 17, 1952, in Bessemer, Alabama
Hired July 14, 1976
Hooks up electrical wires on the Final Line

I WISH I DIDN'T have to pay union dues. Ford pays those union people, so they can only do what Ford tells them to do. I don't vote anymore because none of them help you. They're just getting out of running behind those trucks and cars on that line. All they want to do is lay back and smoke their cigarettes and drink their coffee and read their paper and wait for their checks on Friday, while you are out there doing all the damn work.

You don't need a union. What does the union do? Nothing. One time I was sick with the flu, and they wouldn't accept my doctor's excuse. The company-union review board decided they would let it stand on my record. The union people on the review board sit back on their ass and don't do a thing. They never worked on this production line a day in their life and they tell me they can't accept my excuse?

I'm tired of working hard. If I hit the lottery today, I would tell Ford that I appreciate what they did for me, but I don't want to stay there to get thirty years in. If I have to work the rest of my life, I will. But I don't want to.

I have six sisters and four brothers. My mother raised all of us

Yvonne Sumpter

herself. I never met my father until I was 18. We lived in two rooms, a living room and a kitchen. In the kitchen we had a bed, a stove, and an icebox, but no refrigerator. My mother used to pay 15 cents for a big cake of ice from the ice truck. It would last a couple of days. We had a table, but no chairs, so we would stand at the table and eat. There was no bathtub. We had to take baths on the back porch in a tub. In the living room we had a little closet with the toilet in it and a bed on one side and a baby bed. Me, my mother, and two sisters slept in one bed. Later on my aunt and her boyfriend came to live with us, too.

We didn't even know what a lamp was. We had a socket with an extension cord, and we would screw the bulb in. We would move that socket, and that was our lamp. We used to make a fire when we got up in the morning, all year round, and that would heat the house, and we'd cook on it.

My family got $150 a month from welfare. You weren't allowed to have radio or TV on welfare. But we got surplus cheese, butter, rice, and peanut butter. After my mother started working as a maid and making $20 a week, they cut her off welfare. Then it was rough.

Every afternoon, starting in first grade, I would have to rush home from school. My mother and my two older brothers and one older sister were working, so I would cook dinner. When my mother came home, her kids would be sitting on the porch with their hair combed and clothes clean. Then everybody would eat dinner and clean up. The house was always clean. When my mother had someplace to go at night, I would watch the younger kids.

Food was no problem because my grandmother in Birmingham had a garden and raised chickens. She had pear trees and peach trees. She canned a lot of food. On Saturdays she would go to the grocery store and put groceries for us on the bus, and we would pick them up from the bus driver at the bus stop near our house.

None of us even had a bike, but we were happy. We got something on Easter, Christmas, and the Fourth of July, but nothing in between. I remember at Christmas I got a pair of shoes from Good Fellows. All our neighbors helped each other.

When I was older, they built a housing project on the hill. My mother got a job there washing windows. We figured we were moving up because she was making over $100 a week. One day she came home and said, "I got a town house in the projects, and we are going to move in tomorrow." Boy, were we excited.

In our new house there were four bedrooms, a living room, a kitchen, a gas stove, a refrigerator, and a bathtub. The night we moved in we all stood in line to take a bath. Later my brothers in the service sent money home, and we got a living-room set with a couch, chair, lamps, and end tables. We were living in luxury.

I remember one day in school the people who were with Martin Luther King came with bullhorns and told us to leave. We walked out and marched with them. When they put the hoses on us, we went and got bathing suits and played in the water. But then Governor Wallace brought out the German shepherds, and things got very tense. When those people bombed that church and killed those kids, many of the people in the civil rights movement began to question nonviolence. They said this has to stop.

I would never go back to Alabama to live because people are still doing the same things. There are certain parts of Alabama where blacks don't dare stop. When we visit home, we make sure we don't run out of gas. Behind where my mother lives now is a mountain, and the KKK is still up there at night burning crosses. There's really no change, even though Birmingham has a black mayor now. The South will always be the South.

The people at the plant who are prejudiced are the ones from the South. I can't deal with those kind of people. I was brought up with them, and I know how they are. They'll never get that hate out of their systems.

When I started at the truck plant, there were about fifteen women there. Most of them worked on the Sealer Deck, and that's where they put me. My job was wiping cabs. I had three days to learn it. I was used to working hard, but it was all new to me. I was trying hard, because I was determined to work. I had sealer everywhere. My gloves had holes, and my hands were burning.

On the third day the foreman told me, "I'm going to have to let you go because you can't do the job."

I said, "I'm giving it all I got. I'm doing the best I can."

So he told me to go see the general foreman, and he gave me another chance. After a week the foreman told me he was satisfied with the job I was doing, and he said, "I'm kind of glad we kept you."

Until I got ninety days in, I used to work twelve, thirteen hours a night. When the Sealer Deck closed, they would send me upstairs to paint. They told me I had to do it because I didn't have ninety days in.

They kept hiring more women. I would see them come and go. They just couldn't deal with the work. When this one woman started, they were giving her a hard time, so I told her, "You just have to put it in your mind every time you go up to the next truck and start doing it that you're going to do the best you can." If you do that, the next thing you know you're around the bend.

Every week they put me on a new job until I ended up learning every job on the line. After a while I would train every new person. And because I knew all the jobs, I started relieving for people. I actually used to love to come to work then.

When they suddenly eliminated the second shift in 1980, it was a big surprise. They told us on a Thursday that Friday would be the last day. I said, "Where's the union?" It seemed like the union knew what was going to happen and should have told people. But the union said they didn't know what was going on.

Everyone with five years in got transferred to Wayne Assembly. Wayne Assembly had more women than the truck plant, but half of them were pissed off because the people from the truck plant were taking their jobs. The foremen there were hard on the women. They put me on all kinds of rough jobs that women didn't ordinarily do. They even put me in Underbody, and a guy there said he had never seen a woman in Underbody. Each time I started a new job, no matter how hard it seemed, I would put the thought in my mind: This is my job; I'm never going to refuse a job; I'm always going to try to do the best I can. And I did.

One really hard job I had was building up parts and stock in the Body Shop. The guy who trained me told me how you had to put the parts in the welding machine and then find a wall or a place to hide to keep the sparks off you. There was an old lady in there, about 60, who was bald. The sparks had burned all her hair off. I said to myself: If she can do this job, so can I.

My next stop was building up stock on a feeder line they called the Money Line because everyone there volunteered to work thirteen hours a day. But I told them I didn't need it and I was going home after ten hours. They didn't like that, so they moved me again.

When I worked on the line, people would ask me, "Why are you walking so slow and not running?"

And I would say, "Because it's going to be there when I get there."

When I got called back to the truck plant, there was a lot of tension because they had eliminated jobs and overloaded jobs. People were scared they were going to lose their jobs.

They put me on what was supposedly an easy job, and it was terrible. I said, "There is no way I can do all this." Then I hurt my leg. I worked on it for a week, and it swelled up. The doctor told me I had torn ligaments in my ankle. They put me on medical for two weeks. When I came back, they told me to go on the same job. I refused because I'd already hurt myself once on it. I told them that I came there to work, not to kill myself.

I got the plant doctor to tell them I couldn't do the job. He said, "You're going to have to find her a job she's able to do."

So the supervisor said to me, "What the fuck do you want? Do you want my motherfucking job?"

So I said, "Now you talk to me like I ain't shit and I can talk to you like you ain't shit." All their mouths dropped open. I told them, "I come here to work, and I work for what I get."

The doctor picked out a job I could do, but they didn't want to give it to me. They kept loaning me out every day. I didn't like that, and the foreman and I would have it out. I was mad every day, and I wouldn't smile until I came out the front door. Finally I went over their heads to the production manager, and he told them not to loan me out anymore. That really pissed them off, so they put me on a job that was way overloaded.

I do the job, but I walk at a normal pace. I come in to work, not to run behind these trucks. They can't handle that. I had the union and Labor Relations come down, and I told them, "Tell me where my work area is, and that's where I'm going to be." I'm not going to run down the line while these repairmen and Quality Control people read their papers. They stand there all day and don't help out, but as soon as you miss a screw, they run and tell the foreman.

The jobs are so overloaded that half of these people won't get thirty years in. I see them taking people out of there damn near every day because someone had a heart attack. But I'm never going to fall down on that line with a heart attack because I'm just not going to run.

The way these jobs are going, everybody is scared they are going to lose their jobs. Everybody is out to hurt each other. That's why there is so much hatred in this plant.

A few years ago I thought I would never come back to the factory again because of all the layoffs and the way the economy was. I told myself then, "Well, my mother made it." I don't cry about whether I'm going to have a job tomorrow or the next day because I look back at when my mother had all those kids and she made it. Some people say they can't make it working only forty hours a week. I say, "What do you mean you can't make it?"

I made $32,000 last year. That's probably more than my mother made in her lifetime. I look at that and say, "I know things are changing, but like the old saying goes, 'Where there's a will there's a way.' " If I lose my job, I'm still going to eat. I'm not going to starve as long as there is a grocery store somewhere. I'm either going to steal or going to die, and I'm not going to die.

Chapter Seven
The Battle-weary

I'm so tired
Tired of waiting
Tired of waiting for you.

—*Ray Davies, "Tired of Waiting for You"*

Ed Aubuchon

Born March 24, 1952, in Highland Park, Michigan
Hired April 17, 1972
Installs drive shafts on the Frame Line

I GOT INTO PLANT POLITICS because I care about people, and I thought by doing that I would better my life. I had dignity and self-respect, and I wasn't going to let those foremen take that away from me. I would rather be out on the street than have someone treat me like a dog. And I didn't like other people in the plant being treated like dogs. I saw people taking other people's self-respect away, and that's something I never wanted done to me.

So I stood up for people's rights, and eventually I got involved in a rank-and-file newsletter and became one of the main agitators in the plant. I learned a lot, and I think I accomplished some good for other people. But I got tired of the struggle.

Now I'm comfortable, and my main goal is to relax and have a nice retirement. I'm just trying to live. Unless there was a crisis now, I don't think I'd get involved. There's too much sacrificing involved, too much personal pain. When I was involved in politics, I believed that it was nice for people to share and that everybody should live on a subsistence level. But I was never so sure I wanted to live that way myself.

I also got tired of having people spying on me in the plant all day

Ed Aubuchon

long. And I feel like I've been left alone because all the other people I stirred up trouble with in the old days are on medical leave or on other jobs. People spit on me all day at work. Maybe it's because I'm the only one of the old activists still left on the line, and it's easy to pick on me.

I really don't care to put my neck out anymore because all the people I used to get involved for don't think much of me. I don't deserve a pat on the back, but some people are pretty cruel to me after some of the things I did for them.

I guess I was one of the top guys, and I never realized it until I got the stigma of being a Communist. Now I've gotten tired of being called a Commie and doing things for other people.

There's a guy I used to consider a racist redneck. We became friends by going hunting together. One day I told him, "You know what? I'm tired of doing all this stuff, of being called all these names. I just want to be a regular guy. I'm going to be an asshole just like you."

I still care about the people at the plant on a personal level. I watched *Platoon* recently, and I could see all the guys I work with in that movie. I could see how easy it is for there to be one rotten guy and for other people to learn from him how to kick some poor guy who doesn't look the same as they do. And I could see there are some guys who don't give a shit.

I was watching another movie recently about the Holocaust. That reminded me of the plant, too, because when I first started working there, some of the foremen were so cruel they seemed like Nazi soldiers to me. One Nazi they interviewed in the movie said that most of the Jews were so weak, so undernourished that it was easy for them to march into those ovens because the thought of fighting back never entered their minds. And they were so weak that it was easy for the guards to think of them as less than human. Watching that, I understood how easy it is for some people in the plant to be so passive.

I grew up on Lake Erie near Monroe. I wasn't a farm boy, but I lived in the country and liked the woods. We had indoor plumbing but no bathtub. When we came to Detroit to visit my grandfather, we would take a real bath; that was a luxury. My dad worked two jobs in Detroit. He was a taxi driver by day and a bartender at night. He was only home on weekends. My mother worked, too, and my older sister watched me.

On holidays we all would visit my grandfather in Detroit. A lot of people knew my grandfather, because he'd been a leader in the community a long time. In the depression he had struggled a lot. I remember his stories about going out and catching carp and selling them for 5 cents a pound from a bathtub and stealing coal off the coal cars. He was an old-fashioned working-class kind of guy.

When I was 11, my dad got a job for a construction company, and we eventually moved to Detroit. It frightened me to move to the city because I had heard a lot of bad stories; but we moved into a real working-class neighborhood, and I fit right in. I got into rock and roll. I taught myself some chords, learned some Beatles songs, and started a band. We got to be real good. We played in shopping centers for five thousand people. We even played with Bob Seger once.

My dad taught me to take on my responsibilities, so when my

girlfriend got pregnant, I was determined to support her. I didn't want my parents' help. One day, instead of going to school, I went to work cleaning carpets. I was only 17, but I got married, got an apartment, and started taking care of my responsibilities.

The work cleaning carpets wasn't steady, so I got a job at the truck plant. I remember coming into the plant and looking down the line and seeing all those guys working. I was pretty impressed the way they put the trucks together. I hadn't realized there was that much to it. I was excited to be working at the plant. I saw it as a steady income and a chance to get a retirement—things my dad didn't have.

It was hard work back then, but even worse was the attitude of the supervisors. Some were really mean. There was an Arab guy on the line the foremen used to call "camel jockey" and make fun of and a Scottish guy who also got a lot of abuse. There was a guy from Yugoslavia, another from Romania. I started asking them what it was like where they came from, and it was like the whole world opened up.

The foremen were all under a lot of pressure, and they'd take it out on people. There was a lot of racism. I suppose some of it was joking, but it got to be an everyday thing, and it was more degrading than funny after a while.

The Scottish guy talked me into going to a union meeting. I found it inspiring. Sometime after that I took up a petition to have a shift meeting about harassment and job overload. It was the first of a lot of shift meetings I helped organize.

After we had a few shift meetings, they started watching me all the time. There would always be some guy whispering in my ear, "Watch out." People would come over and tell me to be quiet because some guy was going to tell on me. I'd say, "So what?" It didn't bother me a bit for them to know what I was doing.

I was pretty forward back then. For instance, there was this one guy in the plant whose daughter had a brain tumor. He was worried about her, so he got a restriction, but the foremen were mad about that. One day he was sweeping the floor, and he had some stuff on a piece of cardboard that he was ready to throw away, and I saw this foreman grab the cardboard, throw it back down, and tell him to clean it up. I got so mad that I ended up getting half the line to stay home the next day, and I didn't even work over there.

At first I thought I might have some trouble doing things like that. But after a while I learned the contract and the company rules real well. I found out they couldn't do too much to me as long as I went by the rules.

My job was building windows. I was such a fast worker that I could build all the windows in five hours, so I had a lot of time to go around and help people out and stir things up a little bit. Foremen started calling me the Line Diplomat. After a while I started enjoying the fight more than the reason I got involved in the first place. Maybe I was a smart-ass. A lot of foremen were scared to talk to me because if they said something, it would get turned back on them.

One foreman really hated my guts. I used to play a little game with him. I would come over to his line, and he would come up to me and say, "You're interfering with production. I'm going to have to ask you to leave." So I would go to the other end of the line, and he would walk all the way down to that end to kick me off his line, and just as he got to me, I would leave and go down to the other end. For several weeks I had him walking up and down the line like a yo-yo. I really enjoyed that.

I got involved in the *United Truck Plant Newsletter* by doing a cartoon about that foreman. I had heard about how he'd tell women that if they didn't go out with him, he would fire them. So I went through the whole Trim Shop and asked every woman if the stories were true. I found out they were. So I did a cartoon showing him pointing a finger at a woman and saying, "Either you go out with me or I'm going to fire you."

When I first started going to newsletter meetings, I didn't even know what the term *rank and file* meant, but it sounded good to me. People were talking about how we needed a change, and I agreed. It seemed to me there were a bunch of guys in the union who really didn't care about the people, that all they were concerned about was their own personal gain, being stars and getting an easier job. The things the union was supposed to stand for didn't mean much to them. Meanwhile, the union was getting weaker and weaker. I was tired of all these little strikes because no one was winning. People went back to work with nothing after being out a long time.

The people I got involved with in the newsletter weren't concerned about getting elected. In the paper we would support people in other caucuses, but we didn't run our own slate. And at our meetings people could say what they wanted to say; there wasn't somebody cutting them off like at a union meeting.

At first we wrote in the newsletter about problems in the plant, like the paint walkouts. We'd just describe what happened. We wrote about contract violations and told people they didn't have to run on the job. I don't know why that was considered radical.

After a while we started writing about things outside the plant, too. There were a couple radicals from the sixties who each belonged to different political organizations, and I started to disagree with them about outside things. My opinion was that it was hard for some of the regular guys in the plant who weren't that deep into politics to talk about things that didn't involve the plant. I felt the newsletter was a place for anybody to express their views, and I didn't want it to become a mouthpiece for anyone's political ideology because that would cut people off.

When people first started calling us Communists, I had to ask someone what the word meant. That's how apolitical I was. I thought I was just reacting to some people in management who were really mean, that I was just fighting some rotten people. Later on I understood what I was doing a little more.

I started going to demonstrations. I went to Indiana to an Essex Wire strike and marched in a picket line. I joined Chrysler workers who had a walkout over high temperatures in the plant. I went to a march on the Pentagon.

I went to political meetings and learned things I had never learned in school. I started studying English and history on my own. I started feeling like I wasn't a dummy, that I had talents for cartoons and writing.

As I got more sophisticated, I noticed how people were trying to suck me into their organization with flattery. If I blew my nose, they would say, "Boy, you're doing a fine job. That's the best nose blowing I've ever seen anybody do." I didn't need someone patting me on the back just for drawing a straight line. And when I saw them doing the same thing to other potential recruits, I got pretty sick of it.

I didn't like the manipulation. One time I was at a meeting, and I realized that the woman who was leading the discussion wasn't nearly as interested in what I had to say as she was in trying to get me to answer her questions the way she wanted me to. It was subtle indoctrination.

I also got tired of some of the sloppy work. We'd get in a lot of arguments over the newsletter. Someone would say, "We don't have time to fuss with this," and I'd say, "I don't want to print this because it's not right." I wanted people to enjoy what we were printing, to have it be good-quality stuff, but some others just wanted to get their line out.

As I got into politics at the plant, I learned about women's liberation, and one day I told my wife that I wanted to practice liberation at home, too. So I started doing more around the house, cleaning, watching the kids, changing diapers. And the more diapers I changed, the more closeness I gained; the baby started looking at me. I started to really enjoy the housework. But it became a real problem. My wife began to feel like she wasn't as important as she had been.

What I concluded from that is that you can give somebody freedom, but with that comes responsibility. When women and blacks started getting more freedoms, some of them went wild because they weren't responsible. Instead of using that freedom, they abused it. Sometimes I feel guilty that I'm a little prejudiced. But I see a lot of blacks who don't want to work or who are always crying discrimination. The same thing with women. All of a sudden they get this freedom, so half of them are leaving their husbands.

I can understand now why that happens, and not be so mad about it, even though I got divorced because of it.

I've lived with my second wife ten years now. I have a teenage stepdaughter, and we have a baby son. To the three kids from my first marriage, I see myself as sort of an uncle. My first wife is married again, so they have a stepfather, and I don't want the role of being a part-time dad, because it's too hard on me emotionally. I care about them, and I take care of them. But I know they're in good hands, and I've moved on to a different life.

At one time I thought the union really wanted people who were willing to fight. But it didn't take me too long to learn that just like the company, the union was only looking for guys to suck ass. All these union suck-asses are now sitting down at the Solidarity House. These guys aren't fighters; they just want to get by. And as they sit there, they're going to slowly be picked apart.

The union takes a stand on firings, but that's been the only real good the unions have been able to do since I've been there.

I ran for union office a couple times. One time I ran for president of the local. I took it seriously, though everybody in the newsletter group thought it was funny. I had things in the back of my mind I envisioned doing if I won, and it's almost like that vision now in the plant. Things are much nicer. We have air-conditioned break rooms all around the plant; we have television, even on the line; the areas are a lot cleaner. They put a mat down to walk on so your feet won't hurt. Supervisors treat you a lot better. But all the time I feel like it's a sucking in, and I think everybody in the plant feels that way, that EI is like sticking a carrot under our nose.

Even the salaried guys, the engineers and big shots, are starting to worry. The cutting that these companies are doing is starting to shove down a lot of people. They're starting to cut into people who live in a lot nicer houses than I do. The company would like to get rid of a lot of people.

Deep inside I know that things have got to change. And I know how easily all these things the union fought for can be taken away. People in the plant used to think no one could take away their retirement benefits because it was the law. Under Reagan, they're beginning to understand how easily someone can.

Sometimes I don't want to think about what's coming down the road. I want to think that in fifteen years I'm going to retire, take my boat, and have fun. But I sometimes feel all these crises we used to talk about are going to come true.

I don't look for anyone to protect me or fight for me. I'm just trying to get by myself. I don't see me putting myself on the line for the union. But if I have to go out on strike, I'm sure I'll go out and enjoy it.

I'm glad I learned a lot of things, but sometimes I wish I didn't know all this stuff. Then I'd be a dummy who didn't have to worry so much. Sometimes I wish I could go back to being just a regular asshole again.

Don Mushinski

Born September 18, 1932, in Detroit
Hired April 7, 1964
Inspector

I WAS RAISED with the thought that you work in a plant at the company's blessing. I firmly believe that what we have has been gained through the unions.

My dad is a charter member of UAW Local 900. He was a radical. He helped organize the union at Ford, and his activity got him fired for two years. When the union was recognized as a bargaining agent for the workers, he was reinstated.

In the early days, when the UAW organizers pulled a strike on Ford, the union set up pickets all around the whole Rouge complex, twenty-four hours a day, and forced the workers to stay there. Now and then some of the guys would try to get out. Some of them swam across the river. The union organizers would catch them and take them to a kangaroo court. My dad was a member of the original Flying Squad, which would sit in the court like a troop protection group. Walter Reuther was at many of those trials. They didn't hurt anybody physically, but they'd give them a warning and explain to them what they were trying to accomplish.

When I was a kid, my dad used to take us to union picnics and

Bruno Mushinski and his son, Don

Christmas parties, and I would see all these union activists there. At the time they didn't impress me that much, but they left a big legacy for unionism.

My dad came to Detroit from Texas in the twenties. He was a sharecropper back there; he knew what hardships were. He came up here because Michigan was the industrial hub of the nation with plenty of jobs and good pay. When he first came to Detroit, he worked at Kroger's supermarket. He knew Jimmy Hoffa from the early organizing days in the Teamsters. After Kroger's, my dad worked at a car company called Graham-Paige, and then, sometime in the late thirties, he got a job for Lincoln-Mercury.

While he was working for Graham-Paige, his younger brother visited him from Texas. They went down to the Rouge Plant and waited all night in line to get his brother a job. The way they hired then was that the plant guard would come out to the gate and holler, "Hey, you, you, you, and you." Whoever he picked, he'd let them in. They'd give them a short interview and put them to work right away, even if the guy had stood out there all night. So my dad was waiting in line, and the plant guard came out and picked him. They hired him, and he worked a couple of hours. The next day my dad sent his brother in his place. And they never knew the difference. His brother worked in his place for about six or eight months and then went back to Texas. They had no records or anything. They just wanted a body to move the line.

My dad told me that in the early days at Ford, before the union, they used to have gangplanks on top of the assembly lines. The foreman would walk on the gangplank and holler at people, "Hey, you, get this done. Hey, you, get that done. You're not workin' fast enough." If you had to go to the bathroom, you had to raise your hand. They didn't have doors on the bathroom, and sometimes the supervisor would follow you and watch you. And if you didn't have anything in that toilet, you would get fired on the spot. They had a lot of workers running scared.

My mom worked in the plants during the war years. She worked the afternoon shift, and my dad worked the day shift. She loved working in the plant. That's where she learned how to smoke and to sit around with the girls after work and have a beer.

My dad accomplished a lot of good, but as the years went by, he lost interest in the union. By the late fifties, when he was working at Wayne Assembly, he became complacent like everybody else. Other values, like making money, became more important. He got interested more in his house and his hobby of building homes.

Some union guys keep on going forever. But they have some position in the union. They get so many perks out of it that they remain active. There are very few others who stay very loyal. These days they all go into it for what's in it for them. They want to get off the line.

The union is geared now for the present employees, but very few ever attend union meetings. Very rarely is there a quorum. I remember in the early days how the meetings were always packed. My dad was the sergeant at arms, and when there was rowdiness, they'd just grab the guy and throw him out. And everyone would support that. Now, if a guy wants to dominate a meeting from the floor, people are afraid to stop him.

* * *

I never wanted to make a career out of working in an automobile factory. I just fell into it. I started working in the plants when I was 18. I worked on the dock at Chrysler's old Dodge Main Plant. That was a nice job; there wasn't regimented work production. Then I went to GM's Clark Street Cadillac Plant and started off with stock work there, too. I didn't want to work assembly. I didn't like the notion of not being able to move off your job and go somewhere, that you had to be there all the time. But working stock, I was isolated from everybody, so I asked for a transfer after five days, and they put me on the assembly line. The lines then weren't as fast as they are now. But for somebody who'd never worked on an assembly line, they were fast.

After three days of somebody breaking me in, they cut me loose, and the minute they cut me loose, I went in the hole. When you're in the hole, you have to keep running with each truck down the line and then run back to get your stock. I couldn't catch up. I told the boss, "I can't do this. You have to get me another job."

He said, "That's the best one we could find."

I said, "If that's the case, I'm leaving."

I was young, and I figured I could find another job someplace else. Jobs were plentiful in 1951. If you wanted to do manual labor, you could go to any one of the Big Three and you'd probably get a call.

I was quite a baseball player, so I also considered that as a career; but I went in the service in 1951, and when I came out, I was 23 and figured I was too old for that. I got a job at Burroughs and worked there eight and a half years. I had several jobs there. The last one was as a printed circuit process man, silkscreening circuitry boards. It was a good job; but I got laid off, and my brother, who was a general foreman at Wayne Assembly, convinced me the opportunities were better in the auto industry.

I hired in at the truck plant just when it was starting to make trucks after being converted from manufacturing station wagons. After six months Burroughs called me back. But even though the work at Burroughs was nicer, I decided to stay at the truck plant because I could make a lot more money with the overtime. We started off working ten hours a day, six days a week, and it's been that way ever since, except for a few slack times.

Working as an inspector at the truck plant was a lot different from Burroughs. It took a long time for me to adjust to the terminology. Plus we didn't have much safety then. People were always slipping on the oil that was all over the floor. Maintenance people only took care of a big spillage. They didn't have enough people to do a proper maintenance program then. I used to write so much stuff on inspection tickets I'd get behind on the line and have to start on another one.

They needed a program to see that the vehicles were being built according to specification. So after three months I set up a program to check things like cotter keys, locknuts, and front-wheel bearings, to make sure we're not building a lot of vehicles that are not secured properly. The program developed so much that it's a regular part of manufacturing now. It's come a long way. And so has the plant. The environment is much, much better than when I went in. The autoworker is better off now than before, in terms of wages and working conditions. The only thing is that productivity keeps increasing.

Every time we got raises, management raised productivity. And with the union's blessing. The union understands that if they're going to get the raises they want, they have to create productivity to compensate for the raises. So the work load has gradually picked up. Each assembly operation now is a pretty heavy load.

When a person becomes adapted to his job and does it for a long time, it's pretty easy to give more work to him because he knows how to pace himself. He can adapt to an increase. What that leaves for somebody coming after him is very rough.

The work load for each employee is based on how long the company allows for each job. In 1967 most of the work loads in plant were set at 400 minutes out of the 480 minutes in the t-hour workday. That meant they allowed you 80 minutes for not fitting, dropping stock, lighting up a cigarette, or wiping face. Now they have almost every job up to at least 440 es. That was based on the experience of people who were on for a long time. This has to stop because it's impossible to out of 480. No human can keep that kind of pace. But they t as much as they can.

are no longer any young people in the plant. All of the re are experienced and are so adapted to manufacturing that the company is getting the best possible results I don't see how anybody's going to keep up this type of ing in later years when these people are retired. I can't eople coming from the outside and replacing these t pace.

utoworkers are the best workers in the world when

they put their minds to it. And they've become smarter and more skilled. We don't have uneducated people coming into the plant anymore. Most are high school graduates, and a lot have some college. And a lot of them are already knowledgeable about automobiles; many worked on them at home as young kids. And so they learn much more quickly.

I remember in the sixties and early seventies, especially on the night shift, Fridays and Saturdays and Mondays were a very critical time. Mondays a lot of people stayed home because they were pooped out from working a six-day ten-hour shift. Friday was a payday, and either that was taken off or there was a lot of drinking and smoking grass—not inside the plant, but off the job. Saturday was the same thing. After lunch those guys were getting geared for partying. Their attitude was whatever went went. If the guy missed his operation and nobody caught it, that's the way it went out. They went through the motions, more or less. But it was surprising how many guys could get high and still do a good job.

Whenever there was a walkout, as a union committeeman I was caught in the middle. You would get fired if you were directly involved, and you were expected to walk around with management and tell people not to join the walkout. I refused to do that. I said it was up to each person, and the only thing I would do is to try to tell them to go back to their jobs if they decided to walk out.

Now people are older. They have at least twelve years' seniority, and most of them are pretty well established with their families. So they've become more responsible. They won't take chances anymore. It's similar to the situation when the unions were first organizing. You have a certain number of people who would do anything to keep that income coming in. They'll complain, but they will keep up the production pace because of the seniority they have and the money that keeps them going. I don't think these people would vote for a strike for any damn reason.

All these perks that they've instituted—profit sharing, bonus clauses—are all geared for a person who is pretty well established in life. They have an investment program, called TESP [Tax Efficiency Savings Plan]. A young guy hiring in would have no use for that. He would want the money in his pocket, so he can go out and blow it. But I use the plan as an incentive to sink money away for retirement.

I don't know how we can instill that union loyalty or rebelliousness again. The workers now don't ever get involved unless

something's going to happen to them personally. They're getting close to retirement, and they're looking out for themselves. The loyalty that banded the union together, taking on the big corporation, is gone forever.

I'm looking at it from a different perspective now myself. I used to be a union committeeman and very involved in the union. Now I run classes for retirees, and I play a lot of golf. I'm getting close to retirement. If I feel I'm being violated contractually, they'll catch it from me. But I'll do it for myself. Otherwise I won't make waves with management because I want to keep my job. I probably follow the same pattern as my father.

What's going to develop is a service-oriented economy. Companies get whatever they can manufactured more cheaply in foreign countries. We're drifting toward a two-wage-earner society, husband and wife, at a lower wage scale. The companies say the lower wages are necessary to compete with foreign industry. I think that's a big farce. Big corporations have no loyalty to any country. Their loyalty is to the dollar. They exist to make the buck.

If these big corporations are going to compete with one another around the world, let them take their headquarters out of our country. Here they have all the benefits. They have a stable government that's existed for two hundred years. They have the strongest protective army in the world. If they want those perks, they should have to take care of the people here first. Don't go to those other countries for the almighty dollar.

Chapter Eight

Renegades

Lots of people complainin' that there is no work
I said, "Why do you say that for?"
When nothin' you got is US-made
They don't make nothin' here no more
You know capitalism is above the law
They say it don't count unless it sells
When it costs too much to build it at home,
You just build it cheaper someplace else.

Well it's sundown on the union
That was made in the USA
Sure was a good idea
Till greed got in the way

—*Bob Dylan, "Union Sundown"*

Ramon Reyes

Born August 12, 1949, in Elsa, Texas
Hired July 27, 1972
Spot welder in the Body Shop

IN THE PLANT people constantly call me names. They like to pick on somebody, and I happen to be one of about five Mexicans in the plant. Because of the way I look, they don't consider me 100 percent American. They call me taco bender and wetback and really give me hell.

To me I'm more of an American than anybody in that plant. I was born in this country, and my family goes back three generations in Texas. People yell at me, "Go back to Mexico," but I wouldn't know what to do there. My oldest brother fought in Korea, and I and two other brothers fought in Vietnam. I went there because I wanted to serve my country. When we got home, they still called us wetbacks. We've been to war. For us not to be called Americans is a sin.

Some people in the plant don't like me because of my beliefs. I don't believe in a lot of mushy patriotic bullshit, waving the flag and all that. But I'm still an American.

I was born and raised in Elsa, Texas, seventeen miles from the Mexican border. I was one of ten kids. That was a typical Mexican family. All the Mexican-American families lived on one side of

Ramon Reyes

the railroad tracks, and the whites lived on the other side. The town was only about 10 percent white, but the whites had all the good jobs. The Mexicans worked in the fields. The discrimination was disgusting. If you were white, you had it made. If you were Mexican, you had to struggle like a son of a bitch to make it.

In 1969 we had a little revolution in the town. I was in high school and took part in it. We followed the same steps as blacks were taking and wound up with a little bit of liberation.

These days all the whites are gone, and the area is controlled by Mexicans. Because all the middle-class white folks have fled, it is one of the poorest areas in the country. When I go back home, it makes me sick to see all the ghettos.

My dad worked in the oil fields, about seventy miles away. He'd come home sometimes during the weekends and sometimes on a Wednesday. He made $175 a week, which was good money back then, but it wasn't enough to support us all.

From the time I was 12 until I was 18, my mother and I and all my brothers were migrant workers every summer. In April and May we hoed beets in Idaho. In June we came to Michigan to pick cherries. In July we picked cucumbers around Alma, Michigan.

Then we went to Defiance, Ohio, and picked tomatoes until October, and then we went back to Texas and started school late.

The money we earned as migrants was the extra money we needed for clothes and for college. We all chipped in. All of us graduated from high school, and four of us graduated from college. That was a great accomplishment.

I was a biology freak when I was a kid, and I went to college to be a marine biologist. But I didn't finish. I had always thought I would be a professional person. I never dreamed there was anything like assembly-line work. But I wound up with this job, and now here I am on the line, getting called names by some redneck foremen and my fellow workers.

I got the shaft at the truck plant a long time ago, not because I was a Mexican but because I just didn't give a damn. The more you go against the company, the harder they try to break you. They send you from one hard job to another.

The first few days I worked at the truck plant I was living in terror. They put me on the fan job in the Engine Line. I was trying my hardest because I really wanted to make it. It was a matter of pride. I had a brother working there, and if I quit, it would be embarrassing to him. I thought: He made it, and so should I.

I had come to Detroit on a vacation. My plan was to go up North and work in a factory, come back to Texas, buy a new car, and go back to college. But at the truck plant I made over $250 a week. Back home you were doing great if you made $100 a week. I figured that even if I graduated from college, I'd never make as much money as I was making at the plant. So I stayed, and I've regretted it ever since.

I have two kids now who are in grade school, and I'm already scared for them the way the job market is going. I want them to go to college, and I am going to be on them 100 percent. My biggest fear is that they might turn out to be like me. I was careless about school and never tried my hardest. I don't want them to spin their wheels like I did and repeat my mistakes. My biggest mistake was ending up at Ford Motor Company.

The assembly line is very damaging to your self-esteem. You work hard and build a lot of trucks, and that accomplishes something; but you don't ever learn how to do anything else. You stay and stay, forever and ever.

I stayed on the Engine Line about six years. My job was to put pressure on the fan belt, tighten it up, pull on the alternator, and tighten that up. Doing that enormous amount of pulling for six years eventually got to my elbow, and I pulled a muscle in it. I filed for workmen's comp, and they put me through hell. They tried to fire me. They gave me time off. Eventually they sent me to the Sealer Deck, but I didn't like it there at all. I was getting terrible headaches from the paint. So I got transferred to the Body Shop. They gave me a job where nobody bothered me. I went to work every day, and they finally figured out I was a damn good worker if they left me alone.

But after a while they put me on a job nobody wanted: the bracket job. You climbed on top of the Bronco, got inside the truck, and bent down to put insulation brackets on the side; then you'd climb out. In and out, in and out, all day long.

Eventually my back couldn't handle it. They ruined my back so bad I couldn't even walk, and I wound up with about two years off from work on medical, unpaid. I only made it because I was single then and didn't need much to live on. But I felt like I was dead for two years. Two good years were wasted, and that hurt my pride. It made me a little smarter, though. I found out they were trying to eliminate people who were on medical too long. So I decided to go back to work and bear the pain.

I worked my back into health gradually, through sheer determination. The more I worked, the better it felt. Now I don't have any back problems. The last three years I haven't missed a day. I even got a $500 award for perfect attendance.

The job I do now is reinforcing the rear end of the Bronco roof with about forty spot welds. Soon they're going to use a robot to put in the welds, and we'll be gone. I feel like I'm working to destroy myself. I'm a hell of a good worker; but the harder I work, the more I accomplish, the more profits they make, and they use those profits to buy robots to clear me out.

There's no protest against the robots coming in. When I was younger, I didn't care about keeping my job, and I was radical. That fighting spirit is not there anymore. Everybody who works with me now is about 35. We all have fifteen years in, and we're damned scared. You're afraid to say anything because you might wind up in the street and you've just blown away fifteen years of your life.

I don't have any plans for finding a job someplace else. Ford Motor Company is going to be it. If I'm eliminated from Ford, I don't know what I'll do. Maybe I'll start a group and buy weapons. That's the only thing left.

I think there's going to be a revolution in this country. That's the only thing that is going to stop all this bullshit, stop them from putting so much pressure on people to do slave-type work. This country is going to collapse, just like Chile and Peru and other South American countries that were too dependent on one industry and had too much world competition and all of a sudden the people just wound up on the streets.

The auto companies aren't going to take care of the workers here. That's a joke. Let's see in a few years what happens to Pontiac when General Motors moves everything out. It's going to be a disaster area. That's just what will happen at Ford, too. Eventually they are going to automate everything and get rid of everybody. We're the last people they will let retire from the plants. We're the end of the road. They'll string us along, and then they'll hang us. The company will offer people a little more than the union has to offer, and then they'll get rid of the union. When that happens, we'll be in deep trouble because we'll have to work thirty-five or forty years to get retirement.

I'd get the hell out of the plant now if I didn't know I could retire after thirty years. Retirement, medical benefits, and protection if you get in trouble are the biggest benefits of having a union.

The union has its hands tied in a way during this modernization process. But they also believe this bullshit that Ford is going to take care of the workers, or at least the union.

The company came out with this EI bullshit. That's where they give the worker a lot of rope and he eventually hangs himself. Most people help because they don't think about the future. They think: I got fifteen years in; Ford Motor Company is going to take care of me. That's ridiculous.

I do attend the EI meetings because they pay you for an extra thirty minutes if you go. But in our EI group we don't discuss the plant. We talk about what's going on in the world. I only had to make my point one time at the meetings. We were discussing the little things that we could do to improve our jobs, and I said, "We are going to be eliminated completely. Why in the hell should we help them eliminate jobs. Are we crazy?"

But people are competing for some sort of glory. If something goes wrong in your area, the check and adjust person asks you how to fix it. You give him the information without thinking about it. The guy takes the information and comes up with some way to make everything run more smoothly. He's not thinking about the consequences; he just thinks his idea will put him on a pedestal and maybe get him promoted. He gives the information to the supervisor, the supervisor makes the adjustment, and the line runs a little smoother.

When you have a lot of little problems being solved every day like that by these people, what's the result? They run the line faster. The line has speeded up since EI was instituted from forty-one units an hour to forty-nine units. And we're doing the same amount of work on each unit as we did then. That's eight free jobs for the company. That's disgusting.

There used to be a lot of drugs and alcohol at the plant. There were so many bottles in the parking lot you couldn't drive. Everybody would go out on their break and sit around and drink. You don't see that anymore. I used to drink a lot, but now if somebody offers me a beer, I tell them I came to work, not drink.

People who were hired a long time ago and got laid off are begging to come back. And if they get rehired, they know they have to behave or they'll be out of a job. They screen out anybody who's not responsible. They don't want people anymore who work a couple days and then take three or four days off, like I used to do.

Drugs and alcohol aren't completely gone, but the people who do them are fading away. Soon there will be so few people left that it will be easy for the company to monitor their behavior.

They always tell us we have to become more efficient because we're competing with the Japanese. But I don't know anything about Japanese autoworkers. Maybe they're slaves. Maybe they don't get paid enough. Maybe they're constantly threatened with being downgraded to a much poorer job if they cause any problems.

I wish the Japanese companies that are coming here would just go to hell. They're using our labor, our tax breaks, our money to build plants, and they're just going to rake in the money. It's the same thing American companies have done to them for years, and the Japanese have done to all the South American countries. Now they are going to do it to us.

The Japanese are like a cancer. They control the whole industry. The government should kick them out. U.S. auto companies are making a big mistake by joining them. They're going to control everything from Japan, just like the auto companies here used to control everything from Detroit. And do you think they give a

damn about what happens in the United States, a country that
dropped the atomic bomb on them in 1945?

I trust Ford Motor Company a little bit more than the Japanese.
At least they'll give me a retirement. The Japanese might give you
a rope.

But our companies are screwing other countries up, too. U.S.
auto companies are building plants in Mexico, and not just for
cheap labor. They're going from an extreme amount of government regulations here to absolutely no restrictions in Mexico.
There they can dump all kinds of chemicals in the river, and
nobody gives a damn. In Mexico a plant comes in, and people see
only good-paying jobs, which for them is about 90 cents an hour.
They don't see what we have here, like what happened to the
Rouge River and the Detroit River. In Mexico people are used to
drinking water right out of the rivers and lakes. If they continue
to bring in factories there without regulations, they'll regret it.

If I were Owen Bieber, I'd call for international strikes. I'd say,
"Stop the country for a while. You're going too fast. Let's slow
down and reorganize." The United States is not prepared for
what's coming. They are making this big change, closing all the
big factories, and it's happening too fast. It's going to be disas-
trous, not just for the autoworker but for the whole country.

The company thinks the UAW got too powerful, so they want
to stop the unions and make everything just like it is in Japan. But
look at why Japan is so successful. They don't have any union.
They don't care about their sewage. The rivers are polluted. People live in cardboard boxes. How can you go to that from what we
have had here? For a long time in this country almost everybody
had a home and a job somewhere. Now people are on the streets. I
hope somebody will wake up soon and realize what's happening.

My family is prepared because I've saved up. The house was
paid off a long time ago. I don't owe any bills. I could still go out
and do a little hustling if I have to. But I'm worried about the
neighborhood. I may have it made, but other people who don't
have it made and don't care are going to rip me off. I can't go to
work without feeling scared someone will break in while I'm
gone. I got ripped off recently and lost my $800 microwave and
my stereo. Now I have bars on my house. Sooner or later crime
will destroy me.

There are only a few middle-class people left in my neighborhood. The rest are on welfare. The middle class is dying. Pretty soon it's just going to be the rich and the poor, and it'll be like Mexico and South America, where it's a constant war between the rich and the poor.

I consider myself middle-class. I made about $36,000 last year. As long as I make $30,000 or so, I can afford to hire people to do work around the house and keep the economy going. For instance, I paid a guy $1,600 to put in windows in my house.

People like me who can afford to pay other people to keep the economy going are going to be chopped off pretty soon. And when we fade away, the whole system will fall. The middle-class people are the ones who keep the economy going, who buy the cars and the consumer goods. If everybody is on welfare, how fast and how far do you think this country will go down?

If a man doesn't have a buck to spend, it weakens the country. Things are deteriorating. Unless they can get some more jobs in this city, kids are going to continue to make money the only way they can, by selling drugs and stealing. Pretty soon everybody will be out of a job and walking around like a bum. All the stores will be closed, and my neighborhood will look like a ghost town. Eventually people are going to pick up a rifle and say to hell with it.

Vic Wilkins

Born February 13, 1947, in Inkster, Michigan
Hired December 9, 1971
Operates a computer that monitors stock

WHAT GOES ON IN THE PLANT is completely different from fifteen years ago. The union is just a policeman for the company now. If the UAW wasn't there, the people would organize themselves. It's a big reversal from how it used to be.

Fifteen years ago, when I was a union committeeman, I'd raise hell to help any guy on the line who was having any type of problem. I'd negotiate to get a guy a lousy fifteen minutes of pay that he had been docked because it was a matter of principle. The money wasn't important, but I had to show the boss the guy was right. If I saw I wasn't getting anywhere in the negotiations, I would pick up a chair and throw it at the company's Labor Relations reps and tell them I wanted that time and I was going to get it. It was just a tactic, a setup we had. I would storm out of the office, and my partner would go in and say quietly, "You got him really mad; he really wants that fifteen minutes." He would play the good cop like I played the bad cop.

Now that kind of behavior would be absurd. Nobody would even think of doing anything like that. Now the committeemen write ten grievances and give up on nine of them to win one, and

Vic Wilkins

that one will be for a friend. The man paying his union dues is getting nothing.

The company created this EI program to get in the middle of what the union is supposed to be responsible for. It was a brilliant idea. The same shit happens in the army. You take a know-nothing private and tell him he's in charge, and that son of a bitch will do everything in his power to get his fellow soldiers to do whatever the sergeant wants. That's exactly what they've done here. They give these morons a job as an EI leader, and guys with twenty-five, thirty years' seniority are eating that shit up.

These EI guys once told me that the company took them on a tour of another plant where they have a salad bar in the cafeteria, and they said, "We're going to fight to get a salad bar here." A salad bar! So the company says, "Sure, give them a salad bar," and these guys are running around like peacocks, their feathers sticking way out, because they think they've accomplished something. They got a salad bar. And they think: The company's listening to us, and the union didn't get it for us. And I'm sitting there thinking: You dumb bastards.

Harry Bennett told old Henry Ford fifty years ago, "Give those bastards what they want." Bennett argued that if Ford gave the workers what they wanted, they could make the union dependent on the company. But Ford was hardheaded and wouldn't do it at first. Now, fifty years later, they're following Bennett's plan: "Give them what they want." But I'm not getting what I want. When's the last time we got a pay raise?

Profit sharing sucks. They give you a check and say, "OK, Vic, you worked hard, and you contributed to the cause, so we're going to give you $2,000." Now, wait a minute. I was part of that process; all the guys were. We built those trucks, and there's a profit, sure enough. But you can take your profit sharing and stick it up your ass. Give me a 9 percent raise spread over three years instead. A pay raise connects to my sense of self-worth. I've made a deal with the devil to come in here and sell my labor to you. You're going to pay me for my labor because you're going to kill me in the long run anyway.

The audacity of the UAW to go along with profit sharing is disgusting. Now you no longer can go in there and negotiate with your fists, like I used to. And in the long run the company is getting everything they want. That little bit of money they give you, you would have gotten anyway with a raise, and you would have kept your self-esteem, instead of this peacock-feather stuff they're selling about "I'm a Ford employee." That's what they want you to think. They're blowing smoke up your ass, and you're falling for it.

People fall for it because they can say, "We're part of the company." So now, if a guy takes a day off, it doesn't matter if he broke his arm, hey, he's messing with my profit sharing. That's the company's money he's taking away, and the company's money is my money. It's no longer them versus us; it's we.

I don't know where the hell American workers are at these days. People are working twelve hours a day because it's cheaper for Ford to work two shifts twelve hours a day than to put on a third shift. They do not feel any sense of responsibility to mankind, to the people who have been laid off. It's money, and that's all anyone gives a damn about.

The younger employees, people who have less than ten years in, are so afraid they're going to lose their jobs, they go along with anything. There have been no new people hired since 1980. The hammer's over their head. They know if they don't come to work and perform, they're out. So they're like cattle. They won't fight for their rights. They don't even question things or put up any resistance. They're like I was when I went to Vietnam.

Even some of the older employees, guys with forty years in, are in debt to the company. They have not prepared for anything else. They will die in these plants. And when they die, they will not be replaced. The job is eliminated, and they double another guy's work. The people who are left work their ass off day in and day out and don't complain because they need and want that job. Sure, it's a legitimate fear. We all need work to survive. But they're so afraid to say anything about the extra work being put on them that they work at an incredible pace.

There are some guys who can work at that pace only by drinking a fifth of liquor or taking some other drugs. I'd say a lot of the people in the plant are alcoholics and drug addicts. We have coke dealers walking up and down the line. It's worse now than it was fifteen years ago, when getting high was the thing to do. Back then people were just doing it to screw up. Now they're hooked.

There's a guy in the plant who came to this country as a refugee when he was a kid. He's not young anymore, and he is supporting his wife, his children, his cousins, and all his relatives. He's doing coke every day just to keep working these ridiculous hours at this ridiculous pace. He's half out of his mind. He's really a very intelligent man; but he's screwed up, and nobody knows it.

I remember years ago there was a guy on the line who was into sabotaging the cars. Now there's none of that. I don't know whether it's because the work force is getting older, but they've definitely become more conscious of what they're doing.

There's no room in the plant anymore for people who don't go along with the program. In ten years guys with my attitude will be phased out.

My mother and father are from Dunklin County, in the Missouri bootheel. Nothing's there except some poor people scraping the dirt. People talk about all the prejudice in the South, but our area was different. We were all different colors down there.

I am the eighth of nine children. My father was a sharecropper on the cotton farms, and my mother is the daughter of a sharecropper. They never had a pot to piss in or a window to throw it out of.

During World War II my folks moved to Michigan because there was plenty of work in the auto factories doing war production. My dad worked awhile for Ford at the Willow Run Bomber Plant, but he quit, probably because he was a farmer and couldn't stand working inside. He got a job in the Detroit Harbors, the boatyards.

The house we lived in had no plumbing and one light bulb. My mom and dad paid $800 for it when they moved here.

My dad had a heart attack at the boatyards and died on Christmas Eve in 1948, a month before my younger brother was born. My mom was left with nine kids to take care of. So she took the only skills she had, taking care of kids and cooking, and got a job at the Board of Education as a baker's assistant. After thirty years she was head cook.

She worked very hard. She was always too proud to take General Assistance. She was paid $40 every two weeks, and she had to save very hard because there was no job for her at the schools during summer vacation. In the summer Mom did laundry for other people. We planted a garden in the yard, and that's how we survived. But I never thought of us as poor back then.

I look back now and try to figure out how Mom did it. She is 75 now and has rheumatoid arthritis from her spine to her ankles. She is bowed and crippled, but she gets around better than I do. Her spirit is unbelievable. She is like a rock. When my nephew died recently at age 35, it must have hit her hard, but she just said, "Just because somebody lays down and dies doesn't mean we have to."

I was raised in the suburb of Inkster, which is predominantly black. It's where Henry Ford put the black workers he brought up from the South to work in the Rouge Plant. He set up a store and gave the women sewing machines and gave the men five dollars a day. He put the whites in Dearborn.

There were three white families on our block, and none of us had anything. I remember brand-new homes being built across the street and black folks moving in. They're just little cracker boxes, but when I was a kid, they seemed like really nice homes. Those folks had everything. The most important thing they had, to me, was fathers who could work and provide.

I started working when I was 10. I worked for a black man who owned a gas station about five blocks from my house. I hung out there every day, and finally he hired me and paid me five bucks a week. I learned how to change tires and pump gas and do oil changes, and eventually I learned tune-ups and changing clutches and rebuilding transmissions. I would come by every day after school until I was 15.

I thought the owner was a genius. I was impressed by all the things he could do. He was a hustler. He had the gas station; he painted cars; he did anything with cars you could think of. He also played the harmonica, and I used to go down to this night-club in Detroit and watch him perform. I was the only white person in the place, but I was never afraid. I had never experienced racial fear in my life. I had always been accepted.

At 15, I was still working for $5 a week. By then I was doing everything on the cars. So I got my guts up and asked for a raise. And he told me, "You're too big for me to take care of now. Go find yourself a job that's going to pay you $40 a week."

I didn't like school. I'd fight with the teachers and skip class. I felt trapped. I wanted to be out in the world. It was boring sitting in a classroom when I'd been working since I was 10. I couldn't relate to any of the kids. I never played any sports.

I never committed any crimes, but I was a troublemaker. The big thing was drinking and hanging out on the streets until mid-night, just playing kick the can. You'd go down to the park with a jug of Mogen David, drink that till you got drunk, blow your groceries all over the place, and then at 11:00 try to find your way back home.

We'd get into a lot of fights. I'd always take on the toughest guy in the neighborhood, and every time he'd make mincemeat out of me. But he became my buddy. Kids from southwest Detroit would drive out to fight us. We had rumbles down in the park, but they were more like running for your life than anything else. We didn't have any malice. We never even thought of killing anybody, like these kids today. All we did was stand on the corner shucking and jiving.

When I was 16, I was stupid and naïve. Most of my friends had probably been with everybody, but I had never even kissed a girl. Then I met a girl who worked in a restaurant. She was 19. One thing led to another, and I got her pregnant. So at 16, I was a father. Now, I was raised that you make your bed, you lie in it, and it's your responsibility.

The child was born deaf. I felt a lot of guilt because I had created an imperfect child.

I had to have some money, and I wasn't a crook, so I went to the

Pepsi-Cola bottling plant and lied. I told them I was 17. I got a job and worked there for four years. I made good money on that job, $250 a week, but I never had any because at the end of every week I would give my paycheck to the mother of my child.

I was still living at my mother's house, and every day I'd walk to work and drive the Pepsi trucks all day long. At 4:00, I'd be done, and I'd walk down the railroad tracks to Pioneer Detroit, which was a metal fabricating shop. And I'd work in there until midnight, go home, sleep, and start all over again. I did that for two years and never kept a penny.

What a jerk I was. Here was my mother, who gave so much to me, and I could have helped her out, but I wasn't even thinking about her. I was so full of guilt, so sinful, for getting this girl pregnant. And I figured since I was getting laid, that had to be love. It wasn't, it was just sex, but I was too dumb to know it.

I figured we had better get married. So her mother and father drove her to the federal courthouse in Detroit, and I took a bus from Inkster and met them. We got married; they left; I got back on the bus and went back home. We didn't even start living together.

My mother kept harping on me, saying I was a damn fool, but she never would tell me what to do. Finally I started putting two and two together. I realized I was the one making the money, and I didn't even have a shirt to wear. My girl was running around in a brand-new car and living with her family in Taylor, which in my mind was where all the rich people lived. I mean, compared with my house, if you had carpet and paint on the walls, I was impressed. And I realized my mother was still feeding me and I was doing nothing to help her. It wasn't right. It was time to go. So we found a place of our own. I ended up living with her for less than three years, and we had three children. Legally I was married to her for seven years.

During our marriage my mind started opening up too much. At first I figured I was entitled to things because I worked hard, and soon I figured I was entitled to a lot more. I had always liked to drink because I always liked to bullshit. Drinking was a good time, and I thought I was entitled to one.

I didn't have a car, but one of the first things I bought myself was a motorcycle, an old Harley-Davidson. I was always a good mechanic, so people had me work on their bikes. I started running with a bike club. It was a lot of fun. It was just like when I was a kid, out there on the street shucking and jiving. I didn't think of

hurting anybody. But I found out these guys were serious criminals. They would shoot you in a minute. So I broke away from
them, and my brother and I started our own club, the Scorpions.

The best part of the club was the sense of accomplishment I had
in organizing something. I had finally done something. It wasn't
much, and I regret doing it to this day; but I did it.

Time really started flying for me. That's when LSD was on the
streets, and a lot of chemicals, too. I was introduced to some
freaks in Ann Arbor, and there was also this little San Francisco
scene in Detroit, on Plum Street, with leather shops and candle
shops and flipped-out people running around. That was open
game for us. We'd go down there or to Ann Arbor and sell these
kids acid. I would take it with them and get all wigged out, even
though I was still working for Pepsi-Cola.

I was 21, and the marriage wasn't any good. I didn't even
consider myself married, really; I didn't know what an adult
relationship was. Every night I would sit around smoking dope
and drinking beer and screwing around with somebody's woman.
I had never got to do it before, so I was making up for lost
time.

One day in 1968 we were sitting at a house in Dearborn. Some
members of our gang busted in the door, and somebody pulled a
gun on me. I went out the door to avenge my friends. I walked
down the street in a drunken haze, and all I remember is somebody cracked me across my head. When I woke up, the police had
me handcuffed to the bumper of a car. They told me not to move
and whacked me a couple more times across the head. I was
screaming, "I want my rights." I didn't know my friends had gone
into this house and beaten the shit out of everybody there. And I
was the only one at the scene of the crime. They had me.

They locked me up in jail and put a $50,000 bond on me. I lost
my job at Pepsi. I was charged with felonious assault with intent
to kill, which carries a penalty of two to five years. So I copped a
plea. I said, "I'll do anything to get out of this jail." I agreed to go
into the service under a program they had then. So they carried
me over to the recruiter's office, and I signed up. I was so out of it I
didn't even know about Vietnam.

I was 22, an old man, when I went to Vietnam. I had a twelve-
month tour in 1969 and 1970. When I went there, I thought: This
is my hour of redemption. If I can make good here, I've cleared

any wrong I've done. Maybe I can get my record clean and make my marriage work. I really believed that. I was really naïve.

I was a combat soldier. I didn't finish my tour because I was shot. I went back to Fort Hood, Texas, for rehabilitation and learned how to walk with pins in my leg. While I was there, I got a Dear John letter from my wife. My mind snapped. I had an urge to kill her.

Most guys reenlisted to get out of the line of fire, so they could take the truck-driving jobs or whatever. I went back and reenlisted as a combat soldier just so I could get thirty days' leave of absence. When they gave it to me, I called my wife and told her I was coming home, but she said she had plans to go to Tennessee with her father. I said I'd wait for her.

I was put on a plane, and when I got into Metro Airport in Detroit, somebody spit in my face because I had my uniform on. I took a cab to my mother's house. I sat there in silence for two days, waiting. After two days my wife pulled up, with the children in the car, and without asking any questions, I yanked her out of the car and beat the shit out of her. My mother called the police on me. They in turn called the military police, and they came out and busted me.

I didn't even get my thirty days off. I went right back in the army and just kept volunteering. I never paid any attention to what I was doing. I became a paratrooper. To me it was just another job. I did my job.

I realized later, after I joined the Vietnam Veterans Against the War, that I was part of the problem. I had volunteered for everything without questioning anything. I did a job against people who didn't have a chance against our weaponry. They were fighting a civil war, but I didn't understand that. I did a lot of damage to a lot of people. I and thousands of others just destroyed that country. Had our Congress ever declared war, we could have annihilated that place in a few hours. But thanks to the rest of the world, there was some sanity, and the Vietnamese people eventually gained their freedom.

I was released December 24, 1970, twenty-five years to the day after my dad died. Nobody was at the airport to greet me when I got home. I was by myself again on Christmas Eve. I went to my wife and apologized. I lied and said I didn't know why I had beaten her up. I had a lot of anger in me, and I didn't even know where it was coming from. I took it out on a lot of people for a long time. It's taken fifteen years of therapy for me to understand it.

A year after I was released, I was still involved in the marriage. I was a diehard. I felt the responsibility was mine and I had to make it work.

I got a job shortly after I got out of the service for the C & O Railroad as a clerk. I checked the fuel in the refrigeration cars that came over to the Dearborn yards near the Rouge Plant. I did that for a year and was making no money at all. Meanwhile, my marriage was going down the tubes. So I said, "This is nuts," and I got a job at Ford. I was put on the afternoon shift.

I saw right away that the truck plant was run like the military. There was a chain of command right down to the line foreman, who was just a guy like you who's never going to go anyplace but who had an attitude that he was better than everyone else. I figured, what the heck, I could survive in that. I had survived a lot worse.

I worked at the truck plant for ten years, on the line and in the Material Handling Department. Back then it was hip to smoke joints and get screwed up at work, and I was one of the highest dudes in the plant.

I already knew a little about how to organize people because of my involvement in the Vietnam Veterans Against the War. I was open to the world of plant politics. I knew what unions were because when I worked for Pepsi-Cola, there was the Teamsters and the awesome figure of Jimmy Hoffa. So I saw these guys running around claiming to be fighting for the workers, and it was just a popularity contest to see who could run their mouth the fastest. I figured I could shuck and jive with the best of them. So I ran and became a committeeman and later a bargaining committeeman.

I eventually quit union politics because there was a big guy in the union who I considered to be a gangster. He was no more a union man than Roger Smith, the GM boss. He was there solely to benefit himself and for what he could steal. He was very corrupt. He had a network of thieves. And he could blow you away if he wanted. I was afraid of that son of a bitch, but I was bound and determined not to let him mess with me or anybody around me because I believed in the principle of what we were doing. I figured I would die for the cause if I had to.

See, I always believed, and still do, that we are a very wealthy country and that there's enough to spread around so that we could all live well. We wouldn't all be millionaires, but everybody could be productive. There are things like health care, education, and jobs that we should automatically have, but we don't because the dollar runs everything.

I believed if I got involved, at least I could help protect what somebody had fought for. I am a fighter. But I didn't know that dirty little game of politics. The bastards involved in it can eat you alive. I was so goddamn naïve. I thought the union was committed to principles. But they aren't at all. Eventually I quit, because I figured this gangster would either have killed me or killed some of the other guys if I kept fighting him.

In 1980, when the recession hit, I was one of the first people to be kicked out of the truck plant and sent over to the car plant. There's no doubt in my mind they wanted to get rid of me, but I didn't even question it. I wanted to get the hell out of the truck plant because of all the everyday hassles I was getting, a lot of them from the union. People who I once thought were my closest friends turned out to be the ones who had been stabbing me in the back all along.

I was put to work in the Body Shop at Wayne Assembly. The people on the line there resented me for taking one of their fellow workers' jobs. They treated me like I was the enemy. I thought: Christ, I've given six years to this union, organizing all this stuff, and for what?

One time this woman really got in my face and told me I was a no-good motherfucker for stealing a job. In defense of myself, I told her, "I work for Ford Motor Company. I don't work for any particular plant. It's a vast empire." When I said that, something went off in my head, and some of the stuff I used to preach, that we are all one, really hit me. I realized that none of us knows how vulnerable we really are. You're nothing at Ford. There's no such thing as job security.

Because of my Vietnam injuries, I'm limited to certain movements. I told them at the car plant that I couldn't do the job they wanted me to, and they said, "If you can't do it, hit the road." So I marched up to Labor Relations and threw a fit.

There was a general foreman in there who got a little close to me and put his hand on my chest and started shoving me. I grabbed him by his shirt and slammed him up against the wall. I said, "Don't touch me. Don't even think about it." The veins were popping out of my neck, and I said, "Nobody in this fucking

place is going to touch me." I felt like I had entered a new penitentiary and I was declaring my turf.

My display of anger worked. The next thing I knew I was being
driven in a cart over to the Trim Department. They put me on a
job building up the instrument panels. I had to pick out the
dashboards with the various options—air conditioning, colors,
tape decks, digital clocks. I had to read a computer printout, make
the selection, and pick up the right dashboard.

There were six people on that job, two on days and two on
nights plus relief men. Within six months after I started, they
brought in something that looked like a sophisticated crane that
runs on tracks. It was a robot with an arm. I was told it cost four
million dollars. It had photo sensors to distinguish the colors, and
it was controlled by a keyboard that programmed it to make
certain moves. That eliminated all our jobs. As they installed this
creature, I asked the technicians how it operated, and they
showed me. It was easy.

I didn't know at the time that they were putting it there on a
trial basis. They were recording everything and reporting whatever went wrong. One day the thing broke down, and I went over
to the keyboard and made a few moves on there and got it operating. Someone saw me doing it, and I figured I was in trouble again.
But they ended up giving me the job of baby-sitting the machine.
If it broke down, I had to fix it. I no longer had to do any manual
work. I thought that was cool.

After about a month I was told after my shift ended to clean up,
and they gave me a pair of coveralls that said "UAW" on one side
and "Ford Motor Company" on the other. I saw the plant manager
coming around the corner with this big group of people, including
this little guy with red hair. I knew he was somebody because of
the kind of clothes he had on. He came up to me and asked me
who I was and what I did. He was very nice. He asked me what the
robot did, and I explained it to him. He said, "What do you think
of it?"

I said, "It's quite a piece of machinery, but it's eliminating a
bunch of jobs here."

Then I was cut right off. An engineer stepped in and started
talking, and I was backed out of the way. The following week
there was a $50 bonus in my paycheck and a thank-you from
Harold Poling.

*   *   *

A few months after that the damn robot put me out of work. I went into the hospital for an operation on my foot. I was out less than thirty days. When I came back, I was told the robot didn't need me anymore. A programmer had set it up so it didn't need to be watched. They told me to go back to the Body Shop. I said I couldn't do that work.

When I got hired at the truck plant in 1971, there were two hundred people a day standing out there to get a job. The physical was: Drop your drawers, cough, take your temperature and blood pressure, and that was it. As long as you could crawl or get to that job somehow, they didn't care. It didn't matter to them then that I have pins that run from my hip to my knee and from my knee to my ankle, and I have no muscle control under my left knee. Any continuous bending or stretching of the left side, and it goes out on me.

But now suddenly they said they didn't have any record of my disabilities. So I got a big file from the VA hospital and showed them. I was told they no longer had any work within my restrictions and they were placing me on medical layoff. I figured: OK, I'll collect my couple of hundred bucks a week; I don't care. But after I had been off almost ten months, they told me to file for Social Security. I was 35, and I'm thinking: Wait a minute, these guys are blowing me right out the door. When I filed my Social Security papers and found out I would end up with a couple hundred bucks a month, I said to myself, "That's ridiculous. I can't afford to live on that."

The union should have stepped in and helped me. After all, I was a qualified hi-lo driver at the truck plant. I had worked plenty of jobs there. But everybody turned their heads. I went to the local, then to the regional, then the international, and all of them said take the retirement. I said, "Take the retirement, are you crazy? A few hundred dollars a month, what am I going to do with that? I still have kids in school."

So I went to my congressman's office. They said they would help me, and they steered me back to the VA. The VA told me there was nothing they could do because it was a labor problem. It was a vicious circle, everybody passing the buck. I went back to the VA again and got nowhere, but as I was coming out, I saw the federal courthouse across the street, and I decided I'd go in there and talk to somebody from the U.S. Labor Department.

I ended up talking to someone from the Veterans Affairs Office who told me that a law had been passed in 1971 giving disabled Vietnam vets the right to rehabilitation and priority in job placement. So I filed a complaint, and soon after that they sent a telegram to the Labor Relations office at Wayne Assembly. Labor Relations called me up right away and told me they didn't think I had gotten a fair shake when I had come home from the war and that they were willing to try to place me.

The next day I got a letter from the Veterans Affairs office stating that if Ford didn't put me to work, they were going to be fined $1,000 a day for every day I hadn't worked and every day I remained out of work. They also said they wanted to examine all the veterans in the plant, and after that all the black employees and then all the female employees, and that they could tie them up for years.

So I reported back to work, and the company reps said, "We don't think you got a fair shake."

I thought: You bullshitters.

There were union reps telling me, "We fought for you, Vic, and got this."

I said, "No, you didn't, you lying bastards. You were told I had to be placed, and now you're scrambling to see what you can do."

Everybody was patting me on the back, saying, "We didn't know, we didn't know."

I said, "You didn't bother to ask, and besides, I had eleven or twelve years' seniority. You could have given me a job doing something."

They put me on this job operating a computer keyboard. They were patting me on the back, but they were thinking: Old dumbass Vic, if he can't handle these computers, well, too bad; we tried. Well, I managed to succeed with my one-cylinder brain, quite to their amazement and my own.

Like everyone else, I was intimidated by the computer at first. Most people just sit in front of that keyboard and freeze up. But I was amazed at my memory retention. That's all you need to do the job.

I was trained at Ford World Headquarters on a new program to computerize the material handling system. It's a job that the UAW negotiated for hourly people to do twelve years ago, when they realized computers were coming. I do what a whole lot of people used to do manually. I input information into the computer for the Material Handling Department, which brings in parts from all over the world and gets them to the jobs in the plant. My job is accounting for the parts. Once I enter in the data, anyone can go to a terminal anywhere in the plant and track down the parts.

It's a great system, but what about all those people my job has put out of work? They were salaried people, but they are still human beings. It's ridiculous. Five years ago there were hundreds of clerical people in the front office. Now it's like a ghost town, these vast offices sitting empty.

I'm caught between a rock and a hard place with this job. I argue against taking people's jobs, but that's what I'm doing. I'm working so much overtime that last year I made $52,000, and I'm one of the low-paid ones. It's disgusting.

I have no set hours. I go in when I'm needed and leave when the job is done. I've always been conscientious about my work, and I've gotten caught up in this job. I work twelve to fourteen hours a day. I come in on Sunday afternoons sometimes to make sure the paperwork is done. If the data isn't entered, the workers, the foremen, and the vendors can't get to it and can't do their job.

I've been doing the job over three years now, and the challenge has worn off. It's tedious, it's repetitious, and I could train a monkey to do it. The only difference from other jobs at the plant is that there's no physical labor.

I have learned a lot about parts. When the Escort was first introduced, Ford's PR people called it the world car. It's a world car all right because the parts come from all over the world. It's just assembled in the United States. The whole front-end technology comes from Japan. The wiring looms were shipped out from California to Mexico about four years ago, and it's all junk now. What do you expect? The workers down there get a buck and a half an hour. They get parts from Brazil and even Argentina. "Buy American" is a joke. These vehicles aren't American.

A lot of the white guys in the plant feel like they're being screwed. You could have twenty-three years in, and they could kick you out of your job and put a woman in. Here's a poor bastard who has given twenty-three years of his life, and because he's a white man, he gets booted, so he thinks there is no justice. On the other hand, we haven't created a society that is equal for everybody. Who pays the penalty? Not the hotshot honchos up where I work, but those poor slobs down on the line. They are always going to pay the price. That's the way it is. How do you change that?

The only reason women were hired is that they were forced to do it by law. They hired the women who had the biggest tits. That's literally how they did it. You had union guys who would look over the applicants, like at the meat market. There were a hundred and fifty people standing out there, and if they figured they could get laid, you got the job. I remember a woman who worked in the Trim Department at the truck plant. She told me that a committeeman laid her in the committee room as "payment" for hiring her.

I was always amazed at the attitude some guys had. One guy in the Trim Department, an old union instigator from way back, said, "Get these women out of here. Kick 'em in the cunt."

And I looked at him and said, "Why do you think they're here?"

And he mentioned the law.

And I said, "Well, the law may have helped somebody get a job, but these women in these plants have to take care of their children. They need the job just like you do." I related to that because of my mother having to provide for us.

Attitudes are the same now; there's just a new face on them. The blacks now express their needs more. I think it's ironic because I'm always the one telling some of these black guys, "Do what you got to do." But it's not that simple; there's that slave mentality. It blows my mind. I'm talking to a guy who's fifty years old, who's seen all this stuff go on in our society, but whatever it was in his life that beat him down is still operating, and he still has that fear. It's bred in there. And the racism is still out there in society and in the plant.

I have five children now, three from my first wife, and two after I remarried. My biggest concern is that they're living in a world where they are not going to make it. They're not like me. I'm a survivor. You could put me in the worst conditions, and I'd survive. But my children don't know how to survive.

My biggest fear for my children is that they will live the kind of life I had to lead as a kid, but they'll have to do it as adults. They won't have the chance to get ahead. I've worked since I was a kid. I didn't want my kids to have to do that.

As little as I had when they were young, I gave them everything. One of my sons is now working in a steel fabricating shop in North Carolina for seven bucks an hour. I guess that's good money down there. It's sad, but none of my kids will ever make what I'm making. The jobs aren't there, and the price of everything is so high that they don't have a snowball's chance in hell.

My one daughter is 23 and a waitress in Miami, in one of the worst parts of town. She's struggling. There's nothing wrong with waiting on tables, but they don't give you enough for your labor to survive on. If you get sick, you're in deep trouble.

My youngest daughter is working in western Michigan at a minimum-wage job. She has to drive fifty miles a day to get to it. The job doesn't pay her nearly enough for her insurance and gas. She's living in poverty, but she's too proud to ask for anything.

I want to leave my wife and children something to get them through the hard times if something happens to me. There's always going to be hard times. Life is nothing but a bitch and a struggle.

I saw something on TV recently about these guys in their 20s who are traders on Wall Street. They're multimillionaires driving Mercedes. Most of them are just crooks.

As part of the deal that they negotiated for my job, I got nine shares of Ford stock. But it's not my money. It really belongs to those crooks in New York. You'd be better off taking your weekly wages and saving your money your own way. People have done it for years. But now you have a guy on the line with no education and all of a sudden he has $1,200 worth of stock. He thinks he's got it made. Now he has a vested interest in the company, but he doesn't even know what the stock market is.

When people ask me how I'm doing, I say, "They're killing me." If they ask me what I mean, I tell them, "I'm in here every day of my life, I haven't had a raise in years, and this profit-sharing stuff is the biggest scam you've ever seen, pal. It's a way of ushering you right out the door."

The Social Security system is going to be broke when you retire. There will be nothing for you, pal. And you've paid in that money, every week, $40, $50. If you took that money and put it in the bank, by the time you had thirty years in, you'd have a bundle. But under Social Security, you might get a couple hundred bucks out after you've paid thousands and thousands of your own money into it.

We've created this mess, and there has to be a way of getting out of it. Why do you need a Mercedes-Benz to cruise around? Why do they pay a guy like Roger Smith millions of dollars every year? Look at the money Lee Iacocca's making. Nobody is worth that kind of money. What do you need to cover your ass? Some clothing, food, medical protection if you get sick. It doesn't take a million dollars to provide that, but if we keep escalating the price of everything, it will. The American dream is to have a new house in the suburbs, a couple of cars in the garage, to go on vacations, and have money in the bank. But that dream is getting out of reach for almost everybody.

Take a kid growing up in the inner city now. His biggest idol is the baddest dope dealer on the block. So he'll kill to get what he has. There's nothing wrong with working for something and getting it. But when the work isn't there and your dignity has been stripped away from you as a kid, the mentality is you're going to get it however you can.

We cannot go on this way in this country. The best thing that could happen would be an overthrow of this ridiculous government that we have. I mean that. You can isolate yourself from the rest of the world, but it's going to catch up to you.

Look at the farmers. The very essence of this country has been taken away from us. We have big agribusiness firms owned by foreigners. These are farms that have been in the hands of the same families for a hundred, two hundred years, and now they're gone.

They're going to keep this shit up until we have an entire nation of people on welfare. If society doesn't provide people with an education and some security, people are going to get fed up and say, "Enough is enough." And then there's going to be an armed confrontation, and God knows what will happen.

Berlin Scott

Born October 24, 1938, in Olive Branch, Illinois
Hired June 9, 1969
Painter

IT'S BEEN WORK, work, work ever since I've been at the truck plant. I was working hard when I started, but I'm doing almost twice as much work now.

When I get home, I don't want to talk about my job. I told my wife, "Don't ever ask me about the Michigan Truck Plant because when I leave there, I'm through." We hardly ever talk. She's a registered nurse and works at a hospital. When she gets off work, most days I'm already asleep. I'll go to bed at 6:00 and get up at 2:00 the next morning. I pick up my buddy and go back to the same thing again.

The police stopped me the other night about 3:00 in the morning because one of my headlights was out. They said, "Where are you heading this time of night?" I told them I was going to work.

"You're going to work this time of the morning?"

I said, "Hey, buddy, it may sound funny, but that's where I'm going. I got my lunch in the backseat." He looked at me like I was nuts.

On the line you never can do enough. You never get ahead. The first eight hours I'm OK. But after eight hours I start getting tired.

Berlin Scott

And four hours of work at the plant is about eight hours' worth of work on other jobs. A lot of guys take medical leaves to get out of there. They say their shoulder hurts—anything to get off the job.

Most of the people in the plant don't worry about anything except those big paychecks. As long as they make the money, they don't care how many hours they work. If you try to tell them it's not fair to work so much overtime when so many people have been laid off, they don't listen. When you start talking about cutting that money, they start drifting away from you.

These guys cry about how tired they are, but they'll work fifteen hours. I've seen some work eighteen hours. They don't have to stay there and work that long, so why are they bitching?

Every union election the people put the same guys back in there, and then they cry for three years. They don't really want to change. All they care about is keeping the ten hours going, five, six, seven days a week. That's the name of the game.

A lot of those guys are paying $600, $700, $800 in house payments. They got too far in debt. You can't have boats and cars and things like that without getting in debt. They're used to making that kind of money, but those sixty hours a week aren't going to last. We're working ourselves right out of a job. But nobody wants to admit it.

You have to be at the plant ten hours a day just to keep what you have. So what's the sense in accumulating stuff I can't enjoy? If I got a mobile home, it would just sit in my driveway six days a week. If I got a boat to water-ski, it would just sit all winter. If they cut the hours, it wouldn't bother me.

We should go down to eight hours, quit all that overtime business, quit having people jump around from job to job. The plant's so messed up I get mad when I start thinking about it.

To me, we don't have a union anymore. There is a lot of favoritism. Lots of committeemen sell out a lot of people. The union should get people back to work, just get a straight eight-hour base, try to slow down the line. But they don't have the power anymore.

I stay at the plant because of family and bills. But I'm seriously thinking about moving to California. I know I have to have security for my family, but I'm not going to die for my family. This job is getting to me. If I left, I'd be giving up my retirement, but it isn't going to do me any good anyway. If I stay there another thirteen or fourteen years, I'm going to be dead anyway.

The EI is what really messed things up. That was the worst thing that ever came through the plant. All that did was start eliminating jobs. I'm telling the company what you're doing and you're telling what I'm doing and how many hours you mess around on the job.

A lot of guys like it because you can walk around off the line for a couple hours. But those guys are making it harder for you. I can't get mad at a man if he walks off the floor for two hours, but don't go up to those meetings and make my job rougher. Leave my job alone.

In one of the EI safety sessions they told us to stop using the paint thinner for washing our hands. They told us it wasn't good for us, that it can mess up your liver. I've been washing my hands in thinner for seventeen years. You're telling me now this is bad for my health? I'm dead already; I don't need to see a doctor. When you work in the Paint Booth, you're right on top of each other. You paint the man next to you, and he paints you. How could that be a healthy environment?

Concern for quality? That's a big joke. At 5:30 A.M. the company will come up to us in the Paint Department and say, "They might close this plant if we don't put in a little more quality." Then, when the rest of the plant starts running and they need the trucks coming out of the Paint Department, they stop talking quality and start talking quantity. After 6 A.M. you don't stop the line; you let it run.

Someone in the booth told me he was taking a computer class. I said, "You don't need a computer class to paint trucks." These people don't see what's coming. They're having a great time. But the robots are coming. And when they do, they'll say, "You're just another tired ass, I'm through with you."

People think it can't happen in America, the land of plenty. They think they won't lose their jobs or worry about not making it. But we've been seeing it happen for the last ten years now. I remember how people used to say robots couldn't take their jobs, that no robot could open and close doors. But here are the robots. They're putting them in the Paint Department right now.

It's a hard thing for people to accept. This isn't Germany or Russia; it's America. Things like that aren't supposed to happen here. People don't go hungry. But you see it happening every day. People at the plant used to call some of us Communists for talking about what was going to happen. Now they can see what we were saying. The things we talked about years ago that they said would never happen are happening. Now they're working with their backs to the wall. Everybody is working scared.

The solutions will have to come from ordinary people getting together. We have to work it out among ourselves and quit pretending we're so ignorant. More than in any other generation, people know what's going on, but we're afraid to talk about it. We don't have the courage to say what needs to be said.

As a kid I was hotheaded. I grew up in East St. Louis, Illinois, which was a tough town. I was in a few gangs. I was kicked out of school and ended up in reform school, Illinois State Training School for Boys in St. Charles, outside Chicago. I was there fifteen months, and I fought so much that I stayed in a cell most of the time and wouldn't work. I have always been a rebel.

I had two brothers and two sisters. My dad was a car dealer. We weren't rich; but we always had enough to eat, and I never went ragged. My father and I had a good understanding. We could sit down and talk. He told me it doesn't matter what color a man is.

I've never been prejudiced. I don't look on you as white and me as black. It doesn't make any difference; if you're my friend, you're my friend. I had a lot of white friends when I was a kid, and I still do.

My dad used to tell me that the only way you can make a major change is to fight. If you aren't ready to die, don't mess with it. In order to get a victory, you have to shed some blood. That's the way I am. If you don't want to take the risk, just go along with the rest of the crowd. If you step forward, you have to suffer the consequences, whatever that might be.

There was a lot of discrimination in my hometown. Blacks couldn't go to certain places. So we started a movement called the Black Egyptians. We got in a lot of trouble. I got in a couple of shoot-outs. The police started bugging my mother. I went to jail a couple times. I had a cousin on the police force, and he told me they were going to set me up to kill me, so I left.

I didn't come to Detroit with the intention of staying. I thought I would stay here with my uncle for a while. But I got hired at the truck plant in 1969, and they put me in the Paint Department. The plant was just like East St. Louis. I was going through the same thing. I've had some rough days there.

Racism is still a problem in the plant. As long as they keep us divided, blacks against whites, they can do what they want. Some people think they're better because when the day ends, they're going back to the suburbs and I'm going back to Detroit. So there's a gap, but we're still working on the same line, with the same pace and the same paint, and we are all trying to take care of business. We all go to the store, pay our bills, we all have homes and cars we're trying to pay for, and you don't have any more than I do—the only thing that's different is color. Everything else is the same.

I still consider myself a rebel. That means standing up for my rights, trying to help the next person, not biting my tongue. That part of me will never change. If the cause is important, come and get me, I'll be with you. In the Black Egyptians it was more of a violent thing—what can I do to hurt you? Now I have a broader view. It's time to get things united now.

Lack of jobs and lack of values are what's killing kids in our cities. Everybody sees somebody else getting richer—by stealing or peddling drugs—and everybody wants to be like them, with the silk shirts and the Jordache jeans and the Reeboks. Everybody wants to be like the baddest dude making the money. If you've got a $12 pair of tennis shoes and everybody else has a $60 pair, you're not part of the crowd.

I want a different life for my kids. I want them to get the education I didn't get. And I want them to get involved in movements to help other people, to join some of the struggles. I try to teach them: Whatever you think is right, speak up on it and don't be afraid. Don't be ashamed if you make a mistake because the greatest men in the world make mistakes. If the road gets rough, don't give up, hang in there, get the best life you can.

Joe Roche

Born September 10, 1955, in Detroit
Hired July 8, 1976
Front-end aligner

THINGS ARE NO BETTER or worse at the plant than when I started. It's still the same stuff. The work is degrading for everybody—the repetition, the boredom. And management doesn't understand people. All they know is they have to get that number of trucks out every day. You can't blame them because they aren't getting paid to be human relations people.

You have to understand what you are choosing to do by working in the plant. You're making money, and you just have to put up with that stuff that comes with it. That's the way I look at it.

I used to have a real bad attitude. I used to complain a lot about how they should do this or that. But it is a big operation, and they are not concerned at all about how you feel. They have a number to put out, and once that number is out, they are happy.

I still feel there should be better human relations. They should take people into more consideration. But I accept everything now because I've been there so long. I've put up with it this long; I might as well keep putting up with it.

Management thinks they are better than you. They look down on you. It should be that your boss is just there to see the job gets

Joe Roche

done. He isn't supposed to reprimand you. He should just take your name if there's a problem and send you to the office. It's really childish to raise your voice at somebody you're working with. There is no reason to rant and rave, but they still do that at the truck plant. They think they're like your father, giving you a reprimand.

At Wayne Assembly they give you a big psychology thing. They act like they are your friend, but behind your back they talk about you like you're a dog. When I had gotten called back there after a layoff one time, I was sitting in the production office, and I could overhear some of the managers talking in the next room. One said, "This guy is back to work. He's just come off medical leave. Where should I put him?"

And the other guy said, "Put him back where he came from."

The first guy said, "But he had a heart attack on that job."

So the other one said, "Put him back there anyway; maybe he'll die, and we won't have to worry about him."

And they all started laughing. The guy they were talking about was about 55 years old. They thought it was a big joke: "Maybe he'll die, and we won't have to worry about him." That's their attitude. They don't care. You're just a number to them. You're nobody.

At this plant you don't know if you are going to have a job tomorrow or not. They can just come in one day and say that's it. I know; I've been told that enough times.

I got hired in 1976 at the truck plant and worked in the Body Shop until March 1980, when they gave me a pink card that said, "Your employment has been terminated." I thought that was it. I knew they had shut down one shift, and I figured I was out. I didn't expect to get called back. But in August that year I was called back to Wayne Assembly. They acted like I'd be there for good. I worked there about a year and got laid off again. I ended up working in every department at Wayne Assembly because I was laid off and put back to work so many times. The last time I was laid off was in January 1985. That April I got called back to the truck plant, and I've been there ever since.

Keeping my job used to be my main concern. But I'm not concerned about that anymore. I'm a certified master mechanic now. I could get another job right away. I have had offers to manage a body shop for $400 a week. I stay at the plant only because I have so much time invested already. I might as well try to stick it out as long as I can and get as much as I can out of it. But I doubt that I'll retire from the plant. The plant will probably be closed before I retire.

Now that I have my ten years in, I feel a lot more secure. I don't care if they lay me off because I'll be able to collect what I have coming. Before I got my ten years in, I was always worried that all my time would be wasted because it wouldn't count toward my retirement. When I first got laid off, I already had six years of work invested, and it's hard to walk away from that. You have something coming to you, and you don't want to leave it. It might not be the best money you can make, but it is good money. It is a lot of work, but it pays the bills.

There is no risk of layoffs right now, though it's always a possibility in the future. They could just decide to cut back, and they wouldn't care how far. When the decision is made to cut back, there is nobody there to represent the people who work at the plant. The management's only concern about manpower is whether they can run the line and make their number. When they get an order to cut back, they just cut back.

*   *   *

I started working on cars when I was about 8 or 9 years old. My dad's brother owned an auto repair shop, and I used to work with him, doing tune-ups. I've always been interested in cars. I guess it's in my blood.

My dad works for Ford in a transmission plant in Livonia. He has close to thirty years in and is getting ready to retire. He was a skilled tradesman, but when they cut back, he got a line job. My mom works as a cashier at Farmer Jack supermarket. She's in the AFL-CIO. They just had big concessions. They tore that industry up. The big companies' main goal is profit. If they have to step on people to get it, that's what they're going to do.

I grew up on the west side of Detroit and went to a Catholic grade school. There were five boys and one girl in the family. In 1971 we moved to Westland. I raced motorcycles when I was in high school, and I was so good at it I thought that's what I was going to do for a living. But I got some injuries, and it cost so much to race them that eventually I quit.

My wife and I were next-door neighbors when I was in high school, but we didn't start going out until I was about 19 or 20. We've been married nine years and don't have any kids yet. She works at the school district, and we are not hurting financially. That's why I haven't minded getting laid off so much.

On March 26, 1986, I got hurt. A steel roller fell on my head and knocked me to the ground. I came to a little while later sitting at a table and trembling all over. I didn't even know what had happened to me. I had a concussion.

The hospital sent me to a specialist, and he told me I couldn't work at all. I took his note and gave it to the plant doctor, and he examined me. He said, "Where did you bump your head?"

I said, "I didn't bump my head. A big piece of steel fell on it."

The health and safety engineer saw the thing that hit me and told me I was lucky to be alive. But the plant doctor said I could work, and he sent me back to work with no restrictions.

I took it to the union. The union called up the plant doctor and told him he couldn't overrule a third-party doctor. So they changed it and put me on restriction. There are more guys now than ever working on restriction because of injuries they suffered in the plant.

About two weeks after I got hit, our committeeman told me another roller fell off and almost hit somebody else. The roller that hit me had no nut or cotter pin in it. It was just hanging up there unsecured. It wasn't even being used for anything anymore. One guy told me they had worked on it about 1981 or 1982, but they couldn't get the roller off the rails, so they just left it up there.

I had gotten hurt once before. A welding gun broke and came down and hit me in the back and knocked me down. The plant doctor just said, "Go back to work." That must be his job, to put you back, so that's what he would do.

Recently they put out a newsletter that said, "Safety is your job." They are trying to make you think when you get hurt, it is your fault. But it's not. There just aren't enough maintenance people anymore; they can't maintain all the equipment, so people are getting hurt.

I feel bad about stuff like that, but there is nothing I can do about it. I'd like to run for the union committee, but if I got a committee job and tried to do something, they'd blackball me. I saw it happen next door. A committeeman at Wayne Assembly was blackballed right out of the union. He had more seniority than a couple guys on the committee, but one day they had a hearing on whether to keep him. He was winning the vote until they allowed all these people from the truck plant to vote, too. They voted him out. It was a big scam. I said right out, "This union sucks."

A committeeman came up to me like he was going to beat me up and said, "You watch your mouth."

I said, "Hey, I pay my union dues here, too."

But that's the way they are. It is a big clan. They all stick together; there is nothing you can do against them.

I've always been a union man, ever since I can remember, since I understood what a union was. I have always thought that through people we could be strong and do something for ourselves. But our union isn't much good anymore. They used to do whatever you wanted. Now they don't want to do anything, and you can hardly find them when there's a problem. If you call a committeeman now, he doesn't come down until the next day, and by then the problem is either resolved or you have already been put on a job you don't want to do.

The problem is it's not their concern anymore. They are detached from the line. Once they get off the line, they forget about what they talked about and what their beliefs are. If they took all the committeemen and put them on the line, they'd be screaming like a bunch of babies. There would be something done then. But if it's not affecting them, it's no big deal. They are not concerned about you or me. They have a good job, and they are happy with it.

All the committee guys are chummy with the company. The committeemen come and go as they please. They can leave the plant whenever they want and come back whenever they want. They are hardly ever in the plant. And if they are, and they know you've got a bitch, they'll walk right by you. Their job should be to find out what the problem is and take care of it. They should be unpopular with the company, not buddy-buddy.

They should give everybody a chance to be a committeeman and change the job each month. You'd get bad ones and good ones, but you'd get your problems taken care of. It would be better than letting some guy just stay there forever.

When the union first started, it was real important for everybody who worked in the plant. Everybody was involved, because we needed it real bad. We need it now, too, but they are so far detached from us. People on the line have let it happen. As long as it isn't bothering them, they aren't concerned. But when it's their ass and they are the ones getting messed with, boy, they are right out there.

We have good benefits at the plant, but the sad thing is the people who work there have forgotten about the struggle that it took to get them. They are just handing them back to the company. Every time we get a new contract, we get less and less. Eventually the union will give away so much that they give everything away.

I don't want any more concessions, and most people I talk to will say they don't either. But behind your back they'll say, "We have to do it just to keep a job." People are just happy to be working nowadays, to the point that they feel we should give it back if they want it. I don't have that attitude. I think we deserve what we have right now. We deserve more really because we make the money for the company.

The workingman will eventually get fed up and do something about it. He is going to have to take a stand somewhere. If they keep pushing concessions down our throat, everybody will be affected. It has to get worse before it gets better. When they are messing with everybody's job, then everybody will get pissed off and start doing something.

There is a lot of stuff in our plant that could be done better, safety-wise and job-wise. But they are not concerned as long as the job is getting done. The EI program has done nothing for us. It's not designed to help people. The whole idea is to make the plant more efficient. That's what they want. If they have to eliminate jobs to make it more efficient, they'll do it.

Automation is also eliminating jobs, but there is nothing you can do about that. The union might be able to do something, but I don't think they're too concerned about it.

What the union is concentrating on now is trying to get other industries involved in the UAW so they don't have all their eggs in one basket. Then, if anything happens, they can just go on. They are going to milk us for every penny they can get, and as soon as the company says they don't want a union anymore, they'll move on to something else, wherever they can make money. The union used to be nonprofit. Now it seems like their whole goal is to make money. They are not out to help us.

Most people at work don't want to talk about politics, even though politics is an important part of your life. They just chit-chat about unimportant stuff like the weather. They don't know how to talk on another level. And a lot of them are not concerned about what other people feel.

They treat women like dogs at both the plants. They are treated as sexual objects and put through a lot of abuse. I know it's the nature of a lot of guys to talk abusively to women, but you shouldn't put your co-worker through a bunch of hassles. It has to be on her mind getting bugged like that all the time.

A lot of the guys on the line just don't care. They don't have respect for anybody. They are trying to amuse each other, to do something to break the monotony of the day.

A lot of people say things because they don't know any better. They don't care anymore because they have been in the plant so long that they have lost touch with reality. All they know is the plant. When you work that many hours, you fall behind with human relations. A lot of guys are so far away from regular people that they get the attitude "Fuck it, man." That is the prevailing attitude at the plant.

In a couple of years there won't be a union. If there is, it'll just be symbolic. When that happens, it is going to be a terrible blow to the country. It is going to be like the Civil War. The country is going to fall apart. There will be a huge gap between the middle class and the rich. The middle class will become poor.

Just about everything in this country revolves around the auto industry—petroleum, plastics, electronics. When the auto industry is doing bad, the whole country is doing bad. It is the country's business. It should be our top priority because it's where everybody is employed.

The automobile is what brought our country close together. The freedom of transportation, that independence, made our country what it is today. People can go wherever they want to and can be what they want to be. When it was the horse and buggy, you couldn't go very far. People lived right where they were born. The automobile changed this whole country.

But now the automobile industry is abandoning the country. There are too many imports, and it's the companies' fault. Ford and GM are worldwide companies, and they have their hands in all those countries. Whatever comes into this country comes because they want it here. If GM and Ford didn't want imports, there wouldn't be imports.

I'm not against people bringing their products here at a fair price. But the autoworkers in other countries are exploited worse than we are. In Mexico guys are getting under a dollar an hour to produce the same stuff we do. There should be a law that says we don't want goods in this country that are produced by workers who are being exploited. If they have to live in substandard conditions and do the same job I'm doing, I don't want to buy the cars they make.

Everybody who builds cars worldwide should be in the same union and get the same amount of money, so it wouldn't matter where the cars were sold. They'd all get a good wage.

There will always be automobiles, but they may be made somewhere else. If people in this country let that happen, they are as much to blame as anybody. We've lost the feeling of nationalism. I think "Buy American" because you'll keep somebody working. It's not that you hate somebody else in another country; but hey, we have to make our own, and they should make their own. It's up to their government to help their people.

The idea that there's going to be all these high-tech computer jobs is a big farce. Anybody can fix computers already. You just put a tape in the computer, and it will tell you what is wrong with it and give you a diagram of how to fix it. So where are all the jobs going to be?

If things go on like this, the auto industry is going to be a dead business here. The stockholders at Ford Motor Company could just decide one day that it's not profitable to build cars in North

America anymore. They could build them somewhere else more cheaply. Ford is antilabor. If we would work for a penny wage, they would think that's great.

What I want to know is this: Would the American people still buy Ford products if Ford pulled out of the country?

Conclusion

Rebuilding the Dream

If it can be said that man
collectively shrinks back more
and more from the Truth,
it can also be said that
on all sides the Truth is
closing in more and more upon man.

—*E. F. Schumacher,*
Small Is Beautiful

IN THIS BOOK, workers have thanked Ford, America, and God for the opportunity to rise from poverty to the middle class. They have expressed pride in being able to provide their families with food, clothing, shelter, college degrees, health insurance, cars, and computers. And they have mourned the high cost of those material rewards—debt, divorce, injury, alienation, and assaults on dignity.

These are autoworkers speaking, but their voices are the cry of twentieth-century America, a society in which the trade of lives for dollars has become the essential bargain and has come to define the American dream. By admitting millions of former outcasts into that bargain, the automobile industry—and the economy of mass production and consumption it helped generate—have shaped values that dominate our lives.

Money soothes the pain, but working people have always wondered whether the deal was worth the price. That wondering has turned into deeper questioning now that they have seen friends and co-workers kicked out the door and realize that they could be next. On the edge of a cliff the view of what's behind and what's ahead is vivid. It's no longer just isolated social critics who are raising questions; it's working people who are asking where we went wrong to end up with a society in which children commit suicide or kill for a silk shirt.

Despite their vastly different backgrounds and beliefs, all the workers in this book are certain that their sons and daughters will not have the same opportunities they had. They all know it's the end of the line.

"When I got hired at the plant, I thought it was a guaranteed job because everybody needs cars. I didn't know they were going to lay off people," says Lance Whitis. "Now I know the whole thing is going to fold. This is the last generation."

Where workers once labored in confidence that they were building a better future for their families and the nation, now the future is a blank wall. They know their children won't be able to get good-paying jobs without an advanced education, and they are afraid of what will happen to them. They see the growing numbers of dropouts from the economy as an increasing threat, as life for more and more people becomes a struggle for survival.

Now that the ax is falling on autoworkers, all kinds of people who thought their jobs were safe are afraid they could become the next to be cast aside. "Even the salaried guys ... are starting to worry," notes Ed Aubuchon. "They're starting to cut into people who live in a lot nicer houses than I do."

The threat is not just the loss of jobs. Everything that was sacred is in jeopardy when so many productive workers are being discarded and the future is being mortgaged. It's not only residents of the inner cities who are worried about crime, drugs, and their children's future; it's not just small farmers who fear being foreclosed; it's not just young people who can't find work above minimum wage; it's not just older Americans who are worried about health-care costs and Social Security; it's not just Native Americans who are concerned about the land and the environment.

People no longer feel the age-old hope that the next generation will inherit the earth. Christopher Lasch has noted: "This is the first time the discrepancy between the rhetoric of the promise of American life and the reality has become really glaring. This is the first moment I know of in American history when the confidence that things generally are going to improve is not there."

Al Commons says: "My father, I'm sure, felt he was making a better world for me. I don't feel I'm making a better world for my daughter, but I don't know what to do about it. I'm caught in the stream like everybody else. I'm being swept along with the tide."

Some believe that their own actions contain the seeds of their destruction. Says Ramon Reyes, "The harder I work, the more I accomplish, the more profits they make, and they use those profits to buy robots to clear me out." Others say the best we can do is slow down the inevitable, limit the pain, and cut our losses. "I know that somewhere down the road what we are doing is going to make it easier for them to eliminate someone," says Lee Thornsberry. "But I don't know if I can prevent that."

On the line there is no longer a silent acceptance of the assumptions and allegiances behind the bargain. There is little trust that hard work and sacrifice will continue to bring rewards or that the union will lead the way to a better future. But there is confusion and disagreement about what can replace those principles and who can provide new leadership. Debate has increased over local contracts as the union struggles to define its role in the new culture of employee involvement and teamwork.

The pursuit of money is, for many, the only value to hang on to. "From the time I started at the plant, my kids knew they were going to get whatever they wanted," says Dee Mueller. "I wanted them to have things I never had, and I had the money." But Jim Vernatter says family life has broken down because so many parents are putting the dollar first. "Children need you to be there to guide them, but all they're getting in some cases is material things, and that's not enough." And he condemns the selfishness that pursuit of money can lead to. "The love of money is holding us back. Recently I asked this guy in the plant if he would be willing to give up $1.50 an hour to get back the second shift. And he said no. I said, 'That's the problem. All you think about is yourself.'"

At the Michigan Truck Plant people work overtime while one entire shift has been laid off for almost a decade. When one employee did a survey to find out what people thought about the situation, he discovered: "The overall feeling was: We're not going to have a job very long, so whatever I can work I am going to do it."

The get-it-while-you-can frenzy leads Abson McDaniel to comment, "People don't see what's happening because these days people are not always looking ahead. They are looking for the easy money for themselves. They think they have a good thing going. They don't realize they're making it rougher for you."

How much longer can Americans keep looking out for number one before our number is up? All-out competition seemed to be working for the good of the nation when the goodies were abundant and the only losers were the outcasts at home, the faceless peasants abroad, and the devastated land. But in a world of dwindling resources, competition means Americans fighting Americans. The survival of the fittest means more losers and more outcasts, and the consequences hit closer to home. "There is so much competitive zeal that I think we're losing the fellowship among ourselves," says Commons. "Our free-enterprise system sharpens our appetite for competition and the feeling that we want to be first in every race, and some of us can't be."

Americans have always competed with other Americans, but now the competition is becoming a war of all against all: cities against cities; states against states; regions against regions; union locals against union locals; high-seniority workers versus low-seniority workers; one generation against the next. And the corporations determine who wins and who loses.

"It is going to be like the Civil War," predicts Joe Roche. "The country is going to fall apart. There will be a huge gap between the middle class and the rich. The middle class will become poor."

This is a profound crisis for America, much deeper than the so-called crises that pop up every other night on the evening news. People "respond" to them by waiting for the experts to provide a quick fix—or for the media to forget the crisis and go on to the next one. That behavior creates a dependence on crisis managers and an ethical atrophy of the body politic.

The company, the union, and the workers are responding to the crisis in the automobile industry with altruistic rhetoric that masks self-interest and shortsightedness. The company says its mission is to improve quality and satisfy customers. The Big Three are building better cars, but only because they were forced to improve quality to maintain profits. Automakers are streamlining operations; diversifying into real estate, banking, the military, or computer firms; and joining their overseas competition in joint ventures and import schemes. They are reducing the work force through layoffs, plant closings, attrition, automation, and outsourcing—farming out work to companies outside the Big Three. All these cost-cutting measures—promoted as improvements in quality—are conducted to maintain profits. Multinational corporations' sole allegiance is to their stock-

holders worldwide, not to the well-being of any nation or community.

The union's slogan is "job security." In an era of overseas competition, overcapacity, and a stagnant domestic market, that
means protecting the jobs of high-seniority workers, making life
in the factory more bearable for most of them, and providing
retraining for those facing layoffs. But there is a trade-off. In
exchange for profit sharing and other financial incentives; physical fitness, health, and counseling programs; and limited job
guarantees for some workers, the union accepts layoffs and concessions on wages, work rules, and rights. In the UAW's 1987
contract with General Motors, a provision barring layoffs over a
three-year period does not apply to 75,000 workers on existing or
previously announced layoffs or if new models are introduced or
market conditions change. In addition, the union is joining the
company in establishing plant committees to streamline operations and improve efficiency. The union's own survival now
comes before its historic commitment to solidarity and justice.
The union is organizing other industries and calling on the government to protect jobs with trade legislation and other measures. But when auto companies want to demolish neighborhoods
to build new plants, the UAW succumbs, accepting the destruction of homes and communities for the promise of jobs. On
Detroit's east side, thousands of residents have been displaced to
make room for modern GM and Chrysler plants, which provide
barely half the jobs originally projected.

Workers who are leaders in the new culture of company-
employee cooperation say profits are good for everyone. But while
quality and pride may be heightened by Employee Involvement
programs and profit sharing, someone must suffer in order for the
paychecks to be fatter. Using such strategies as overseas invest-
ments, outsourcing, and automation, companies get profits, in
the final analysis, from job elimination. With profit sharing, the
men and women on the line, whether they realize it or not,
unwittingly become the cheerleaders for the destruction of their
co-workers.

How the company, the union, and workers are responding to
the crisis in the auto industry is emblematic of the futile search
in old places for solutions to deepening problems that plague
today's society. While workers fight for a piece of the pie, the
company talks quality and the union cries out for security. These
are seductive concepts for people who see disintegration in their

neighborhoods and who fear for their family's future. Quality and security are more than workplace concerns; they are life-and-death issues for all Americans. This country was built on the opportunity for prosperity and citizenship that is threatened now by deindustrialization, violence, individualism, and the disintegration of community and family. We are searching for lasting values, and we want to believe that the institutions which once kept us secure and hopeful can continue to take care of us.

People are concerned with quality nowadays because of the growing sense that we have less control over our lives and the things around us. We spend more time repairing things, returning things, going back and forth to doctors and therapists, filing complaints, and getting the runaround. Because quality is so rarely found, it has become more sought after, so we hear about "quality education," "quality products," "quality time," and "quality of life."

Quality seems rare these days because for years we have accepted the primacy of quantity, speed, and cost efficiency—the values of mass production and mass consumption. People have come to define their own worth in terms of numbers: incomes, IQs, weights, net worths, grades, miles run, computer capacity, and the price of homes and clothes. When everything is measured, human beings are reduced to parts of the equation.

"The standard of efficiency displaces and destroys the standards of quality because, by definition, it cannot even consider them," writes Wendell Berry in his essay "Discipline and Hope." "Instead of asking a man what he can do well, it asks him what he can do fast and cheap."

Efficiency in our society, says Berry, "means cheapness at any price. It means hurrying to nowhere. It means the profligate waste of humanity and of nature. It means the greatest profit to the greatest liar. What we have called efficiency has produced among us, and to our incalculable cost, such unprecedented monuments of destructiveness and waste as the strip-mining industry, the Pentagon, the federal bureaucracy, and the family car."

When production is put first, quality suffers. Mander "Lee" Thornsberry notes: "Quality at the plant was pathetic in the past. Guys back then were instructed by supervisors: 'Get it out of here. We don't care what kind of shape it is in, as long as we get our quota.' . . . I once saw a truck leave here with an automatic transmission *and* a clutch in it. People didn't care back then. We worked a lot, and the trucks were selling even though they were

bad trucks." Numbers brought profits; all other concerns were secondary. You couldn't stop the line to put the screw in right; you let it go. The attitude reflected a society that measured its worth by its gross national product. The company didn't care, the workers didn't care, and the customers didn't seem to care either. Standards and judgment were destroyed by the numbers game.

Now people are looking to restore meaning, to give their work and their lives a measure of quality and dignity. Car companies that once produced shiny and shoddy goods are now saying that quality is their mission. Consumers who gobbled up hamburgers and fries now flock to salad bars at the same fast-food restaurants. Parents are buying educational programs for fetuses to give their children a head start in the race for a quality degree.

In the plant the new concern for quality is reflected in the Ford slogan, "Quality Is Job One," and in workers who participate in EI meetings, help the company root out the source of production problems, and willingly cross job-classification boundaries to get the job done properly.

These developments show a widespread recognition of the importance of quality. The desire to do good work and have meaning in life is part of what makes us human. Everyone has the potential to contribute something to society and leave something lasting.

However, when mass production and mass consumption set the agenda, quality is only an option, not an overriding principle:

- Quality in automobile production doesn't mean that we apply all our technology and skills to make a car that will last as long as possible with as little service as possible. Such a change would, as Harold Coleman points out, spell trouble for an economy based on planned obsolescence.

- Quality can't seriously impede production or interfere with other measures to cut costs. As Larry Poole observes, mandatory overtime, overloaded jobs, and line speedups are inconsistent with real quality.

- Quality of work life can't be measured by external trappings. Improvements have been made in conditions at the factory—from floor mats to exercise rooms, from psychological counseling services to free health checkups—but workers are working faster and harder, and their jobs are still monotonous and difficult. While the rhetoric says that the worker is now a human being, the reality is that the worker is a more efficient and adaptable tool of production.

Just as quality of work is subservient to production, so quality of life is placed second to consumption. Take the notion of quality time. The desire for quality time with loved ones is motivated by the fact that more people are spending more time making money or spending it. In the little time remaining, we want to have the best possible experiences with our children, partners, grand-parents, or friends. We want to make up for our long absences by being fully present. We want to be both money machines and loving persons.

But quality time defines our relationships in terms of getting the maximum out of the time left over. It's defined by the lan-guage of cost efficiency. And it's a poor substitute for sharing all your life and your experience with the people you love. What is missing when you share only quality time is the everyday experi-ence of the struggles, slow times, and spontaneity that make up life. It is a synthetic and controlled and therefore deficient envi-ronment, and the recipients of quality time get the message that they are being squeezed in only after more important things have been taken care of.

Just as the search for quality is a desire to restore meaning in our lives, the search for security is a drive to restore order. Security is a buzzword these days. Banks advertise security for investors. Unions demand job security for their members. Corpo-rations promise stockholder security. The aging are concerned about Social Security, and everyone worries about the security of home and family. And all kinds of foreign policy decisions are defended in the name of national security interests.

The drive for security is the attempt to gain control over a complex world. It is a reaction to the many threats facing society and individuals—from nuclear war to chemical contamination, from automobile collisions to airplane crashes, from the hitch-hiker on the expressway to the stranger in our neighborhood, from the uncertainty of the economy to the dangers of drugs and alcohol for our children. In the midst of all these dangers, in response to their fears about the future, more people are looking for safe havens.

It is a hopeful sign when more people join together to try to get safer neighborhoods and more secure jobs rather than accept crime and chaos or corporate abuse. The search for security is a way to start to take responsibility for the world around us. But when security is sought at the expense of others, it becomes a danger to all, obliterating compassion and community:

- Unions are making job security a rallying cry, hoping to protect those who are left in the plants. "If a guy can make a decent living and then get his retirement, that's all he wants," says Walter "Jeff" Washington. But job security doesn't mean anything to millions of unemployed or to the hundreds of thousands of former union members who have lost their recall rights.

- Workers are trying to get secure futures by making as much money now as they can. Not only do they work the overtime agreed to in the company-union contract, but many volunteer for extra overtime while friends and neighbors are jobless.

- Cities are trying to gain economic security by offering tax breaks and incentives to corporations to lure new plants or keep plants from moving, creating a situation of corporate blackmail. After taxpayers spend millions of dollars financing new roads, sewers, bridges and even job training programs, they can be left high and dry whenever another city comes up with a better deal. This game of "Let's Make a Deal" has no long-term winners except the companies.

- People are looking for security at home by fleeing to enclaves to get farther and farther away from chaos. But looking the other way doesn't solve the problem; the flight of capital only multiplies the woes of the people who are left behind.

In fact, there is no quick fix to traumas created over a period of years by policies and choices dictated by self-interest rather than concern for the public good. The legacy of corporate and individual decisions made for the purpose of maximizing profit and mobility is the devastation of our cities and the hopelessness and violence of our children.

In Detroit 365 young people 17 or under were shot in 1986, 43 of them fatally. Members of the community responded to this deepening crisis in several ways:

1. They put more bars on their homes, more German shepherds in their yards, and more guns in their cars and bedrooms.

2. They demanded handgun legislation, harsher punishment for criminals, weapons searches in schools, stricter curfews for youth, and more job programs.

3. And, finally, a few parents of the victims started discussing in schools and neighborhoods the need to change the values by which children were being raised, to say it was time to teach kids to value human life over $100 tennis shoes.

The first type of response to the crisis is to circle the wagons in the hope of protecting yourself with security devices. That behavior reinforces the culture of violence and ups the ante. The second type of response relies on experts to make policy changes that will manage the crisis and mitigate its worst and most recent effects. Both responses are, at best, short-term solutions that may alleviate the crisis for some people or for some period of time without getting to the roots of the problem. But the third type of response breaks through the cycle of dependence on things or authorities to provide answers and starts to examine values and collective responsibility.

When the parents in Detroit formed SOSAD (Save Our Sons and Daughters) and started talking about how the problem was more than jobs, prisons, money, social agencies, and weapons, they took a leap from being passive consumers of the twentieth-century American dream to becoming active participants in its remaking. SOSAD members have started to discuss how their community can have real security—not just the temporary protection of locks and guns and laws—and how their families can instill quality and meaning in the lives of their children—not just the desire for designer jeans.

In this questioning, there is a recognition that quality and security cannot be purchased like commodities, bestowed like educational degrees, or stolen by hustling on the streets or speculating in financial markets. There is a fervent desire for meaning and order, for a life that is more than producing and buying things.

In America the car has represented freedom from restraints of time and place—from the dead-end poverty and isolation of the past. With "wheels" we believe we can go where we want when we want. With a job we believe we can buy what we want and live where we want.

In our pursuit of individual freedom we have come to value convenience over tradition, speed over taking time, getting there over appreciating what's in between, and independence over interconnectedness. Instead of taking a walk to the corner store and stopping to chat with neighbors, we pile into the car and go to a shopping mall full of strangers.

Today we spend more time than ever before getting places, and there are more places than ever where we feel unsafe. Our world has become smaller and smaller; our ability to protect ourselves and our families requires a watchful eye and close proximity; we have lost track of our traditions and lost sight of the future.

We cannot control time and place with the technology of speed and power. We cannot get quality relationships by speeding up the process of human interaction and compressing the panorama of life into a few precious moments. And we cannot get lasting security by moving from place to place or by staking out a place for ourselves and surrounding it with defenses.

The Chinese spell the word *crisis* with two characters—one which means "opportunity" and one which means "danger." There is danger in responses that attempt to buy our way out of this crisis with individual solutions and in responses that rely on those in power for the answers. Such things may give us temporary security and quality in our lives, but at the cost of more chaos and disintegration in society. Short-term solutions pit our welfare against the rest of society and risk destroying our own humanity. In acquiescing in the elimination of our neighbors, we destroy our own sense of compassion and responsibility for others; we take on the characteristics of the faceless corporation, concerned only with our own survival.

The dangers of our present course are clear. Without a change in direction, our cities will continue to crumble, our schools fail, our communities dissolve, and our children die. We will become a nation where the minority who have jobs live in enclaves, serviced by a vast force of minimum-wage earners and surrounded by a sea of predators.

If the concepts of quality and security are dominated by the bottom line and the enclave mentality, they are dangerous notions. Quality in the service of profits ignores the human costs of the bargain and lets multinational corporations define the terms. The enclave mentality means temporary and limited security for a few at the price of permanent insecurity for growing numbers of outsiders labeled as scapegoats and blamed for their own plight.

But the crisis can be an opportunity to remake the American dream. As long as good-paying jobs were plentiful, we could evade the hard questions about the bargain and could continue to believe that technology would solve our problems and money would buy solutions. Now that competition and self-interest have taken us to a dead end, we have to look beyond quick fixes and old solutions to regain meaning and purpose. Now that the have-nots cannot have the American dream of jobs, prosperity, and economic security, what will we mean when we say quality and security?

In this book many autoworkers criticize the agenda of the dollar and feel trapped by their own outmoded priorities. But amid the frustration and fears and feelings of powerlessness there are a few whispers of hope that point out how we could rethink and rebuild the American dream on some solid principles. Here is what those whispers are saying:

· There are more important things than money. "I know I need bread on my table and decent shelter, and I need an automobile; but I know there is more to life than just that," says Al Commons. And Bernard Clifford tells his daughters: "Don't do work you don't want to do just for the money. It's not worth it."

· Family and community are more important than production and consumption. Betty Foote thinks overtime should be outlawed. Yaser Awadallah doesn't spend much money on material things because he wants to save it for his son's future. After years of working overtime, Gary Shellenbarger is taking some time off now to be with his kids.

· Everyone deserves respect. "I would rather be out on the street than have someone treat me like a dog," says Ed Aubuchon. Lorenzo Sharpe adds: "I don't let people at the plant harass me. . . . I look for respect and I give respect." And Debbie Listman tells co-workers who are harassing her: "I'm not here to be a plaything for you. I'm here, same as you are, to make a living and support my kids. . . ."

· Our happiness should not come at the expense of others or the destruction of the environment. "I get angry about people working overtime," says Sheryl Jackson. "Why not split it up and let somebody else get some of that money?" Commons adds: "I can't justify what we make in our industry when so many people are out of work." Joe Roche says: "There should be a law that says we don't want goods in this country that are produced by workers who are being exploited." And Ramon Reyes worries about what is happening to the rivers and lakes of Mexico that are being used as dumping grounds for factory sewage.

These whispers can be heard today throughout America, among people of all races and classes who are beginning to question the unrestrained materialism that has made fools and victims of its disciples. The crisis in our culture touches everyone, and our lives depend on recognizing our interconnectedness and the long-term consequences of our choices. The public good can be created only by our respecting and understanding the values and the visions of the many cultures that make up America. We can no longer pay mere lip service to quality and security or compromise them for corporate profits or the prosperity of the privileged.

Native Americans took a view that extended back through generations of ancestors and far into the future for generations to come. They found meaning and safety in harmony with nature. They learned the lessons of the past and practiced clear thinking about the future. We need such clear thinking now.

The challenge is to dream an American dream that our children can build upon. For us to have hope in their future, we need to give them more than quality educations and material security. We need to build upon the life-affirming principles of community and the public good as we remake the American dream.

In trying to create a new society, we can draw on the legacy of the dreamers and builders of the past. Just as the descendants of sharecroppers and slaves, of coal miners and farmers wrested dignity out of the assembly line, so today, as Berlin Scott says, "The solutions will have to come from ordinary people getting together. We have to work it out among ourselves and stop pretending we're so ignorant."

Bibliography

BOOKS

Adair, Margo. *Working Inside Out: Tools for Change.* Berkeley, Calif.: Wingbow Press, 1984.

Altshuler, Alan, et al. *The Future of the Automobile: The Report of MIT's International Automobile Program.* Cambridge, Mass.: MIT Press, 1985.

Babson, Steve. *Working Detroit.* Detroit: Wayne State University Press, 1986.

Bensman, David, and Roberta Lynch. *Rusted Dreams: Hard Times in a Steel Community.* New York: McGraw-Hill, 1987.

Benyon, Huy. *Working for Ford.* Middlesex, England: Penguin Books, 1973.

Berry, Wendell. *Recollected Essays 1965–1980.* Berkeley, Calif.: North Point Press, 1981.

Bluestone, Barry, and Bennett Harrison. *The Deindustrialization of America.* New York: Basic Books, 1982.

Boggs, James. *The American Revolution: Pages from a Negro Worker's Notebook.* New York: Monthly Review Press, 1963.

Boggs, James and Grace Lee, and Lyman and Freddy Paine. *Conversations in Maine: Exploring Our Nation's Future.* Boston: South End Press, 1978.

Buss, Fran Leeper. *Dignity.* Ann Arbor, Mich.: University of Michigan Press, 1985.

Collins, Sheila. *Rainbow Challenge.* New York: Monthly Review Press, 1986.

295

de Tocqueville, Alexis. *Democracy in America.* New York: New American Library, 1956.

Ezekiel, Raphael. *Voices from the Corner: Poverty and Racism in the Inner City.* Philadelphia: Temple University Press, 1984.

Gilk, Paul. *Nature's Unruly Mob.* Millville, Minn.: Anvil Press, 1986.

Halberstam, David. *The Reckoning.* New York: William Morrow and Company, 1986.

Iacocca, Lee, with William Novak. *Iacocca, an Autobiography.* New York: Bantam Books, 1984.

Illich, Ivan. *Tools for Conviviality.* New York: Harper & Row, 1973.

Lacey, Robert. *Ford: The Men and the Machine.* New York: Ballantine Books, 1986.

Mann, Eric. *Taking on General Motors.* Van Nuys, California: Labor Distributors, 1987.

Meiklejohn, Alexander. *What Does American Mean?* New York: Norton, 1935.

Neihardt, John. *Black Elk Speaks.* New York: William Morrow and Company, 1932.

Rae, John B. *The American Automobile Industry.* Boston: Twayne Publishers, 1984.

Rifkin, Jeremy. *Entropy.* New York: Viking Press, 1980.

Schumacher, E. F. *Small Is Beautiful.* New York: Harper & Row, 1973.

Serrin, William. *The Company and the Union.* New York: Vintage Books, 1970.

Swados, Harvey. *Standing Fast.* Garden City, N.Y.: Doubleday, 1970.

Terkel, Studs. *American Dreams: Lost and Found.* New York: Ballantine, 1980.

Widick, B. J. *Auto Work and Its Discontents.* Baltimore: Johns Hopkins University Press, 1976.

Wright, J. Patrick. *On a Clear Day You Can See General Motors.* New York: Avon, 1979.

JOURNALS

Labor Notes, Labor Education and Research Projects, 7345 Michigan Ave., Detroit, Mich. 48210.

Manas, P.O. Box 32112, El Serene Station, Los Angeles, Calif. 90032.

Monthly Review, Monthly Review Foundation, 122 W. 27th St., New York, N.Y. 10001.

Multinational Monitor, P.O. Box 19405, Washington, D.C. 20036.

North Country Anvil, Millville, Minn. 55957.

Save Our Sons and Daughters Newsletter, Box 32421, Detroit, Mich. 48232.

Solidarity Magazine, United Auto Workers, 8000 East Jefferson, Detroit, Mich. 48214.

PAMPHLETS

But What About the Workers! (1973); *Manifesto for an American Revolutionary Party* (1982). National Organization for an American Revolution, P.O. Box 2617, Philadelphia, Pa. 19121.